sorted

sorted

GROWING UP, COMING OUT,
AND FINDING MY PLACE

a transgender memoir

jackson bird

TILLER PRESS
NEW YORK   LONDON   TORONTO   SYDNEY   NEW DELHI

TILLER PRESS

An Imprint of Simon & Schuster, Inc.
1230 Avenue of the Americas
New York, NY 10020

First Tiller Press hardcover edition September 2019

TILLER PRESS and colophon are trademarks of Simon & Schuster, Inc.

For information about special discounts for bulk purchases, please contact Simon & Schuster Special Sales at 1-866-506-1949 or business@simonandschuster.com.

The Simon & Schuster Speakers Bureau can bring authors to your live event. For more information or to book an event, contact the Simon & Schuster Speakers Bureau at 1-866-248-3049 or visit our website at www.simonspeakers.com.

Interior design by Patrick Sullivan

Manufactured in the United States of America

10 9 8 7 6 5 4 3 2 1

Library of Congress Cataloging-in-Publication Data has been applied for.

ISBN 978-1-9821-3075-6
ISBN 978-1-9821-3076-3 (ebook)

to my mom

For always letting me be myself,
even when you didn't understand.
And to all the trans people
who came before me, who fought
tirelessly for their rights,
and without whom this book, and
my life as I enjoy it, would not
be possible.

I sometimes think we Sort too soon.

~~—J. K. Rowling~~
Albus Dumbledore

contents

a note on language

TRANSGENDER...PERHAPS ONE OF THE MOST CONFUSING
AND MISUNDERSTOOD WORDS IN THE ENGLISH LANGUAGE.

—Julia Serano

I spent the better part of my childhood and adolescence grappling with intense feelings that I didn't have the words to explain. If someone had presented me with a simple glossary like the one that follows, I could've sorted things out a lot sooner.

While this book will take you on my journey of discovering most of these terms, I thought it might be helpful to have a place to flip back to that defines them in clear language and adds some context beyond just my own story.

Transgender: Someone whose gender does not match the sex they were assigned at birth.

Cisgender: Someone whose gender matches the sex they were assigned at birth.

Nonbinary: Someone whose gender is beyond the binary of male and female, whether that means being neither, both, somewhere in between, another gender entirely, or some combination of any of those. This can include, but is not limited to, people who are genderqueer, bigender, genderfluid, agender, and more. In addition to being an umbrella term, *nonbinary* can also be used as its own singular identity. Some nonbinary people identify as transgender, and some do not.

Transition: The act of socially, legally, or medically adapting to live life as one's affirmed gender. This might include coming out, changing your name, undergoing hormone replacement therapy, or more. Further exploration of this in chapter thirteen.

Trans Man: Someone who was assigned female at birth but is male. Note the space between "trans" and "man," indicating that "trans" is an adjective. Trans men are men, even without the adjective. They are not a separate category of "transmen."

Trans Woman: Someone who was assigned male at birth but is female. Note the space between "trans" and "woman," indicating that "trans" is an adjective. Trans women are women, even without the adjective. They are not a separate category of "transwomen."

FTM: An initialism for Female-to-Male, which refers to people who were assigned female at birth but are male.

MTF: An initialism for Male-to-Female, which refers to people who were assigned male at birth but are female.

Transsexual: Someone whose gender does not match the sex they were assigned at birth, usually in reference to binary trans women and trans men who undergo some type of medical transition. It has gone out of favor with many people in the current and upcoming generations, but remains an important identity marker as distinct from *transgender* for older generations.

Transmasculine: An inclusive way to refer to people who were assigned female at birth and fall along the masculine spectrum with regard to expression, transition, identity, or more. This can include trans men as well as some nonbinary and gender-nonconforming people.

Transfeminine: An inclusive way to refer to people who were assigned male at birth and fall along the feminine spectrum with regard to expression, transition, identity, or more. This can include trans women as well as some nonbinary and gender-nonconforming people.

Intersex: A person who was born with any number of conditions in which their sexual or reproductive anatomy does not adhere to the typical definitions of *male* or *female*. This is *not* a type of transgender identity, though some intersex people are also transgender.

Gender-Nonconforming: Someone whose gender expression does not adhere to typical expectations of their affirmed gender. Not all gender-nonconforming people are transgender, and not all transgender people are gender-nonconforming. Binary transgender or transsexual people in particular (i.e., trans women and trans men) *conform* to their affirmed gender and are therefore not gender-nonconforming. This term is often used in reference to historical figures whose gender identity we cannot be certain of, cisgender people who subvert their gender in one way or another, and children who may be exploring their gender (other terms for children include "gender expansive" and "gender creative").

Gender Dysphoria: The anxiety or unease experienced with regard to the incongruence between one's innate sense of gender and one's assigned sex—including how one is perceived by others, one's relationship to one's body, and more.

Hormone Replacement Therapy: The administration of androgens or anti-androgens to induce secondary sex characteristics of an individual's affirmed gender. Sometimes referred to as cross-sex hormones, HRT, or simply hormones. You may also hear it referred to as E for estrogen or T for testosterone.

Binding: The use of a compression device to flatten one's chest. To combat unsafe practices like tape or compression bandages, many companies produce safely designed nylon compression vests called binders for transmasculine people to wear. For more on binding, see chapter ten.

Gender Affirmation Surgery: Any number of surgical alterations trans people might elect to undergo as part of their transition.

Many trans people never undergo any type of surgery due to cost, extenuating health concerns, or personal choice. No type of medical procedure is required in order be trans.

Top Surgery: The procedure some transmasculine and non-binary people undergo to remove their breasts. It can also refer to the breast augmentation some transfeminine people undergo. For more detailed information about transmasculine top surgery, see chapter twenty-three.

Passing: The act of being assumed by others to be a particular gender or identity, regardless of how you identify. While a useful term and popular milestone for some transgender people, it's not without controversy. The term can imply that a person is simply playacting as a gender and not *actually* that gender. It also puts sometimes unnecessary emphasis on a connection between physical appearance and gender. In many cases, a good alternative is to say that one has been *read* as a particular gender.

Stealth: A term describing someone who is not open about being transgender in some or all parts of their lives.

LGBTQ+: An initialism for Lesbian Gay Bisexual Transgender Queer (or Questioning). The plus sign refers to the many more identities that can fall under this umbrella term. Sometimes you'll see other letters or numbers included, such as "A" for asexual, "I" for intersex, "2" for Two Spirit, and more. For clarity and brevity, I've chosen to use LGBTQ+ throughout this book.

For more transgender terminology (including more on transfeminine and nonbinary experiences), I suggest visiting www.transstudent.org/definitions or reading *The ABC's of LGBT+* by Ash Hardell (published under the name Ashley Mardell).

When asked about how to keep up with the sheer number of terms we use in the LGBTQ+ community without offending anyone, I always have two pieces of advice:

1. Be compassionate and show you're really putting forth the effort. Small flubs will be excused if it's clear you're trying and willing to learn.

2. Take a moment to think about what you're saying. These terms have been created to make language more precise, not more confusing.

For example, are you talking about an issue that broadly affects lesbian, gay, bisexual, and transgender people? Great! LGBT is the right thing to say. Does what you're talking about refer only to sexual orientation and not gender identity? No need to include the *T*, then.

Are you discussing an issue that affects nonbinary people, like the ability to put an *X* instead of an *F* or an *M* on identification cards? Don't include trans women and trans men as people that applies to. Binary trans women and trans men are women and men who would use *F*s and *M*s on their identification.

Throughout this book, I occasionally use terms that I personally would prefer to phase out but which are useful in explaining concepts, illustrating my interpretation at the time, or reflecting how society currently operates.

For example, I occasionally refer to women's/girls' clothes and men's/boys' clothes. I believe anyone can wear whatever clothes they want. Clothes shouldn't have a gender, in my opinion. To quote comedian Eddie Izzard when confronted about the clothes he was wearing during an interview: "They're not women's clothes or men's clothes, they're my clothes. I bought them."

However, our world still separates clothes by gender in most stores, and, for me, as a trans person growing up and discovering himself, those distinctions were extraordinarily significant. It's important to remember that for binary trans people, certain gender markers can be very validating. While attempts to make everything gender neutral are generally the most inclusive routes, such neutral assumptions can sometimes be disappointing to the point of being offensive for binary trans people who have worked so hard to be seen as their authentic gender.

Finally, one last disclaimer: This book will discuss dysphoria, sexuality, and body image at length. There are also brief mentions of sexual harassment, mental illness, substance use, and suicide. There is nothing too graphic or intense, but I know from personal experience that anything about these topics can be triggering at certain times. Do whatever you need to do to feel okay while reading. Take breaks, go for a walk, call a friend, eat some chocolate, or maybe even don't read it. That's totally okay. My feelings won't be hurt at all.

Transgender vs. Transsexual

While *transgender* is the current accepted term for binary and nonbinary trans people alike, this wasn't always the case. The term *transsexual* predates *transgender* by a few decades and was first used by medical professionals Drs. Magnus Hirschfeld and David Oliver Cauldwell. It referred to people who were assigned one gender at birth but affirm their gender to be another, and who desire medical intervention to align their innate sense of gender with their physical body.

Transgender first came into use in the 1970s and was popularized in a few forms by various people, but most notably by cross-dresser Virginia Prince as a way to distinguish herself from transsexual people—in other words, from those who, unlike her, sought some form of medical transition. Through the 1980s, the term continued to be used in reference to people whose gender identities differed from their assigned genders but who did not desire any form of medical transition. Sometimes the term was used in an intentionally queer political context to subvert the very idea of gender. By the mid-'90s, *transgender* was being used as an umbrella term for any type of gender expression or identity that differed from one's assigned gender or from typical notions of gender, including, in some circles, transsexual people. This frustrated many transsexual people who were not gender-nonconforming and saw their legal and medical needs (such as access to hormones and surgeries) as distinct from those of transgender people.

Over the years, *transgender* has remained strong as an umbrella term and *transsexual* has fallen further out of use—due in part to its clinical origins, which some wish to shake off. Many younger binary trans men and trans women on hormones who would have self-identified as transsexual forty years ago now call themselves transgender. Yet for older generations, using the term *transsexual* remains an important distinction. For them, transgender implies a nonconformity of gender that they don't express as binary men and women.

If you're worried about offending someone in either direction, a safe option is to use the abbreviation *trans*. Personally, I find *trans* to be less awkward than *transgender* or *transsexual* anyway—not to mention it takes up fewer characters if I'm tweeting.

introduction

This book began as a zine I wrote titled *Free My Nipples: The Story of My Chest*. It was meant to be a lighthearted gift to say thank you to people who donated to support my top surgery. I thought it would be a quick essay about my relationship to my chest that I could whip up in a couple of weeks and send out to donors before the fund-raiser even ended.

How wrong I was.

As I began to write, I realized just how much I needed to get off my chest—pun one thousand percent intended. Beyond the obvious physical protrusions, there were a lot of memories and emotions I hadn't dealt with, things I had never shared through this lens before.

I generally spend a lot of time thinking about my gender. I mean, when you're both trans and prone to overanalysis, it kind of comes with the territory. I also make YouTube videos and give talks on transgender topics and am constantly speaking with other trans and nonbinary people about their experiences. But the act of narrowing my own thoughts down to one specific topic ended up bursting open a well of memories.

Words flowed with a raw mellifluence unlike any I'd experienced before, but there were so many of them, so much I wanted to explore. I needed the story to be complete, and I needed to do it justice.

The zine ended up taking many more months and about seventy more pages than originally anticipated to tell my story as I wanted to— and even then I wasn't entirely satisfied. Though it got a wonderful reception from my fund-raiser donors and other people I showed it to, the story felt incomplete. I had opened up an old wound that I'd been ignoring, and I needed to spend some time caring for it before it could begin to heal and close up again.

While I puzzled over how I could make this story feel complete, I continued to hear from people, trans and cisgender alike, about how much the zine had moved them. I started thinking that maybe I could do more with this little zine, to help more people understand the transgender experience or find resonance in a familiar but too often untold story. So I decided to expand the zine into a full-length book, reaching beyond my chest to bare my full body, mind, and soul.

That said, I'm a bit nervous to be publishing so many details about my life and my innermost thoughts. A lot of people are under the impression that I already share everything with the internet because I make videos that are, ostensibly, very personal. Maybe discussing my sexuality and the medical procedures I've undergone *is* more personal than the videos in which I've set waffle irons on fire, but the fact of the matter is that even when broaching the more personal topics, I have very sturdy, deliberate boundaries that I established online from the very beginning. While I share the occasional personal anecdote, the vast majority of what I discuss online is hypothetical or academic in nature. When asked to publicly discuss sex or dating, for example, I share facts as well as experiences I've heard from others generalized into anonymity. This book, on the other hand, is indisputably about me. The fences do remain, albeit lowered at times. I've carefully chosen what I'm sharing and how I'm sharing it. It's all been meticulously considered and, importantly, is all being told in my own words, on my own terms.

• • •

I do remain slightly wary, however, because telling my story necessitates telling *other* people's stories as well, the stories of those who have entered and exited my life over the years. To avoid spreading unkind or revealing stories about people, skewed in their telling by my memory, I've endeavored to keep this book as introspective as possible—only bringing other people into the story when I absolutely must. Even then, names have been obscured or changed, and some identifying characteristics have been altered as well.

In addition to protecting the privacy of people in my life whom I care about, it makes sense that this would be an introspective story because the process of sorting out your gender can be a very solitary, internal one. For much of my life, I felt much more alone than the loving family and friends surrounding me would lead outsiders to believe I could possibly be.

Relationships with other people might affect a transgender person's path of transition or discovery, but they do not affect who the person is. There is no parent or partner who misstepped in some way to "make" me transgender. It was always, only, about who I am and who I can be. Nothing more.

In reflecting on my past and working to fact-check what I can, I read through over five dozen physical journals dating back to age six and hundreds more digital diaries. I don't have *all* the journals I once recorded in my possession anymore. Some are lost—lost in moves, left behind on trips, misplaced during Hurricane Sandy. But I pored over the ones I still had and have scanned many of them to share with you. They reflect everything from my passing interests and the banality of my middle-class suburban life to searing struggles with my innermost demons. They also caused me a fair number of cringe attacks to read through as an adult. I was a terribly obnoxious child. And preteen. And teenager. Those tendencies mostly mellowed out by college, but then the entries became unbearably sad.

It's very possible that when I look back on this book in a few years' time, I might feel a similar embarrassment—at my naivety, at my style of writing, at opinions I no longer share. I mean, some of the earliest videos I posted on YouTube are downright mortifying. Heck, there are videos I made just last year that I can't bear to watch. In the constant cycle of content creation there is a pressure to be consistently posting. I realized early on that if I held myself to a standard of perfection for every video, I would never complete any of them. I have had to learn to let things go. I tell myself that my videos, my writing, anything I'm producing is not just the content itself but also a snapshot of who I was in that moment. It's frozen in time, a portrait of all my beliefs, interests, shortcomings, and bad haircuts from that exact moment.

•   •   •

Just as I could never be anyone but myself, I don't think I could ever tell anyone else's story as well as I can my own. My story is not the *whole* story of the transgender community. I strongly believe the individual is universal, but I also know that every transgender person's experiences are different, so alongside my story in this book you'll find sidebars filling in the gaps, providing peeks at other people's experiences, and giving newcomers a starter pack of transgender knowledge.

These are meant to be jumping-off points to guide your further learning and contextualize my story, not an exhaustive summary of every issue affecting transgender people. The information comes from years of casual research and lived experiences (my own as well as those shared with me by other trans people), and has been fact-checked against up-to-date sources. Despite that, it's important to note that I am not a doctor. Nothing I say in this book should be taken as medical or legal advice. You can view sources and suggestions for further learning at the back of the book. I especially recommend the resources on trans women and nonbinary people's experiences because, while I occasionally touch on more general issues, this book is written first and foremost from my own perspective—that of a white, able-bodied trans man.

While I stand by the way I've presented information here, this field is complex, with many nuanced distinctions of opinion, and is always rapidly evolving. I strove to provide historical context and to leave room for growth, but it's very possible certain language will be outdated by the time you read this. For that reason, I especially encourage you to peruse the digital resources listed at the back, which will be updated much more frequently than the printed ones.

• • •

In addition to peeks at my personal journals, I've also elected to include numerous photos of myself growing up. Sharing pre-transition photos is not something that most trans people are comfortable with and is never something that should be expected of us. Seeing those pictures can often bring up a lot of emotions about a difficult time in our lives or cause dysphoria about how we see ourselves now versus how we physically looked then. Depending on the situation in which the photos are shared, they can also open a trans person up to harassment or humiliation. In a broader sense, the sharing of before-and-after photos contributes to society's fixation on the visible transformation of our bodies, implying that gender is merely physical; that transition is a linear, one-step process; and that our trans identities are the sum of our beings.

While trans people fought for many years against featuring "before" photos in articles or other media coverage, there has recently been a reemergence of sharing before-and-after photos—not from tabloids or daytime talk shows but from trans people themselves. Younger generations especially are posting lots of photos on social media showing their transition timelines, childhood and pre-transition photos often included. I've spoken with older trans people who are flummoxed by this behavior, concerned that it could lead cis people to believe they are entitled to see these photos from any trans person they encounter.

Having posted these types of photos myself in the past, I've spent some time trying to reconcile my reasons for doing so with my desire to protect my own and other trans people's privacy. In my case, the ability to watch transition timeline slideshows on YouTube gave me the confidence to transition. I was worried I would never be read as male, even with hormones. When I saw trans guys who were many years into their transitions, I would often think, "Well, he probably looked that masculine before he transitioned. There's no hope for me." Seeing people in those timeline videos who had maybe presented just as feminine as I once did grow into themselves and into the kind of guys I desperately wanted to look like gave me hope.

I also think there's a certain amount of agency younger trans people are hoping to achieve in posting these photos on their own terms. Unlike earlier generations, most of us had social media accounts documenting our lives before we came out and started to transition (some have even grown up with their parents posting photos of them since birth without their consent). It's much more challenging to wipe our histories from the public record than it used to be. Electing to share pre-transition photos ourselves is a way of owning something we may feel a lack of control over.

I do share the concern that this popular trend could lead cis people to feel entitled to see our pre-transition photos, and I do think those of us with public social media accounts should exercise a little more forethought and discretion when sharing photos (or any personal information). However, I also believe transition timeline photos are useful tools within the trans community, and I hope that cis people receive them graciously, seeing the variance among trans people and how there is no typical path of transition. While I become more and more wary about sharing my childhood photos as I get older, it's for these final reasons that I ultimately chose to share them in this book. Plus, I was a dang cute kid.

And now, as I consciously stall the inevitable of your reading so many intimate details of my life, I'd like to address one final item: the title. Much of its meaning will be illuminated throughout the story, and perhaps you'll come to more conclusions or revelations about it than I even intended, but here are a few bonus thoughts.

Growing up as someone who felt different but didn't have the words to describe or understand that difference, I was drawn to labels that could define me in other ways. I liked being a part of clubs and wearing uniforms. I liked taking personality tests in magazines—anything that could mark me as something definitive and provide indicators about the type of person I was.

SPELLING PRACTICE, AGE SIX.

Yet despite that desire, my natural personality traits often resisted sorting. When we took a test to see if we were more right- or left-brained in fifth grade, my results were straight down the middle. The same thing happened with the introvert-versus-extrovert test. I even do many things as well with my left hand as I do with my more dominant right hand. I believe a part of my long-held resistance to accepting the label of bisexual was not wanting yet *another* part of me to be right in the middle.

Labels can be so important to understanding who you are, finding a community of people with similar experiences, and gaining access to resources you might need. But they can also be oppressive and limiting, like when they come attached to laws restricting rights or when they leave no room for growth or variance between binary options.

I was sorted into the female category at birth, and that defined the name I was given, the clothes I was dressed in, the way I was spoken to, the roles I was supposed to have in life, the amount I would get paid when I grew up, and so much more.

Like so many others, I've resisted and fought to redefine the limitations of some labels that have been put on me, but I've also chosen to change some of those labels. I've found new ones that better reflect who I've been all along, or sometimes who I've grown to be. I've re-sorted myself.

I've heard from many cisgender people how the increased visibility of trans people has not only caused them to examine and unlearn their own prejudices but also liberated them from rigid gender statutes. They've considered re-sorting themselves too, not necessarily with regard to their gender but perhaps in other aspects of their lives that they were sorted into. The growing awareness (and more-slowly-but-still-growing acceptance) of gender fluidity is allowing more and more people to question their own relationship to gender and resist some of the societally defined requirements of that gender. Even when that questioning keeps them solidly in Camp Cisgender, many feel free to experiment with how they express themselves or fight back against defined roles and stereotypes.

We have a long way to go in the fight for acceptance of people who are different from those in power, but the only way forward is to keep resisting, keep challenging, and keep telling our stories. Our humanity is our common denominator, but prejudice can make people forget that.

So, in the same way I realized that by homing in on one specific topic I suddenly had so much more tell, I offer this one story of one person. There are a zillion stories to tell, but I hope that in the laser focus of my story, you will find similarities to your own, challenges to your assumptions, and that thread of humanity that unites us all.

CHAPTER ONE

sorted

It's a testament to the all-consuming pervasiveness of gender in our society that the very first thing we do to babies is sort them into genders. In fact, for most, it's the very first words ever spoken about you. When you're born, the doctor or midwife shouts, "It's a boy!" or "It's a girl!" and from color-coded hospital hats to the balloons greeting your arrival in the recovery room, your life is predetermined.

My parents didn't want to know the genders of me or my brother before we were born. With my older brother, my mom was pretty certain throughout her pregnancy she'd be having a boy, but when he finally arrived after an agonizing thirty-six-hour labor, she didn't ask about his gender. The very first thing she said as my newborn brother was swaddled into a blanket was, "Is the cafeteria still serving food?"

My mom, God love her, knew that getting a solid meal was way more important for her capacity of being a good mother than knowing whatever gender her baby apparently was.

ME AND MOM

Still remembering how hungry she'd been after my brother's birth, she took no chances with my labor. When her water broke on a sunny Kalamazoo afternoon about a week before my expected due date of Mother's Day, she was in the kitchen fixing lunch for herself and my brother.

"Austin," she calmly told the two-year-old as she chopped watermelon, "we're going to have to go to the hospital soon to have a baby, but first we're going to finish lunch."

She finished with the watermelon, spread mayonnaise on their bologna sandwiches, and they sat down to enjoy their lunch while my dad sped home from work to drive them to the hospital.

As determined as she was to get one last good meal in, by the time my dad arrived, my mom admitted that things seemed to be moving fast. The three of them headed to the hospital as my mom's contractions came closer together.

There had been a whole list of friends and family members who volunteered to watch Austin during the birth, but my unexpectedly early arrival on a Friday afternoon meant nearly everyone on the list was busy. The person able to get there the quickest was my dad's mom, coming from a two-and-a-half-hour drive away.

So Austin joined them in the hospital room, where the nurses turned on the TV to pass the time and my mom did her best to hide her pain from the toddler—even after being told things had moved too fast for her to receive an epidural.

Her labor continued to progress rapidly, and eventually Austin was taken out to the hallway by a nurse and given some toys to play with. Shortly thereafter, our grandma arrived to keep him company, and within the hour my mom had started pushing.

The whole labor lasted less than five hours and went so quickly that the nurses didn't even pause to switch off the TV. I entered the world at 5:25 P.M. on May 4, 1990, to the static murmurings of *The Oprah Winfrey Show* playing in the corner.

My mom says that throughout the entire pregnancy she wasn't sure what gender I was. While she'd had a preternatural knowing that her first child would be a boy, she insists she never had a clue about me. She was so stumped, she even considered asking the doctor at her ultrasound appointment, despite her and my dad agreeing they didn't want to know. (She didn't, though.)

It wasn't until she was admitted to the hospital to give birth that she finally got the definitive sense I was going to be a girl—at least as far as we were all concerned for the time being.

Assigned Female at Birth?

Assigned Female at Birth, or AFAB, and Assigned Male at Birth, or AMAB, are the preferred terms to use instead of "biological male/female," "born male/female," "natal male/female," "male/female bodied," "genetic male/female," etc.

When you break it down, it's a lot more difficult to distinguish what a male or female body actually is, or what it means to be "biologically male/female" or "born male/female." Is a male body one with a penis? What about men who lose their penises due to injury or illness—are they no longer men? Does "biologically female" mean someone with XX chromosomes? Not to be presumptive, but have *you* had your chromosomes analyzed? Most people haven't. And what about the one in one hundred intersex people in the world? Many of their chromosomes, reproductive organs, or external anatomy don't match with our cultural expectations of male or female. There are countless examples of men and women not lining up with the typical definitions of male and female—even before we get into discussions of transgender people.

The terms *AMAB* and *AFAB* are also useful because lots of trans people bristle at the phrase "born male/female." We were born as ourselves. Just because we didn't realize we were the gender we are right at the beginning doesn't mean we weren't this gender all along. Additionally, the "assigned" part of these terms emphasizes that we were sorted into a particular gender before we had any say in the matter.

One last note: Knowing this accepted term, some people might be tempted to ask trans or nonbinary people what sex they were assigned at birth. This can quickly turn into a faux-polite way of asking what's in their pants. Consider why you need to know. Even when you're using the "accepted" language, your question can still be rude and invasive.

Prior to having kids, my mom had promised herself she would raise her children as free from the binds of gender stereotypes as possible. She'd grown up with the strict gender roles of the 1960s and '70s and was fed up. Especially if she had daughters, she wanted to make sure they knew they could be tough and self-reliant, and that they had more choices for their futures than just being wives and mothers.

So when I showed signs of boyishness even from the beginning, it wasn't immediately a cause for alarm. My mom was happy to see that I was an independent spirit. Her first inkling that maybe there was something more going on, however, took place when I was just over two years old.

We were swimming in a kiddie pool she'd set up for us in the backyard on a hot summer's day when my brother Austin got out to pee in the bushes. I toddled behind him, trying to do the same. When it wasn't working, I got upset and my mom gently explained how girls' bodies are shaped differently than boys'.

This in and of itself is not a unique moment. All toddlers have to be taught at some point that girls' and boys' bodies are different. And I think plenty of toddlers would be upset to find out they can't do something as cool as peeing in the bushes like their big brother can. But I wasn't just throwing a normal toddler tantrum, my mom says. I was telling her, very soberly, that it was wrong. It was wrong that my body couldn't do that.

She tells me now that she had a brief moment of thinking maybe there was something more to my words then, but again, I was a toddler, and toddlers say all kinds of weird things. So she let it go.

But moments like that kept happening. My mom, a talented seamstress, often sewed my brother and me custom outfits, especially for special occasions. One Easter when I was three, she made me what she thought was an absolutely darling dress (it even had pockets!), but when she dressed me in it and pulled out the family's camera to mark the occasion, I gave her the dirtiest look she'd ever seen. She was taken aback, but got the message loud and clear. "I'm not spending any more time on dresses this girl isn't going to enjoy," she thought to herself.

Easter 1994.

So instead, she sewed me vests. A themed vest for every holiday. Little waistcoats with snaps down the front and printed designs all over them for Easter, Valentine's Day, and Fourth of July. Unlike the dresses, I *loved* those vests. I even made her remake a couple of them when I outgrew them on subsequent holidays.

My Fourth of July vest.

The vests weren't the only part of my wardrobe that changed when I started preschool, around the time I started throwing a fit anytime my parents tried to put anything remotely girly on me. Gone were the pink dresses and ruffled blouses. From three years old onward, my day-to-day wardrobe consisted of my brother's hand-me-downs and clothing from the discount rack at Bugle Boy.

While my parents allowed me to run around in ripped blue jeans and polo shirts on most days and even to school, there were still a few occasions on which I was made to dress like a girl, namely school picture days, piano recitals, and church.

One of them would come at me with a dress bunched up in their hands, trying to force the neck hole over my head as I screamed bloody murder. The whole affair would last several exasperating minutes and end up with either me in some type of semi-androgynous wardrobe compromise or me wearing the dress paired with a tomato-red face from tears and embarrassment.

Neither outcome made me too happy. Even at a young age, I knew that the wardrobe compromises, which usually consisted of shorts or pants instead of a dress and some type of shirt with flowers on it, looked dopey and out-of-place. Meanwhile, wearing a dress made me intolerably uncomfortable. I felt so naked wearing only one article of clothing over my underpants and extremely, *extremely* embarrassed. I felt the eyes of everyone on me wherever we went. Surely someone would notice how wrong I looked, how wrong it had been of my parents to make me dress this way. But of course no one ever did. Instead, strangers usually told me I looked "sweet" or "cute as a button." Until I scowled at them.

On one memorable occasion, I placidly told my mom that I wished God didn't exist so I wouldn't have to wear dresses to church. She was, understandably, shocked to hear her three-year-old sharing such aggressive atheist convictions, and I'm sure said something about how God was wonderful and we should be grateful to him. I don't really remember what she said. I just remember realizing that I had offended her, so I switched course: "Well, then I just wish church didn't exist."

Unlike church, which I was probably never going to enjoy as a toddler, there were many other events in my young life that I think I would've looked forward to much more if they hadn't come with a dress code I couldn't wiggle out of.

A good example is the Daddy–Daughter Dance when I was seven years old. I was excited to attend a special night for just me and my dad, but resolutely told my mom I wouldn't wear a dress. I wanted to wear a suit. Knowing me, I probably even tried to convince her that the point of the dance was to dress like our dads. To compromise, my mom sewed me a bright blue skirt suit, complete with big gold buttons and shoulder pads. I looked like a baby Hillary Clinton.

R_{EADY} TO HIT THE DANCE FLOOR...
OR RUN FOR OFFICE.

Like the holiday-themed vests and so many other questionable fashion decisions of my childhood, my insistence on wearing a suit to the Daddy–Daughter Dance didn't faze my mom. Maybe if I had been growing up now, with so much more awareness of and resources for gender-nonconforming kids, she would have thought to question some of my behavior. But back then, she just thought I was being myself— unabashed, independent, tomboyish, and a bit of a weirdo.

• • •

In many ways, these early revelations about my gender may make it seem like I experienced the most stereotypical transgender narrative— the kind you often hear on daytime talk shows: *I knew from my earliest memories that I should've been born a boy. I felt trapped in my own body. My life was nothing but misery until I transitioned.*

This is not one of those stories. While there may be some incidents my family and I can point to in hindsight as clues about my gender, none of it was so clear when it was happening. Yes, I felt different growing up, but as far as I knew it could've been just as much because I was a total dork as it was because I was kind of boyish. Maybe I looked at the boys in my class with envy, but I never felt for certain like I *should* have been one of them, only that I sometimes *wished* I were.

This is not a story about a lifetime of hating my body or knowing with absolute certainty that I needed to transition. Those stories exist and those people's experiences are valid, but they aren't everyone's. Some people don't have any inkling that they're transgender until later in life. Some people have a much more fluid or back-and-forth relationship with their gender. Some people are very much aware of who they are, but have no desire to physically transition. All of these and more are true, valid transgender experiences.

If you've met one transgender person, you've met one transgender person and that is your basis for transgender fact until you meet another, with a possibly different story. The trouble is, many people haven't even met one transgender person. So that leaves much of the world, trans and cis alike, believing the few stereotypical narratives about transgender people we see in the media, from an overemphasis on medical procedures and an obsession with shocking before-and-after photos to even more damaging language about us, especially transgender women, being villainous figures out to trick poor, unassuming cisgender people. Transgender people are rarely shown in a positive, accurate light or as having rich lives outside of being transgender.

For cisgender people, the danger of hearing only the same narratives is not affording transgender people with different stories the dignity of respecting a most basic part of their being. But for transgender people, the danger of hearing only the same narratives, when theirs differs from those, is not knowing there's anyone else like them in the world—not knowing they could be transgender, and not knowing what they can do to ease the feelings of gender dysphoria they may be experiencing.

That was the case for me. My story is not the one the media was peddling in the '90s, which consisted mostly of hyper-sensationalized and demeaning representations of trans women and almost none of trans men, especially not queer trans men. So I believed myself to be all alone in my struggle. While media coverage of transgender people has improved by leaps and bounds in recent years (in large part thanks to the agency social media platforms provide trans people themselves), it has only underscored just how many different ways there are to be trans and how important it is that those stories are told. So here's one story. It might not be the most unusual or the most incredible, but it's mine.

CHAPTER TWO

a hairy situation

My mom was a hairdresser by trade. When we lived in Michigan, she used to go to work at Toni & Guy most days while friends or relatives babysat me and my brother. But when I was two and a half, my dad's job as a salesman moved us from Michigan down to Texas, where my mom became an independent, freelance hairdresser. Or at least that's probably how we'd describe it in today's gig economy.

What it really meant is that people would come over to our house, or sometimes we'd go over to theirs, and my mom would cut and style their hair right there in the kitchen. Many of our bathroom towels were stained with splotches of bleach and hair dye, and to this day, the number-one scent I remember from my childhood is the ammonium thioglycolate used for perming hair.

Sometimes after a client had left, before she had swept their hair off our yellow laminate floor, my mom would plop a booster seat on the kitchen chair the client had just vacated and cut my brother's and my hair in turn.

I loved the feeling of her hands running along my scalp and of the water from the squirt bottle cooling my warm head to prep my hair for trimming. I found the squirt bottle endlessly funny, and sometimes my mom would spray it in my face to make me laugh.

What I didn't love were the actual haircuts. While my brother got regular crew cuts, my mom pushing his head forward to run the buzzer across the back of his head, all I got were trims to my bangs and long hair.

Mid-haircut at our home hair
salon, circa 1993.

Around kindergarten I started speaking up and asking for shorter hair. I wanted a boy's haircut, like my brother and the boys in my class had.

"But if you dress like a boy and you have a haircut like a boy, how will anyone know you're not a boy?"

I stared at my mom, asking this of me as we sat on the picnic table in our backyard, after this conversation had been brought up for what felt to me like the hundredth time.

I didn't understand what she was saying. Why would people need to know I'm not a boy? Did she mean that if I got a boy's haircut, I'd have to wear girlier clothes every day?

That latter possibility scared me enough to stop fighting so hard about the hair. In the end, I was given a bob haircut that slowly turned ever more into a bowl cut as we negotiated inches off of it every few months. It never went above the earlobes, though. That was my mom's rule.

While there might have been a lot of little girls in other parts of the country with the short, gender-neutral hairstyles that were in style at the time, there weren't any of them in the suburbs of Dallas, Texas. Southern women in general tend to emphasize their femininity and get dressed up more for lesser occasions than their Northern counterparts, but in the Dallas area it's on hyperdrive. Big hair, heavy makeup, lots of jewelry—and that's just to run to the grocery store.

The gendered wardrobes and expectations in Texas are so extreme that a professor of mine at NYU once noted how some people perform their gender so intensely it becomes comical, almost like they're performing drag of their own gender. Her example of the number-one place to view this phenomenon? Dallas–Fort Worth International Airport, which just so happens to be partially located in the town where I grew up. I say partially because it's so big that its seventeen thousand acres actually expand across four cities. But the point remains that, at least according to that professor, I was brought up in one of the most hyper-gender-obsessed towns in the entire country. So from a young age, I was exposed to pretty extreme gender presentations, and I had no examples in my life of other boyish girls or masculine women.

With my thick blond hair chopped crudely at my earlobes, I knew I looked ridiculous, and I eventually resigned myself to never winning the fight for a crew cut. So around second grade I decided to grow my hair out, thinking that maybe if I could pull it back into a ponytail, I would look more like a boy.

I didn't look anything like a boy, of course, but I sometimes thought I could pass as one better than I really could. I would try to style my bangs in the different ways that were fashionable for boys at the time—gelling them into a little flattened swoop at the front or growing them out and combing them over so they'd fall into my face just on one side. I thought I looked just as cool as Leo DiCaprio or Jonathan Taylor

Thomas, but of course no one ever noticed my efforts. It just looked like I had messy hair.

THINKING MY HAIR LOOKED SUPER COOL.

For most of elementary school, I existed in this weird middle ground. I knew I was a girl, of course, and if the teacher asked us to line up girls and boys, I'd go with the girls. I knew I was a sister, a daughter, a granddaughter. I attended Girl Scouts. I used the girls' bathroom.

(I DID ONCE QUESTION WHETHER I SHOULD BE IN THE GIRLS' RESTROOM AFTER MY JURASSIC PARK HIGH-TOPS VISIBLE UNDER THE STALL CAUSED A GIRL IN MY FIRST-GRADE CLASS TO SCREAM THERE WAS A BOY IN THE BATHROOM. MY FEET WEREN'T EVEN FACING TOWARD THE TOILET! IT WAS SIMPLY BECAUSE MY SHOES DIDN'T MATCH WHAT SHE THOUGHT GIRLS WERE ALLOWED TO WEAR.)

But socially, when our class would divide between boys and girls for recess, I automatically went with the boys.

The girls would always ask me to join them as we walked out toward the playground. They'd try to strike deals with me. "Just come play with us today." "How about on Wednesdays you play with the girls?" They knew, even if I didn't, that I was supposed to be with them. In my head, though, I thought they were flirting with me. I'd be coy in my responses and then run off to the soccer field with the boys.

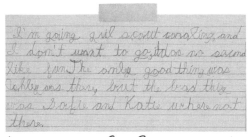

I'm going girl scout wraling and I don't want to go tdoo no second like fun. The only good thing was Ashley was thre, but the bad thing was Sofie and Katie where not there.

I SKIPPED OUT OF GIRL SCOUT MEETINGS SO REGULARLY AS A SIX—YEAR—OLD THAT MY TROOP LEADER NICKNAMED ME "THE COMEBACK KID."

I *was* aware that I wasn't quite a boy. I knew I was different enough that new people needed to be told what to do with me. When a new boy arrived on the first day of second grade, whose held-back status and silver loop ear piercing automatically coronated him as the new leader of the boys, I went straight up to him at recess and said, "Hey, just so you know, I play with the boys. Not the girls. I'm one of you." He said, "Cool," and that's how it was for the rest of second grade.

In November of that year, our teacher told us we'd be putting on a Thanksgiving play for our families. It followed the usual mythical whitewashing of the holiday that most children in America are taught: The Pilgrims traded with the Native Americans, Squanto taught the Pilgrims how to grow corn, and they celebrated their friendship by feasting together on turkey, cans of cranberry sauce, and a cornucopia, whatever that was.

To cast the show, our teacher had us each write down the three characters we most wanted to play and then she'd assign them based on our preferences.

I wrote down all three Pilgrims with speaking roles, regardless of gender.

I don't know why I was so fascinated by the Pilgrims at that age. It could have to do with the fact that my mom was really into Native

American culture and, in my seven-year-old brain, I thought anything she was into must inherently be girly, ergo I had to like the opposite. Or maybe I just liked their hats. I probably just liked their hats.

Whatever the reason, I was absolutely crushed when my teacher announced the cast list and I was to play an unnamed Native American. I had written down three Pilgrims as my choices, and she'd ignored all of them!

Luckily, I overheard the boy who'd been cast as Edward Winslow freaking out over how many lines he would have to perform. I asked him if he wanted to trade and he heartily agreed. Our teacher had told us ahead of time that we could trade roles so long as both students were in agreement, and we definitely were, so there was nothing she could do about it.

Throughout the days of preparing for the play, my teacher made a few comments about how we could rename the character "Elizabeth Winslow" if I wanted, but I would just stare at her blankly and go back to cutting out my construction-paper buckle hat.

I had some sense that she thought it was weird that I wanted to play a male character, but I was still salty about her ignoring all my top choices and giving me a role with so few lines when I was *clearly* one of the best readers in the class. I

Edward Winslow

wanted her to know that my choice to play Edward Winslow had more to do with all of that than with wanting to play a boy—and I tried to tell myself that too. Deep down, I was thrilled to be playing a boy outright, but on the surface I was embarrassed of what people might think of me.

When the day of the play arrived, I

woke up sick. I told my mom I couldn't go to school. She told me to think about how let down everyone would be if I didn't show up to perform in the play we'd been rehearsing. I mulled it over for a bit, weighing the consequences of being embarrassed by everyone's families seeing me playing a boy and my excitement at actually playing a boy. I also took some time to consider whether I was really sick. I *felt* sick. My face was hot and my stomach hurt. Ultimately, I decided that after everything I had pulled to get this role, I couldn't back out now. The show must go on.

I distinctly remember still feeling sick to my stomach when the play started and being disappointed in myself for not acting to my fullest, but despite that, I still got a chuckle from the audience after one of my lines. That chuckle, and the whole exercise of memorizing lines and then acting them out to a crowd, captivated me. I wanted to do it again. I wanted to perform in more shows, and maybe, if I played my cards right, I'd even get to play a boy again.

• • •

So my mom signed me up for acting classes at the local rec center, where I was promptly cast as Gladys Herdman, the tomboy ragamuffin in *The Best Christmas Pageant Ever*. Throughout the whole production, from the rehearsals to closing night, I was in heaven—and not just because Gladys spends half of the show dressed as the Angel of the Lord for the Nativity play within the play.

After flexing my acting chops with such roles as "Younger Sister" and "Barbara Faulters," I was ready to take on my most challenging role yet: convincing my acting teacher to cast me in a boy's role in the next play. It probably had more to do with the fact that there's always a surplus ratio of girls to girl roles in theater than it did with my actual talent, but in the next play, *Saving the Old Homestead*, I was cast as scrupulous attorney Lawyer I. M. True, a definitively male role. I got to pin my hair up into a hat, draw on a mustache with my mom's eyebrow pencils, and even wear a suit.

At the first dress rehearsal, I was admiring my costume in the mirror in the bathroom that served as the rec center's makeshift dressing room when the lead actor, a boy my age who went to an elementary school the next town over, came up behind me.

"You did that wrong," he said, pointing at my brother's hand-me-down clip-on tie hanging from the collar of my white oxford shirt.

"Huh?" I sputtered, equally disappointed I had failed at doing a boy thing correctly and suddenly nervous that this cool boy was talking to me. He was an amazing actor and had perfect fluffy Shawn Hunter hair. I didn't know if I had a crush on him or if I simply wanted to be him, but I do know that as he reached over and pushed the corners of the false tie knot under my collar, my face got warm, my breath caught in my throat, and it took the full capacity of my brain to stammer out a "Thank you."

CHAPTER THREE

transitioning for the first time

Sort of

I suppose I always liked dressing up and putting on costumes, so long as I didn't have to dress like a girl. When I went over to friends' houses and they pulled out their dress-up boxes, I would make a bee-line for the cowboy costume, the doctor's jacket, or their dad's old ties. Anything not to have to don their My Size Barbie princess dress.

Big #2   10 5-99
A present I do not want
is a barbie. Eww.
Disgusting

For Halloween, my mom would usually sew my brother and me a costume for whatever we wanted to be that year and then get out her old tackle box of stage makeup from her cosmetology school days and paint our faces to match. Big white puffs of powder for the ghost costume, a drawn-on widow's peak and some fake blood when my brother was a vampire, a spot around my eye to go with my *101 Dalmatians* outfit.

Every now and then we'd buy our costumes from the store, like in 1995 when I saw a shelf of Power Rangers costumes while we were grocery shopping and I *had* to have one. I immediately spotted the lone blue Power Ranger suit under an overflowing stack of the popular red and pink ones. No one wanted to be Billy, the nerdy blue Power Ranger, and that was part of why I loved him.

I loved him so much that I had named the doll I got for my birthday that year after him and, when my cousins tried to play a prank on our second cousin who we were all meeting for the first time at a family reunion by switching our names around, I ruined it by insisting my name was Billy. My brother tried to reasonably explain that I needed to lie and say my name was Brooke, like our dog, because it was a girl's name and I was a girl. I didn't understand why, if we were playing pretend anyway, I couldn't just be Billy. But as I started digging under all the red Tommy and pink Kimberly costumes for Billy's blue one, I hesitated. Mom would never let me dress up as a boy Power Ranger. Austin would make fun of me for it, just like he had after the family reunion. I sighed and picked out one of the pink Kimberly costumes, holding it up to my mom.

She looked surprised. "You're sure this is the one you want?"

I nodded, thinking that being a Power Ranger at all was cool enough. I could suck up wearing pink if I at least got to be a Power Ranger while I did it.

I had never dressed explicitly as a boy for Halloween. I wore boy*ish* costumes like monsters and grim reapers, but somehow the thought that I wouldn't be allowed to be a boy, even just for Halloween, stuck with me.

My brother rocking the Scarecrow costume I would wear several years later. Apparently, looking at the camera wasn't cool that year.

In black and white, I could have been the blue Power Ranger and you'd never know!

By the time I was in fourth grade, the Harry Potter books had recently been published in the United States, and Potter frenzy was at an all-time high. I had gotten the first book from the Scholastic Book Fair and, after spending a week drudging through the first chapter of backstory, I was hooked.

One of my favorite things about Harry Potter was how, at the beginning of the series, he's just this average, if sometimes weird, kid at a normal school, but then on his eleventh birthday, a giant of a man comes out of nowhere and whisks him away to a magical world that he was meant to be a part of his whole life.

I used to dream about that happening to me, that one day Professor McGonagall or Sirius Black would show up at my front door to take me away to the Wizarding World. It was my destiny and they needed me, but . . . oh . . . they'd have to use magic to disguise me as a boy. Would that be okay?

Even escapist dreams aside, there was a lot to love about Harry Potter. It took place at a boarding school, for starters, something entirely foreign and enticing to me at the time, and that boarding school was filled with eccentric teachers, delicious food, and classes far more interesting than Math and Grammar. It was funny too, and occasionally gross or scary—three of my favorite things at that age.

So of course when Halloween rolled around, the first one at our new house in a nicer neighborhood, I wanted to dress up as someone from the Harry Potter books. I'd seen on the news that pretty much every kid in the world was dressing up as the boy wizard himself. Appalled by the idea that I would have the same costume as anyone I ran into while trick-or-treating, I decided to be unique and go as Hermione.

This was several years before the movies came out, so interpretations of what Hogwarts students wore still varied widely, especially in the United States, where we didn't have the same concept of school uniforms with striped ties and sweaters that they do in the United Kingdom. So my mom and I had picked out various fabrics from the store—solid black silk and gray chiffon with shimmering purple spiderwebs. My mom sewed them into a cape and cloak, paired with a matching black witch's hat.

I had been so excited throughout the whole process, but when I put the costume on a few hours before trick-or-treating, I hated how it looked. The cloak was too short, the sparkling fabric too girly. We'd teased my hair a bit to give it Hermione's trademark bushy look and I thought it made me look stupid.

I was panicking, tears in my eyes, because I was supposed to go trick-or-treating with the cool girls in our new neighborhood and I was too mortified to be seen wearing this costume.

SHOWING OFF MY *Wizard of Oz* POP-UP BOOK
WHILE SPORTING SOME QUIDDITCH-THEMED OVERALLS.
I WAS *THAT* COOL.

Fortunately, we still had a box of all the costumes my mom had sewed for Halloween over the years. The only one that still fit me, and barely, was the Scarecrow costume my brother had worn when he was six. Before Harry Potter came along, the Wizard of Oz had been my favorite book series, so it was a happy trade. I got to wear my regular jeans with the blue-and-white plaid shirt from the costume box. I felt comfortable. Everything was working out.

But then I met up with the neighborhood girls and they, without having mentioned anything to me, had all decided to dress up as "movie stars," which was really an excuse for each of them to wear their fanciest dresses and lots of makeup that they wouldn't usually be allowed to wear. I felt completely foolish next to them, with my squashed straw hat and fake hay sticking out of my too-small flannel shirt.

At one of the houses we went to, the woman there held me back after the other three had gotten their candy and skipped off giggling to the next house. She looked me in the eyes and told me how brave I was for being myself, and then she gave me an extra handful of candy. I appreciated the sentiment (and the extra Snickers bars), but it didn't change anything. I was still stuck wearing an ill-fitting Scarecrow costume while everyone else in the group flounced around in glittery dresses with feather boas. Not that I would've been caught dead dressed like them. I just wished it wasn't so strange for me to be different.

This would be my first exposure to the idea of Halloween, for some people, being an excuse to dress in the most revealing clothes possible with nary a whiff of an actual costume. Throughout my childhood and teenage years, I joined in the public outrage about sexy Halloween costumes, but in reality I was just frustrated that the costumes I worked so hard on and that were never revealing or sexy at all would be judged against those that were. I felt they were giving Halloween a bad name and spoiling my fun.

This came to a head in my junior year of high school, when on the Friday before Halloween we had Goblin Day, a day on which we were allowed to wear our costumes to school and had a big Halloween-themed pep rally, complete with a costume contest.

That year, I decided to be Peter Pan, a character I'd dreamt of dressing as my whole life. Like years past, my mom and I had worked together for weeks designing and sewing an intricate costume. Unlike some of my missteps in previous years, this costume was *actually* impressive. It was a short green tunic decorated with silk leaves in various earthy tones, complete with a brown suede belt for my wooden dagger and a green felt hat.

Walking through the school hallways the morning of Goblin Day, I got a ton of compliments on my handiwork from classmates, which I'd reply to in character with Peter's trademark rooster crow.

When it was time for the costume contest, they divided us (as they did for everything) into boys and girls. The boys' costumes were varied and creative—caricatures of teachers, a group of Village People, a passable Captain Jack Sparrow. The girls, on the other hand, were an endless sea of sexy bunnies, sexy fairies, and sexy cowgirls. I lost the costume contest to one of five sexy Little Bo Peeps and was apoplectic.

Since then, I've cooled down my outrage about sexy Halloween costumes. If a woman—or anyone for that matter—wants a chance to look hot and express herself, why should anyone judge her for that? I don't want to deny anyone their right to wear what they want or tear someone down for wanting to show off their body.

I *will*, however, judge someone who appropriates part of another group's culture or makes light of a tragedy with their costume. Give me a sexy ladybug over an "Indian Princess" any day.

•   •   •

But back to fourth grade. The summer after that embarrassing Scarecrow Halloween, I was at Main Street Days with my mom, watching my brother perform with his middle school's jazz band.

Main Street Days is our hometown's annual festival to kick off the summer. It has carnival rides, live music, lots of fried food, and a ton of local beer and wine for the adults. This was the first night of proceedings, before the festival would begin for real the next morning, and it was raining so hard that barely anyone had shown up.

I, however, was stoked about the rain. It gave me a legitimate excuse to wear the new bucket hat I'd recently gotten, along with my favorite blue-and-yellow pullover windbreaker.

When my brother's band, performing inside a big white tent to keep out the rain, made their usual transition from "My Girl" to "The Pink Panther Theme," my mom slipped me a few dollar bills and told me to go get us a funnel cake from the truck just outside the tent.

I pulled my bucket hat farther down over my forehead as I exited the tent and made my way to the truck, raindrops pummeling my hat and coat. I gave my order to the man and woman inside the truck, handed over my cash, and waited.

"Here you go, young man," said the vendor, leaning down out of the window to carefully place the warm pastry in my small hands.

I scrunched my eyebrows up at him, not saying a word as he handed me extra napkins.

Young ma'am? What kind of phrase is that? Who calls kids young ma'am?

Unless he had said . . .

Suddenly I felt a firm hand clasp around my wrist, nearly knocking the flimsy paper plate out of my hands.

My mom's voice was hissing in my ear, "See? You dress like a boy, you'll get mistaken for a boy."

A boy! He *had* said "young man." Wow. I knew this was a good hat.

But my mom didn't seem to share my excitement. I felt her words searing into me as she led me back into the tent, the loud brass of Austin's jazz band competing with the roars of thunder.

How could she think being mistaken for a boy was such a bad thing? Didn't she realize that was, at least partially, my goal in dressing like this?

I mulled over her reaction as I picked at the doughy funnel cake, licking the powdered sugar off of my fingers after every bite.

The shame of not fitting in had been building for a while, and this was the moment that the dam broke. If even my mom, my great defender and confidante, was embarrassed by my appearance, then what must everyone else think? How silly or pathetic must the rest of the world think I was? This little girl trying so hard, and failing, to look like a boy.

Doing THE GIRL THING ON MY ELEVENTH BIRTHDAY.

I decided it was time to grow up. On our next trip to the mall, I asked to shop in the girls' section. I got spaghetti-strap tank tops and baby-doll T-shirts, choker necklaces and lip gloss. I started wearing braids instead of my trusty ponytail and practiced sitting with my legs crossed at the knee instead of with one ankle over my other knee.

Except for the fact that I was forcing myself to conform instead of feeling freed and happy to be myself, I've always thought that summer when I changed my appearance was ironically similar to the steps transgender children take when they transition. Despite what some sensational media might lead you to believe, trans kids are not given hormone injections or subjected to other medical procedures. When they approach puberty, they might be given hormone-blocking injections that pause the onset of puberty while the family decides if hormone treatment will eventually be right for the child, but until then all transgender kids do when they transition is start going by a different name and pronouns, wear different clothing, and get a new hairstyle. The latter two of which I had elected to undergo myself that summer after fourth grade when I decided to give being a proper girl a shot.

It worked pretty well. I was still made fun of because I was the nerdy kid who listened to Harry Potter audiobooks on my Walkman and liked to practice stunt work in the hallways by pretending to run into walls or fall down flights of stairs, but at least I looked more like people thought I should.

Being treated more like a "normal" person was a great boost for my everyday confidence. I was happy dressing the way people expected me to and picking up the social brownie points that came along with it, but the miracle of puberty was just around the corner and without knowledge of or access to hormone blockers, I was in for a rude awakening.

Hormone Therapy vs. Puberty Blockers

Transgender adults pursuing medical transition might elect to undergo hormone replacement therapy (HRT), which is the administration of medications that cause us to develop secondary sex characteristics. These are similar to the changes you undergo during puberty, such as hair growth, breast development, and fat redistribution. It's important to note that hormones can give, but they can't take away. For example, while transmasculine people on HRT will experience their voices dropping, transfeminine people on HRT will not see as extreme a pitch change in the opposite direction. And while transfeminine people will develop breasts, transmasculine people's will not shrink significantly. HRT will also not change an individual's height.

Some changes from HRT are permanent (such as facial hair growth and breast development), while others will revert if you stop taking hormones (such as body fat redistribution). HRT is undergone on a regular basis for a trans person's entire life (unless they elect to stop).

Transgender children, however, do not undergo hormone replacement therapy. After a child has been living socially as their affirmed gender for a prolonged period of time and as they approach puberty, they might be prescribed puberty blockers, which are intramuscular injections or implants that suppress and delay puberty. If the use of blockers is stopped, puberty goes forward as it would have. Delaying puberty can give the child and family more time to make decisions about which path forward is right for the child, whether that includes future hormone treatment or allowing puberty to commence.

Blockers have been used on gender-nonconforming children for over a decade and on children with other conditions (such as precocious puberty) for much longer. They are, however, prohibitively expensive for most families.

Blockers are not right for every child and are never the first step when you think your child might be transgender. The first step is talking to a professional gender therapist. They'll encourage you to be on the lookout for insistence, consistence, and persistence. Just because a child might be a little gender creative—for example, a boy who wants to wear princess dresses or a girl who begs for a short haircut—does not mean they're necessarily transgender. Curiosity and exploration are natural in young children.

How do you determine if it's just a phase? By talking to your child regularly and letting them explore. Try out different clothes or hairstyles, even a different name and pronouns. Ask them how it all feels. Let them explore and be themselves. Letting them try things out won't "make" them transgender. Plenty of children play with gender and never turn out to be transgender. Allowing them the space to experiment helps them—and you—figure out who they really are and what the right path forward might be. Possible social pressures aside, there is no harm in letting your child discover who they are.

Another point to consider is that your child may be some form of nonbinary, meaning they don't identify exclusively as one of the binary male or female genders at all, and it's possible (though not guaranteed) that hormone blockers and eventual medical transition is not the right path for them.

It can seem like a lot, but the most important things are to learn as much as you can, seek out professional assistance, keep an open line of communication with your child, and make sure they know that you love them no matter what.

CHAPTER FOUR

straight AAA student

I remember the day, early in fifth grade, that I got my first training bra. I think I was kind of excited, mostly by the idea of growing up. Every kid can't wait to grow up, and puberty—as much as parts of it terrified and disgusted me—meant I was growing up.

But as soon as my mom and I got to Target and headed toward the girls' underwear section, I was mortified. I can't even remember the process of choosing one, but I do remember that with every step toward the register, fresh white Lycra training bra in hand, I was more certain that I couldn't face the cashier. I couldn't let anyone know that I needed to wear a bra—which, honestly, I didn't at that point. My chest was as flat as it had been for years and would continue to be for a couple more to come. It was more a rite of passage that my mom had decided it was time to perform than an actual necessity.

I don't know why I was so embarrassed, but I remember raw emotion boiling up in my stomach and turning my cheeks red, tears pricking the corners of my eyes. I was telling my mom that I couldn't do it. I wanted to turn back. I didn't want to be caught buying a bra.

With frantic panic, I also realized that one day I would have to do this. So not doing it that day would just be delaying the inevitable.

My mom thought I was being stupid, but she eventually acquiesced. She handed me the car keys and told me to wait in the car while she checked out. I remember feeling bad. Not because of how I acted, but because I was leaving my mom to do the deed without me. Surely she had to be just as embarrassed as I was to be buying that flimsy undergarment on its tiny plastic hanger. I was a coward for making her do my dirty work for me.

By the time we got home, however, it was a whole other story. I reverted to being proud of growing up. This training bra was the mark of a fledgling adult and I wanted people to know I was wearing it. All evening as my brother and I lounged in the living room watching *Conan*, I kept trying to discreetly pull the neckline of my 'NSync T-shirt to the side as I flopped boisterously around the room, hoping he would spot the shiny white strap of the training bra.

At only two and a half years older than me, my brother had started puberty at the ripe age of eight and therefore had been solidly in a grown-up body for several years now. He had been a five-foot-nine fifth grader who regularly shaved his face. Going through puberty that young is pretty traumatic, especially for a gentle, artistic kid. As a result, it had put a palpable distance between us. He had withdrawn a bit into himself, and my obnoxious nature probably didn't help matters.

I thought that if I was "growing up" now too, perhaps we could be friends again. I didn't think much about how I didn't really want boobs. I'm not sure I even understood that I wouldn't be going through the same puberty as Austin (I still thought I would grow a beard when I got older), but I knew that this training bra was a mark of growing up, and I wanted him to know that I was growing up like he was.

I REMEMBER BEING TALLER IN THIS PHOTO...

He never said anything, of course, and the whole excitement of the training bra wore off within a few days. I don't remember if I ever wore it to school in fourth or fifth grade. I really had no reason to, as I told my neighborhood friend Veronica (the one who had organized the movie star costumes the previous year) one balmy afternoon when she slapped me on the back and was stunned to realize I wasn't wearing a bra. I laughed it off with the self-deprecatory excuse that I didn't need to yet. The real truth was, it made me feel weird and girly. Even though I was still in that phase of trying to be more like a girl, I could only stomach so much.

Plus, there were rumors that our gym teacher paid more attention to the girls who wore bras. He would pat you on the back and, if he felt a bra, he would talk to you more and pull you to the front of the class as an example.

My insistence on not wearing a bra in order to avoid his attention was less about understanding that he might be a potential sexual predator and more that I didn't want to be asked to demonstrate how to spike a volleyball for the class.

I also didn't like the idea that it would mark me as one of the girls. I still sat at the boys' end of the lunch table most days, and the idea of Coach Walker coming over while on his lunch duty to pat my back— something everyone at school knew was code for a Bra Check—was humiliating, because then the guys would be thinking about me wearing a bra. If I just never wore one, maybe Coach Walker would give up on me.*

---

* It should be noted that it's entirely possible we elementary schoolers fabricated the myth of the Bra Check and that Coach Walker—whose name by the way I can't even remember, but who most certainly was not named Coach Walker—was a perfectly ordinary, not-creepy man.

So I told myself that was the reason I didn't wear a bra. Not because it made me feel weird. Not because I had no reason to. Not because I simply didn't want to. Nope, it was an act of moral objection and personal safety.

●　●　●

But soon it was time for middle school and middle school meant locker rooms, which meant taking my clothes off in front of girls my age and wearing a bra every single day of school.

Except for the occasional day I straight-up forgot to put a bra on in the morning, changing in the middle-school locker rooms played out largely without incident. Until the scoliosis test.

The week before the school would be conducting scoliosis exams on each of us during gym class, we were shown a PSA about the dangers of poor posture and then instructed on proper undergarments to wear for the test.

The teachers kept emphasizing that you could wear a bikini top instead of a bra—a well-calculated message to girls who didn't wear bras yet. There was only one girl in our third-period class who didn't wear a bra, and she was one of the girls who needed to more than most of us. I got the impression her mom didn't think eleven-year-old girls needed to wear bras and wouldn't let her until she was a certain age.

Parents can be weird about stuff like that sometimes. I once had a friend whose dad wouldn't let her little brother shave until he was sixteen even though he had a very prominent shadow above his lip that would've looked ten times better if he'd just shaved it off.

Anyway, the day of the scoliosis test came. When my name was called, I went to a closed-off nook in the locker room where a nurse I'd never met before was waiting for me. She had me bend in a couple of different ways, put a little plastic scoliometer at various points along my spine, told me everything looked good, and I returned to gym class.

Later that day, I noticed a bunch of the girls in my class huddled together, speaking in sharp tones. I joined them to find out what they were talking about.

"That nurse from the scoliosis test. She was a lesbian."

"Huh?"

They explained that several of them had felt the nurse got a little too handsy with them during the exam and that she had been looking at their chests too much.

I was skeptical. None of us had ever had a scoliosis test before. How did they know what was standard protocol and what wasn't? Plus, "She didn't do that to me."

"Well," the girls exchanged looks, pity evident in their shrugs. "You don't really have anything for her to look at."

I was stunned. Apart from having no clue how to navigate this new social terrain of breast-related anxiety and McCarthyistic homophobia, I was positively tickled that everyone appeared to think I was so flat-chested.

At that point, I was solidly in Stage Two of breast development, according to my copy of American Girl's *The Care and Keeping of You*. I could feel the buds on my chest move every time I ran up or down the stairs at our house. I thought this was extremely noticeable to the general public. So being told I was still able to slide under the radar as a flat-chested person was an absolute gift.

You see, even this minuscule amount of development was terrifying to me. The fact that there was *anything* growing on my chest freaked me out. And now that my breasts had actually-really-for-sure started growing, who knew when they would stop?

The trials and tribulations of my big-bosomed aunts and elder cousins was a topic of regular conversation among my female relatives. I regarded their hereditary endowments with terror.

Starting with my graduation from training bra to AAA, every trip to the store for a larger-sized bra was accompanied by my insistence to my mom that if they got any bigger, I was getting a reduction.

This probably puzzled my mom. She had grown up very flat-chested herself, the only one among her sisters, and only a few years prior had actually undergone breast augmentation surgery.

This had been back when I was eight years old. A few days before the surgery, she sat down on my cloud-printed bedspread to tell me the news. It wasn't really a boob job, she told me. She just wanted them to be less saggy, not bigger—and it was entirely her choice. It had nothing to do with her friends' or my dad's opinions, she assured me. Not that I had asked. I hadn't asked anything. I still thought boobs were kinda funny, and that was about as far as my brain was going with this one.

Mom AND me, 1993.

I hadn't even received The Talk from my mom yet. I think it was clear from my typical last-place ranking in the annual school height assessment that I was going to be a late bloomer. So, despite the fact that she had started her period at nine without any idea of what it was, my mom seemed to think she was safe keeping this wonderful knowledge from me for a bit longer. She was right. Even telling me all about periods at age ten proved to be several years too soon.

But this meant that back then, at eight years old, I was still running around the house without a shirt on, not understanding what my dad meant when he told me I wouldn't always be able to do that.

So when my mom told me she wanted surgery to augment her breasts, I didn't think much about it one way or the other. Maybe she'd get bazookas installed in them too, like the fembots in *Austin Powers*.

Her reason for getting this surgery was something I didn't understand at all at the time, but a decade and a half later, when I finally mustered the courage to tell her I planned on getting top surgery to remove my own breasts and I wanted her to be there, my mom's breast augmentation would turn out to be a blessing.

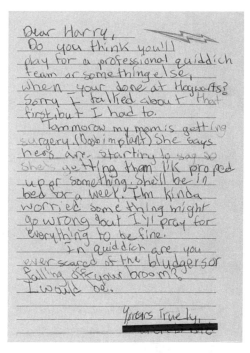

Dear Harry,
Do you think you'll play for a professional quiddich team or something else, when your done at Hogwarts? Sorry I talked about that first, but I had to.
Tommorow my mom is getting surgery (boob implant) She says hers are starting to sag so she's getting them lik proped up or something. She'll be in bed for a week. I'm kinda worried something might go wrong but I'll pray for everything to be fine.
In quiddich are you ever scared of the bludgers or falling off your broom? I would be.

Yours Truely,

FOR A PERIOD OF TIME LEADING UP TO MY ELEVENTH BIRTHDAY, I ADDRESSED ALL MY DIARY ENTRIES TO HARRY POTTER IN THE HOPE THAT IT WOULD HELP MY CHANCES OF RECEIVING A HOGWARTS ACCEPTANCE LETTER.

When I called her to discuss it at age twenty-five, I was certain she would try to talk me out of it or at least be very uncomfortable with the idea, but it turned out to barely faze her. In hindsight, I should have guessed this. After all, my repeated remarks about wanting a reduction and complete resistance to ever showing them off were solid signs that I was a human who did not want nature's gift of boobs, thank you very much. My mom had had a front row seat to my antics, so my plans for top surgery didn't come as a shock to her. Nor did the grisly details of the procedure deter her since she knew exactly what it was like to undergo outpatient chest surgery.

My complete memory of her breast augmentation when I was eight amounts to having to be picked up from school by my dad on his blue Harley-Davidson Heritage Softail while she slept for a solid two days. So I was pleasantly surprised to learn that my mom knew all about handling drains, changing bandages, not moving your arms, and everything else I had been prepared to explain to her. She talked about it all as if she were an old pro. I was at ease.

We may not have understood each other's perspective when it came to chests, but we were able to find common ground in the experience of not having what felt right and undergoing major surgery to feel more at home in our bodies.

My mom PATIENTLY WAITING FOR ME TO PRANK HER WITH BUNNY EARS.

A Note on Trans People's Access to Health Care

It's important to point out that while my mom and I felt an emotional bond over our procedures, our two experiences cannot be conflated. Apart from gender dysphoria being entirely its own beast when it comes to body image, my mom didn't have to get a psychiatrist's letter confirming some sort of diagnosis for her surgery, like I did. While more and more trans people are able to access hormones and gender affirmation surgeries through informed consent (in other words, without a letter from a psychiatrist) thanks to the incredible decades-long work of activists, in many states, countries, and individual practices, jumping through several bureaucratic hoops of diagnoses and red tape is still the norm. While therapy can be a helpful process for some trans people, it creates an additional barrier to access to medical transition, and many feel the requirement is discriminatory, since there are so many similar procedures cisgender people can elect to undergo without psychiatric approval.

This is further complicated by the fact that many jurisdictions still require some level of medical transition to have occurred before a trans person can change their name and gender marker on legal documents—not only an empowering step in transition but also one that provides trans people a better chance of safety, housing, and job opportunities by aligning their identification documents with their appearance. For the trans person wanting to change their legal documents, it can be a yearslong process of finding providers, seeing a psychiatrist, gaining a diagnosis, undergoing medical procedures, securing the documentation proving that those procedures occurred, appearing in court, and taking those finally approved documents to the DMV, the

Social Security office, the bank, the library, and anywhere else trans people have ever submitted their name and gender, forcing them to out themselves in awkward conversations every step of the way.

While there remains a lot of work to be done in the United States, the situation is far better than it was in the second half of the twentieth century. Despite pioneering work by Dr. Magnus Hirschfeld at his Institute for Sexual Science in Berlin in the early 1900s, proving the efficacy of hormone treatment and surgery on transsexual people (and the continued treatment of transsexuality as such in Europe even after Dr. Hirschfeld's institute was burned to the ground by the Nazis in 1933), the medical community in the United States maintained for many decades that sex-reassignment procedures were not acceptable solutions. The 1966 publication of Dr. Harry Benjamin's *The Transsexual Phenomenon* argued that a person's gender identity is immutable and the only salve is allowing them to live fulfilled lives as their identified gender. This groundbreaking work ushered forward a new era of hormonal and surgical treatment for trans people in the US, yet medical professionals still sought to approve as few transsexual people for treatment as possible. At the outset, Benjamin and his contemporaries affirmed a broad variance in trans people—in their expressions, sexualities, personalities, etc. However, as transsexuality and the medical treatment for it became more widely known and public fear of trans people increased, there was mounting pressure to approve of only those trans people who would blend into society after medical treatment, agreeing to leave families and lives behind through a string of carefully constructed lies.

Only those deemed "true transsexuals"—people who were heterosexual, aspired to assimilate visibly and socially, and who exhibited stereotypical, sexist traits of their identified gender—

were approved for medical transition, and even then it was only after years of costly sessions with psychiatrists and researchers. As part of their "therapy," many had to show they could live as their identified gender for a year or two, a test that occurred before hormone treatment. Many trans people find it impossible to be read as their identified gender without the assistance of hormones or other medical procedures, so this test exposed them to possible danger, put them under unnecessary emotional strain, often made them incapable of finding employment to pay for continued treatment, and was essentially set up to make them fail—thus ensuring even fewer trans people would be approved to undergo medical transition.

In addition to accepting only a fraction of applicants into their practices (already narrowed down from the pool of trans people with the means to pay) and the carefully crafted assessments and tests meant to highlight only heterosexual candidates with the best assimilation potential, these early gender specialists focused almost entirely on trans women. The reasons for this could be anything from the fact that trans men, living as women, usually lacked access to financial resources to pay for treatment to the specialists' belief that trans men weren't actually transsexual—an assumption couched in misogynist ideals disregarding "women's" assertions, as well as viewing "men" expressing femininity as more sensational than the relatively benign opposite.

It's been a long road to get as far as we have in the United States, but there remains a lot of work to do before trans people are treated with the same respect, dignity, and awareness as others.

CHAPTER FIVE

these hips don't lie

By eighth grade, my breasts were growing in earnest, now out-pacing those of several of my peers, and they weren't the only things expanding beyond my control—my hips were too.

I had tried sticking to feminine clothing for a few years after the big Funnel Cake Revelation, but my tomboyish ways had crept back in toward the end of sixth grade. I don't know if it was because I had finally made friends with girls who didn't care about appearances as much as my elementary school peers or if I was subconsciously re-belling against my changing body (probably a combination of both), but my motivation to fit in as a societally accepted image of a girl was steadily waning.

I'd returned to my regulation ponytail and began venturing back into the boys' section of the store for the uniform khakis and polos we were required to wear at my school. The problem was, those clothes from the boy's section weren't fitting my body like they used to.

No matter how much weight I lost, my hips still protruded in a way that made me feel awkward. My body was supposed to be straight up and down, no curves. Why didn't it get that? Why did it insist on grow-ing hips and thick thighs that made everything I wanted to wear look form-fitting? I just couldn't feel right in my body.

Around this time, I was sitting in French class while our teacher sat perched on a bar stool at the front of the room, reading to us from *Le Petit Chaperon Rouge*. I had never taken too much notice of her appearance other than to note that she was fairly petite and at least a generation younger than all my other teachers. She often sat on that bar stool when she read to us, but that day I noticed something I never had before: When she was sitting, her hips compressed to become nearly twice as wide as her waist, wider even maybe than her shoulders! How could her hips possibly be that big all of a sudden? Surely they weren't when she was standing up. And indeed, when she stood up again to write some vocabulary words on the whiteboard, her hips had gone back to their normal size, though even that was wider than I had ever noticed before.

Did my hips look like that when I sat down? If they didn't now, would they one day? I was horrified. It was like having the smacking realization that my breasts might grow to the size of my well-endowed cousins all over again.

Maybe some women and girls want to be curvy, but I certainly didn't. I just wanted my cargo pants from the boys' section to fit me correctly. Was that so much to ask?

Given how dismayed I was by my changing body, it's not altogether surprising that I lacked confidence in my appearance. I had never thought I was a particularly attractive person. When you insist on wearing ripped jeans and flannel shirts on family outings, you don't get many grown-ups fawning over how cute you are. The only times they did gush over me had been when I was forced into girly outfits I despised, so their comments were just salt in the wound.

Now in middle school, engulfed in an environment of increasingly image-obsessed preteens, I doubted very much that anyone would find me pretty. I didn't *feel* pretty. My body refused to stay the shape I wanted it to and I wasn't interested in putting in any sort of effort to look stylish or appealing. While girls in my class were beginning to experiment with makeup and hair straighteners to impress boys, I was far more concerned with finding the brightest-colored Converse high-tops and reading theories online about what would happen in the next Harry Potter book. So that made my next discovery all the more alarming.

I was thirteen and backstage for the opening-night performance of *The Best Christmas Pageant Ever*. Yes, the same show I'd performed in when I was eight. Only this time, I'd graduated from the carpeted halls of the rec center to the glitz and glam of the local community theater. When I auditioned, I had hoped to likewise graduate from the role of the tomboy Gladys to her still-super-tough older sister, Imogene. Instead, I ended up as Alice Wendleken, the prissiest, meanest girl in school.

I wasn't thrilled about the role, but I was determined to prove my maturity and professionalism, so I sucked it up and gave the character my all—even when the costumers put me in a vintage lacy pink dress.

On opening night, after donning said dress and being put through hair and makeup, I caught a glimpse of myself in the vanity mirror and saw a very striking young woman staring back at me. I paused in shock. The girl looking back at me looked much more like my character Alice Wendleken than myself, but she was definitely pretty.

Huh. I guess I had some potential to be attractive after all.

BACKSTAGE DURING *THE BEST CHRISTMAS PAGEANT EVER*.

I wasn't about to start making immediate changes to my appearance or wearing heavy makeup to school, because I knew I wouldn't be able to stomach it on a daily basis (or explain to my classmates what caused the sudden change in presentation), but I did wear a sparkly dress and heels to my eighth-grade graduation—a drastic departure from my usual collared blouse and slacks for formal occasions. A male classmate of mine told me the next morning that all the popular girls had been complaining during the ceremony that the twerpy little tomboy looked better than them. I'm not going to lie: Their envious reactions made all my personal discomfort worth it.

Even with such brief forays into feminine fashion for special occasions, I remained in my T-shirts, jeans, and regulation ponytail in my daily life. The one change I did make was to start wearing boyish clothing made for women, instead of actual boys' clothes, which didn't flatter my natural body shape. At least then I wouldn't look as frumpy, even if I did have to swallow the awkwardness of dressing in true women's clothing with all its capped sleeves, darted seams, and useless minuscule pockets.

Apart from a general confidence boost, I was half-hoping that the subtle change in my wardrobe would stop the accusations that I was a lesbian.

I definitely wasn't *bullied* for my masculinity, but every now and then a barb would be thrown my way that cut deep. The jeers from boys on the bus barely affected me (they called every person, thing, and intangible concept "gay"), but one time an older girl from the community theater told me with sage wisdom that I was absolutely a lesbian. She "could just tell these things," she told me.

For a preteen in suburban Texas, being gay was just about the scariest thing that could happen to you. We didn't have Gay–Straight

Alliance clubs in our schools or teachers with discreet rainbows and equal-sign stickers on their doors denoting safe spaces.

Instead we had abstinence-only sex ed that never mentioned same-sex relationships, sparse punishment for the use of the word *gay* as a slur, and relentless bullying directed at anyone, student or teacher, around whom a large enough conspiracy of homosexuality had been built up.

I *wanted* to support gay people. *Will & Grace* had been my favorite TV show since I was in fourth grade, and I had become inexplicably angry when I heard President Bush say on the news that marriage was something that could only exist between a man and a woman. My parents weren't explicitly homophobic, nor was the new age-y church we had started attending a few years prior. There was no reason for me to disapprove of gay people, but somehow at least a part of me had been ensnared by the gay panic of the South. I was genuinely frightened by displays of deviation from what I had been exposed to as normal gender roles (despite the irony of frequently resisting them myself).

Such was my and my peers' fear of homosexuality that at a sleepover with my two best friends in eighth grade, one of them asked with utter fear in her voice, "What if one of *us* turns out to be gay?"

We all looked around at one another silently, eyes wide with fright. She might as well have just revealed, after a lengthy round of Whodunit?, that the true murderer was one of us.

It was as if homosexuality was something that could be spontaneously inflicted on one of us in the future, not something we would've already had an inkling about. We'd been brought up to think it was this tragic thing that just happened to some people inexplicably, like getting into a car crash, and we desperately didn't want it to happen to us.

At that point, I'd knowingly met only one gay adult in my life and I had regular nightmares about his feminine clothing, his long hair, and his varnished nails. Growing up in a culture thick with stereotypical gender roles, and battling so much internalized fear of my own deviations from those norms, actually caused me physical anxiety when I saw people openly expressing gender nonconformity. If only preteen me could see the company I keep now.

Years later, as an adult, I would be reminded of these childhood fears when I saw them expressed in a ten-year-old girl I was talking to at a conference. I had been invited to speak on a panel at TED Women, which at twenty-two was the most impressive event I'd ever been invited to, and yet I still considered turning the opportunity down. No one knew at that point that I was a transgender man. I still presented as a woman, albeit one that most people mistook for a butch lesbian, but I knew that I wasn't really a woman. I feared that when I inevitably came out, people would be upset at me for having invaded this women's-only space—or that I would simply be uncomfortable being in that space.

It turns out TED Women is *not* a women's-only space. Men regularly speak at and attend TED Women, but I didn't know that at the time. After going back and forth on my decision for a few weeks, my ego ultimately won out and I agreed to speak on the panel.

The panel went well, but I felt out of place all weekend. It wasn't just the vast majority of female attendees or the general girl-power vibes—I love all of that—but rather the lack of queer representation. None of the programs so far had featured visibly queer women or people discussing LGBTQ+ issues. I didn't feel like I belonged among the older, wealthy women with their chunky jewelry and fancy handbags. On the final day of the conference, however, I noticed a talk titled "Fifty Shades of Gay" being given by someone named iO Tillett Wright, and knew I needed to snag a seat for it.

iO turned out to be a tall, spritely photographer who was presenting on his Self-Evident Truths project, a photography-based endeavor that took him across the United States documenting the infinite variances of sexuality and gender expression among people. iO additionally shared photos of his own upbringing, showing how his gender expression ping-ponged drastically throughout his youth and adolescence, and refused to put a label on his present identity.

I was awestruck. I no longer felt alone at the conference. Among all the older women with their quiet gasps of surprise at iO's childhood photos, I knew there was at least one other gender-nonconforming person with me in the building.

When the day ended and audience members flooded back into the main atrium for drinks and a dance party led by *Vagina Monologues* playwright Eve Ensler, I kept my eye on iO. I wanted to let him know how much I'd loved his talk and maybe buy him a drink. He was so cool and self-assured, even being slightly out of place among the strongly heteronormative crowd. I wished I could be like him.

As I watched him mingle with friends across the atrium, I was interrupted by commentary from the ten-year-old girl I'd been palling around with that weekend. She was the daughter of one of TED's employees and had taken a liking to me early on that weekend. I thought she was a clever kid and preferred keeping her entertained to having to network with people twice my age, so I indulged her. In that moment, however, I was finally wishing I could join the adults. It didn't seem appropriate somehow to go chat someone up at a bar with a ten-year-old tagging along. She'd seen the talk, though. Maybe she would be excited to meet one of the speakers? Before I could even bring it up, the girl caught my gaze and said with a shudder, "That person scares me."

"What?" I exclaimed, shocked. "I think he's awesome." As the girl kept talking, either about iO's ambiguous and confusing gender expression or likely just moving onto another topic, I got lost in thought.

She was reacting exactly how I used to about androgynous-looking people when I was her age—with genuine fear and skepticism.

I want to believe that kids are born without judgment and that gender variance seems natural to them, but I suppose the prejudice of the world can seep in at a very early age. By the time kids hit the precocious preteen years, so frightened of their peers' judgment and wary of the oncoming changes to their bodies and lives, any variant from their normal can be unsettling.

I never did work up the courage to introduce myself to iO that night. I don't know if it was the girl's comments or my own social awkwardness that put me off, but I did get to share a few moves with Eve Ensler on the dance floor later, so the night wasn't a total bust.

PARTICIPATING IN iO's SELF-EVIDENT TRUTHS PROJECT A FEW YEARS AFTER THE TED WOMEN CONFERENCE.

CHAPTER SIX

the transmasculine invisibility cloak

I was always boy crazy as a kid. Or at least, that's how I tell it.

From preschool onward, I always had a crush on at least one boy, but more likely half a dozen male schoolmates and celebrities at once. Looking back, it's tough to determine how many of those were real crushes and how many were simply fascinations with boys I wished I could be—or even my posturing as if I had crushes when I didn't, because I knew that's what was expected of me.

I'll never forget the time I was listening to music on my Walkman during a long drive with a friend's family around age ten. Determined to prove to her that I was just as cool and grown-up as she was, I leaned over to her and said that the guy in the car next to us was hot.

Suddenly her entire family broke out laughing and her older brother told me, face streaked with secondhand embarrassment, that I had just yelled that to the entire car.

So much for looking cool.

Random "hot" dudes on the interstate aside, I'm sure some of my crushes on boys were legitimate. They at least felt so at the time, and that was good enough for me. I did *not* want to be a lesbian.

While I maybe had some curiosity about women's bodies here and there, I never consciously had a crush on a girl. Stacked up against my endless crushes on boys, this seemed to be definitive proof. I *couldn't* be a lesbian.

I was so determined to not be interested in girls, and so scared that I might be, that when I finally got a hint about what might be going on with my curious and unwavering desire to be a boy, I completely overcomplicated things.

One day after middle school while both of my parents were still at work, I happened on an *Oprah* special about transgender kids, most of whom were trans boys. They were kids just like me who had begged their parents for short haircuts, ran around the house with their shirts off, and wore button-down shirts instead of ruffled dresses on Picture Day.

I watched the episode in a trance, forgetting to breathe as I stared at family photos splaying across the television screen, each one looking more and more like my own. My throat tightened watching one of the older boys at the doctor's office being given hormone-blocking shots to prevent him from having a period.

I started imagining how I would tell my mom about this discovery, how I would ask my parents if I could live like these boys. My heart was pounding with trepidation and excitement.

At the very end of the episode, about the time I started keeping my finger on the remote's return button to quickly change the channel at the first sound of the garage door opening, Oprah asked the older boy if he liked girls. He turned red and shyly confirmed that, yes, he did.

The lump in my throat dropped to the pit of my stomach. I didn't like girls. Or at least, I had spent a lot of time convincing myself that I didn't. I definitely didn't *want* to like girls.

Did all transgender boys have to like girls? I didn't think I could sacrifice my interest in boys in order to be the boy I'd always felt I was.

I let out the breath I had been holding with a mixture of relief and defeat. I wouldn't have to have a tough discussion with my parents or go down the long, hard road of being transgender, but it was back to the drawing board in terms of figuring out what I was.

• • •

Even though that *Oprah* episode made me feel like my interest in boys disqualified me from being transgender, as time went on I started thinking that maybe I *was* transgender, but that I was also gay—as in I was a guy who liked other guys, living the life of a teenage girl by some curse of fate.

The problem was, Oprah had implied that wasn't possible. That didn't stop me from believing it was how I felt, but it did make me think I was some extra-special kind of freak. I must have been unlucky enough to inherit two separate deviant genes working against each other. There was no way there was anyone else like that in the world. I mean, I had never seen anyone like that before in my life or in the media, so, as far as I knew, I was alone.

A few years after that landmark *Oprah* viewing, I went to see the Adam Sandler movie *50 First Dates*, where I witnessed his usual slew of transphobia, homophobia, misogyny, and cultural appropriation—none of which really seemed problematic to me at the time, as a thirteen-year-old from conservative Texas. Until one scene.

There was a character credited as Jennifer, played by a cisgender man, who was flamboyantly gay and introduced as a man who had had sex-reassignment surgery. It was clear by the lilt in his voice and the limpness of his wrist that the implication was that he had made a mistake. It was a classic case of that phrase that was casually sprinkled into so many sitcoms and movies in the '90s, "Oh, sex changes never work out!"

I watched this character's brief scenes with terrified fascination, trying to parse it out.

Okay, so either A) he's being lampooned as having made a mistake, meaning he's not actually transgender because he's gay and, as I had already decided from that *Oprah* special, being both isn't possible, or B) he *is* both gay and transgender, but he's being made fun of because that's such a rare anomaly that people are highly disturbed by it.

I had been shown someone like me, a queer transgender man, for the first time ever in the media, and the lesson I was being taught was that either I didn't actually exist or I was a total freak.

Now I know this was a shock-value comedy, not an educational film. I shouldn't have been taking such strong cues from it, but I didn't have anything else at the time. Not to mention the fact that an Adam Sandler movie was going to tell me a heck of a lot more about how most people actually feel about trans people than a soppy *Oprah* special about little kids.

So hidden are trans men from the media that even recent articles lambasting the transphobia of *50 First Dates* don't mention this character, instead focusing on the butch female character who's comedically implied to have been assigned male at birth because, naturally, cisgender women can't be masculine—the transmisogyny of which is a whole other issue. I actually had to watch the damn movie again to fact-check my preteen memory of the trans male character.

It's a problem across media that people from marginalized communities are tokenized, stereotyped, or completely absent from mainstream media and that (lack of) representation has real consequences. People outside of those communities learn from the few exaggerated characters they see and think everyone of X identity is just like that. People within those communities, especially young people, might grow up thinking that people like them can't hold certain professions or achieve certain livelihoods.

For those of us with lesser-known gender and sexual identities, or other "invisible" identities, struggling to put a label on what makes us feel so different, this dearth of representation tells us there's no one else like us out there at all. Whatever it is that makes us different, that makes us who we are, doesn't exist beyond our own minds.

My experience isn't uncommon. Countless trans men talk of having known all about transgender women growing up, just as I did, but never realizing it could "go the other way," so to speak. I grew up idolizing transfeminine and androgynous gender benders like David Bowie, Dr. Frank-N-Furter, and Eddie Izzard—even though the gender subversion that gave me goose bumps didn't quite resonate.

Some trans men are introduced to butch lesbian culture and find an outlet for experimenting with masculine hairstyles, clothing, and roles. Yet they too often suffer from the misconceptions of society around transmasculinity. It's an all-too-common refrain in certain lesbian circles that trans men are confused butches who are betraying women—and the very institution of feminism—by transitioning. This stigma kept many men closeted and dysphoric and still exists in niche circles to this day, in ever more organized and harassing capacities.

Where Are All the Trans Guys?

While some people's individual experiences and filter bubbles might vary, the truth is that mainstream media, medical professionals, and even some community spaces have historically focused far more on trans women than on trans men. There are a number of possible contributing factors to this, and most of them come down to the power that men and masculinity are given in our society.

First is the matter of "passing" as a certain gender, or being read by society according to society's stereotypes, regardless of how you identify or wish to be seen. This is a broad generalization, but it can often be easier for transmasculine people to pass in society as men than for transfeminine people to pass in society as women—depending on who you are and what your transition journey is like. This is partially because testosterone is a helluva drug that can give some transmasculine people far more drastic, visible changes than hormone replacement therapy usually does for transfeminine people. Even without hormones, some female-assigned-at-birth people find it easier to pass as—albeit substantially younger—men in society than male-assigned-at-birth people find it to pass as women. This is important to keep in mind when you consider how many people assigned female at birth successfully lived quiet, mostly unrecorded lives as men throughout history,* while people assigned male at birth who attempted to live as women or even just dared to don feminine clothing were more often ostracized, arrested, harassed, and worse. Western society writ large is much more willing to accept what they see as a woman being masculine than what they see as a man being feminine.

How does this relate to the lack of transmasculine visibility? Because if you can pass—if you can live "stealth"—it's very tempting to do so, if for no other reason than for life to be a little bit safer. So what's ostensibly happened over generations is that trans men tended to live stealth more often than trans women—disappearing into mainstream society, unrecorded in history, and not participating as heavily in community spaces or activist movements.

Today this is changing, as we see countless transmasculine people sharing their stories online and being active in the

---

* For examples of some of these people and more on this phenomenon, check out *True Sex: The Lives of Trans Men at the Turn of the 20th Century* by Emily Skidmore.

movement. However, there is still a pattern of drop-off when folks hit a point of stability in their transitions: when it isn't dominating their minds anymore, when they can go about life and not be misgendered constantly, when they can live whatever feels like a normal life to them. They don't need the community as much as they used to. This pattern creates a perpetual lack of visibility of older transmasculine people farther along in their transitions—and makes it even more important to listen hard to the few willing to remain visible.

While there's something to be said for using your privilege and security to fight in solidarity with your trans siblings, I can't completely blame transmasculine people who want to be totally stealth, because we've seen what the visibility has done to trans women. They're plagued by stereotypes, ridicule, and violence. Trans homicide rates are staggering, and the majority of the victims are trans women of color.

Even with the uptick in visibility of transmasculine people in recent years, I have a hunch that it still won't become as bad for us as it is for transfeminine people, since we live in a society that sexualizes femininity, quakes when masculinity is threatened, and seems to get why a "woman" would want to be a man but not why a "man" would ever give up his privilege and demean himself to the level of a woman. To quote Julia Serano:

> The media tends not to notice—or to outright ignore—trans men because they are unable to sensationalize them the way they do trans women without bringing masculinity itself into question. . . . This reflects the very different levels of privilege men and women have in our society . . . since most people cannot fathom why some-

one would give up male privilege and power
in order to become a relatively disempow-
ered female, they assume that trans women
transition primarily as a way of obtaining
the one type of power that women are perceived to have in our society: the ability
to express femininity and to attract men.

This blend of transmisogyny and fetishization means that
salacious, usually wildly inaccurate and dehumanizing stories
about trans women have always dominated the tabloids. In
fictionalized media, while trans men may be largely absent, trans
women are nearly always presented as the butt of the joke, or as
someone trying to "trick" men, as fake, deranged, or evil.

All of these representations unfortunately educate society
and therefore lead to the dangerous world transfeminine people
have to navigate, which could be one reason there tend to be
more women and femmes in trans spaces. They have a huge need
for support from one another and a lot to fight for. That's not to
discount the needs of transmasculine people; we deserve a seat at
some of the tables too. But we're not being ridiculed or murdered
on nearly the level that transfeminine people are.*

The tides are changing, but visibility will always be a double-
edged sword. While it's wonderful that more people continue to be
aware of trans men's existence (meaning more transmasculine
people can articulate what they're feeling, be supported by
the people in their lives, and access care from providers who
are educated about their needs), we've also seen the kinds

---

*A 2018 report from the Human Rights Campaign on trans
violence shows that 82 percent of the trans people
killed in 2018 were trans women of color.

of discrimination and violence that can come from increased visibility. As trans men continue to speak up more, it's vital that we also remain aware of our newfound male privilege and don't use it to speak over trans women, nonbinary folks, or our elders. Liberation cannot be achieved without everyone at the table.

I didn't have any older gay or lesbian people in my life who could expose me to these ideas or show me the possibilities for identity and expression out there. Even as I entered high school, there still weren't any LGBT clubs, openly gay teachers, or any resources whatsoever to help me sort out what I was feeling.

So I continued through high school and early college with these cultural misconceptions looming over me, still confused about what exactly my feelings meant. On occasion, I hinted at having a Big Dark Secret to my closest friends, without actually revealing what it was. I wanted to tell someone, but I barely had words for what I felt and was truly scared that divulging my secret would lead me to be locked up in a psychiatric ward.

So I kept my feelings to myself and suffered in confused silence.

CHAPTER SEVEN

the tank top incident

While I was trying to sort out how I really felt deep down, there was still the matter of existing in my day-to-day present reality and the social pressures blossoming around me.

At fifteen, I had never had a serious boyfriend and had only kissed a couple of guys. I was still pretty grossed out by the idea of sex, but the hormones sizzling through my teenage body, combined with a natural curiosity and a desire to act mature, made me really want to try it.

Unfortunately, this was also the time that guys my age were hitting the particularly smelly parts of puberty. Even though I still wished I could look as effortlessly attractive in a simple button-down as even the most sartorially challenged boys in my class and even though the occasional good haircut, roguish smile, or display of solid acting talent could make me weak at the knees, teenage boys were generally, from my vantage point, greasy, sweaty slabs of meat with just enough hair to make you uncomfortable.

They all smelled, most of them were oilier than any of the girls, and I was supposed to want them inside me? As. If.

Particularly as I finally learned the grisly mechanics of sex, I had the revelation that, for the first time in my life, I was glad I had not been assigned male at birth. Their puberty was so much grosser than the one I was experiencing at the time, and I never wanted to be that gross.

I took this total disgust with the teenage male body as evidence that I didn't *really* want to be a boy. Which was good, right? That meant I was normal. Yep, definitely a girl. Definitely not transgender. Can't want to be a boy if you don't want to go through a sweaty, smelly, greasy, hairy puberty. No sir-ee, bob.

And if I wasn't transgender, well, then that meant it was time to suck it up and be a girl. A perfect girl. The kind of girl boys would be tripping over themselves to date. I never did things by halves, after all. If this was who I had to be, then I was gonna do it better than anyone else by far.

Spoiler warning: I was still a totally awkward nerd no matter how hard I tried.

• • •

My sophomore year of high school I joined the speech team or, as it's known at many schools, Oral Interpretation. At our school, it functioned basically like the varsity acting team. The Theater Department's elite would spend every weekend of the school year competing in humor, drama, poetry, and more in exchange for trophies and national qualifying points. Like so many extracurricular activities in large, hypercompetitive Texas schools, it was an all-consuming lifestyle, which meant built-in friends.

Most of the other students in my year on the team had come from the same middle school where they had been the most popular kids in their grade. There was no reason we would've ever become friends outside of Oral Interp., but between the early morning bus rides to competitions and the long nights in strange school cafeterias waiting for rankings to be announced, they had grown to accept me as one of their own.

The main three girls I hung out with lined up perfectly with the trifecta in *Mean Girls*, the Plastics. The blond, cunning, undisputed leader. Her darker-skinned, power-hungry second-in-command. And the third girl, also blond, whose alleged stupidity is played up for laughs.

Though the last girl couldn't tell the weather by groping her own boobs like Karen in *Mean Girls* (as far as I know), she did have a well-known tendency to take her clothes off. She regularly went commando at school, and it wasn't uncommon to wake up at sleepovers with her uncovered boobs right in your face. She always shrugged it off by saying, "It's just flesh." While there were certainly some people at our school who saw this trio as the Plastics incarnate, I remained in fun, pleasant spirits with them throughout high school. I enjoyed their friendship and the antics we got ourselves into.

In the early days, however, there was definitely a lot of insecurity wrapped up in my newfound role as their friend. They were all gorgeous, incomprehensibly thin, and knew how to dress to perfection—not to mention how to do their hair and makeup.

I had figured out how to do my makeup well enough for my desires, thanks to watching the stage moms who applied it for me when I acted in plays, and I was decently satisfied with simply running a straightener through my hair every morning, but I still dressed like a frumpy dweeb and was battling some mad body-image problems.

For one, there was the way my body had changed from puberty. It felt lumpy in all the wrong ways and didn't look the way I wanted it to in the clothes I'd determined were my style. The only solution I could come up with to lose the curves was to lose weight. If I got thin enough, surely my hips would eventually disappear.

Part of my logic for this was the fact that all the girls who were thinner than me didn't seem to have hips. I didn't quite realize that some people are just built curvier than others because, unfortunately for someone who was barely over one hundred pounds, I spent a lot of time around girls who were thinner and less curvy than me.

Growing up acting on stage usually means also growing up in dance classes, especially for girls. It's one thing to be pressured into ballet as a preschooler when all you want to do is build pinewood derby cars and go camping with the Cub Scouts, but quite another to be trapped in a form-fitting leotard during puberty.

Every afternoon as my body was betraying me, I went to dance classes with thin, gangly girls and saw my shapely hips in the floor-to-ceiling mirror beside their ramrod silhouettes.

I poked at my stomach rolls while eyeing their abs enviously. It didn't seem to matter that we all did the exact same exercises every single day; my body just wouldn't look like theirs. I wasn't ready (and in many ways am still not ready) to accept that people's bodies are just built differently, and mine wasn't built in the shape I had decided was my ideal.

So as I became closer to my new friends on the Oral Interp. team, I did a lot of staring at their lithe waists and wondering when they would decide to kick me out of the clique for being too unattractive and awkward. I really thought I had nothing going for myself compared to them. I couldn't dress myself well, I couldn't do my hair or makeup as well as them, I was too pudgy, and I wasn't attractive in the least.

I said as much to them one time, in a jokingly mournful way, and their response was earth-shattering.

"You're joking, right?" one of them asked.

"Uhhh . . . no?"

All three of them went on to say that I was beautiful and that they sometimes resented me for it because it was clear I didn't make any effort. Maybe they were just saying it to make me feel better, but I clung to their comments, hoping there was even a tiny kernel of truth to them.

> I bought a new pair of Lucky jeans.
> Size 2. Dark wash. I love them
> I also got an awesome new knit hat.
> I need to stay in the 0-2 range because
> when I buy pants that size, the length actually fits.
> I hope I stay motivated to go to the gym
> afterschool. I need to be size 0 and 100 lbs. That
> would be amazing.
> My goal for my first yr of JU should be a backwards
> freshman fifteen. Hopefully since I won't be working
> that first semester I'll have lots of time to work
> out.
> I'll have to find a place to do my ab workouts
> and calisthenics. There will be people everywhere
> in college. Hopefully, if anyone makes fun of what
> I look like when I do my workouts, I'll just
> be able to show them my ridiculously ripped abs
> and then they'll just be jealous.
> That is why I have to go to the gym, until I
> start losing weight w/ serious cardio, my abs will
> never look like anything.

DECEMBER 11, 2007: A TYPICAL ASSESSMENT OF
MY PRIORITIES IN TWELFTH GRADE.

Sure, I knew I could be kind of pretty when I really made myself up, but were they saying I was competitively attractive against them even when I showed up to school in a last-season blouse and jeans three sizes too big because I hadn't figured out how jean sizing worked yet?

I wasn't sure I bought it, but it was a good token of potentially placebo-effect confidence to have in my back pocket as I continued trying to fit in with the popular kids.

• • •

That confidence wavered a few months later. The entire Oral Interpretation team was staying over at the lead girl's house for the weekend. The annual state competition was being held at a school too close to our own for travel and lodging to be justified in the budget, but we firmly believed in the necessity of team bonding and undeterred focus during the big competition, so our parents had allowed us to all stay at the girl's family's house and pretend it was a hotel for the weekend.

While her parents would still be in the house and we would be busy most of the time with the tournament, it was still exciting that we would essentially be having a three-day-long coed slumber party.

After our first successful day of preliminary rounds, we all returned on a high and were taking turns showering as others made dinner. I had changed out of my black skirt suit, the kind we all wore for tournaments, and into some pajama bottoms and one of my favorite spaghetti-strap tank tops and plopped myself down at the kitchen island with a bowl of SpaghettiOs.

As I was eating, two boys in my year, a mischievous, inseparable duo, walked into the kitchen, took one look at me, and burst out laughing so hard they had to leave the room.

My face flared up in horror. Did I have a boob hanging out? Unlikely, since I was rocking a large-cupped bra *and* a built-in bra inside the tank top. Had I spilled SpaghettiOs all over myself? Very likely given my clumsiness, but nope. Not this time. Was I just . . . that ugly in a tank top? We had a very draconian and decently misogynistic dress code at school, so that evening was probably the first time the boys had ever seen me in a shirt that revealing, and I guess it had been my mistake for wearing it.

I tried to act on the outside like I wasn't bothered while internally imagining their faces on every piece of tomatoey pasta I speared aggressively with my fork.

Later that night, it was revealed to me, as if it were obvious, that the guys weren't laughing *at* me, per se. They were nervously laughing

Approximately thirty seconds before the Tank Top Incident.

because my tank top apparently made my boobs look *massive*. I was then informed that the size of my boobs was a regular topic of conversation among the guys on the team and that the Tank Top Incident was an unexpected and overwhelming treat.

My first reaction to this was to feel bummed. Bummed that my favorite style of tank top had betrayed me by making my boobs look bigger instead of hiding them. And bummed that my boobs were apparently big enough to be a topic of conversation.

My second reaction, however, was that I had been given a gift. Maybe *I* hated my curves and thought they made me look unappealing, but the guys evidently felt the opposite. I could use this to my advantage. Even if I couldn't be certain my hair, makeup, or fashion sense were alluring, at least I now knew I could attract boys with my impressive rack.

So later that night when the boys asked to touch my boobs during a game of Truth or Dare, I let them—giggling all the while. In an unexpected way, being sexualized gave me the permission I needed to be proud of my body. Or, at the very least, positive attention from my peers discrediting the negative feelings I'd always had about my body gave me the confidence to show it off and enjoy doing so. My brain's jury is still out on whether it was actually empowering or just objectifying.

CHAPTER EIGHT

the id, the ego, and the alter ego

By junior year of high school, I was gaining confidence in this game of being a girl. My style had become more and more feminine. I shed my regulation ponytail and started wearing more makeup. I had established a solid place in the inner circle of the popular theater kids, and had formed other groups of friends to boot. I'd broken up with one guy over the summer in order to date another and was slowly starting to learn that lingering stares from men weren't because I'd forgotten to zip my fly.

Not that they were looking that low. No, they were probably looking at my chest. Despite recent revelations, I never wore low cut tops and unconsciously did everything I could to hide that part of my body with my choice of shirts. Yet the bulbous masses on my upper torso still stuck out way more than I was comfortable with.

While I spent days at school reapplying my lipstick after lunch and sitting with my legs crossed at the ankle (in the way I had learned from Julie Andrews in *The Princess Diaries*), my evenings at home were retreats into my own private world of gender exploration.

With my family safely watching TV downstairs, I would tear apart my closet to find every sports bra I'd ever owned. Putting them all on, one on top of another, I'd look myself over in the mirror, hoping to see a flat chest reflected back.

It never worked. Even four sports bras just created one big hump on my chest. Not a single soul would mistake that monoboob for pecs, or even an AA cup.

Plus, it's not like I could wear that outside my bedroom for any period of time. I could barely breathe for the two and a half minutes I spent trying it on (plus an extra seven for trying to escape the sports bras, Chinese finger trap–style).

I'd been inspired to try flattening my chest after seeing the 1998 Academy Award upset *Shakespeare in Love*. I was a pretentious theater kid who loved reciting my favorite soliloquies, writing my own sonnets, and telling people how actually I preferred the works of Christopher Marlowe to William Shakespeare, so of course I, unlike seemingly everyone else in the country, loved that movie.

And really, looking back on it, a movie about a talented, beautiful blond-haired woman who dresses as a man in order to star in a play and hooks up with a super-hot William Shakespeare speaks so much to my adolescent feelings at the time that it's almost embarrassing.

One of my favorite scenes in the movie is when Will Shakespeare and Viola, the aforementioned blond beauty, are about to get it on and Will twirls her out of the chest bindings she'd been using to disguise herself as a young man. Not because the scene was sexy (I mean, it *was*) but because it revealed just how Viola had flattened her chest and gave me hope that I could do the same.

Alas, my chest was a bit larger than hers and I lacked access to the movie magic that really made it work, so my chest-binding attempts remained in a state of arrested development.

Blundered binding endeavors weren't the only evening activity I juxtaposed with my feminine-presenting school days. I also spent almost every night writing in my journal (well, usually a Microsoft Word doc) about what my day would've been like if I had been a boy.

I wrote about what I would've worn, what gender-specific clubs I would've joined, who I would've been dating. The more I repressed my masculine expression and identity outwardly, the more desperately I longed to magically be turned into a guy. At the time, I was writing it as a sort of alternate-universe fan fiction of my life, starring my very own self-indulgent alter ego: Jack Starkey.

I don't know where I came up with the name Jack, but Starkey was inspired by a fusion of Tony Stark and Ringo Starr's legal name.

Jack was in theater, just like me, but he was much more talented. He was a gifted singer and got lead roles in all the school plays. He was secretly dating the probably-gay-but-not-yet-out boy at school I had a crush on and he was even related to some of my favorite celebrities. But more so than all those fantastical qualities, I loved Jack because he wasn't afraid to be himself and for the very simple reason that he was the boy I thought I could never be.

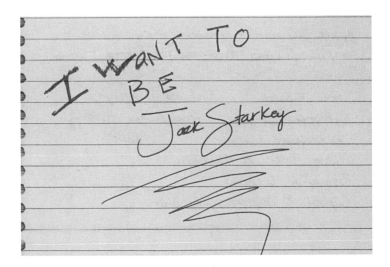

Through all these daydreams, I remained slightly confused about my gender and sexuality, but absolutely convinced that there was nothing I could ever do about it. I believed becoming Jack was impossible, so I let writing be my one outlet and spent the rest of my time working on becoming the perfect, desirable girl. And despite my deep sense of something not quite being right about the body I'd been given, my comfort with showing off that body only continued to grow.

•　•　•

In my junior year, I was inducted into the BC Biker Club, or Breakfast Club Biker Club, so called because we met at Waffle House every Friday morning before school. There were no motorcycles (or even bicycles) involved. Just waffles and cool biker nicknames like Crowbar Curly, T-Bone, Black Mamba, and my bequeathed moniker, Engine Joe.

I have no idea why they decided to call me Engine Joe. None of the nicknames were based in any reality—except for Crowbar Curly, who at least had curly hair—and they were all nonnegotiable. As soon as the others decided on your nickname, that's what you were stuck with.

Although we later allowed some girls in our surrounding friend group to join us at our sacred Waffle House visits on occasion, I was the only girl who was a full-fledged member of the BC Biker Club. Whenever this was challenged by girls wanting to join, the guys defended their stance by saying that I was a dude and that's just the way it was. Bless them.

I couldn't tell you why I was given dude status per se, but I think I'd been grandfathered into the club by being an attendee of the Waffle House breakfasts before the BC Biker Club was formalized as such— and I'd only been invited to those through my boyfriend at the time, Joel, aka Crowbar Curly.

I had barely known any of the other guys before he invited me along and when we broke up a few months later, my biggest fear was losing my place among these guys I had become so close to. But by that point, they had all joined the Theater Department and were effectively much more my friends than his. Post-breakup, the guys invited both of us to every social affair. At first, I politely declined, knowing they were his friends first, but after a while it was evident that I fit in with the group much better than he did. I still feel guilty that I effectively stole his friends, but the time I spent with the BC Biker Club remains some of the fondest memories of my life.

In addition to our five A.M. Waffle House escapades, the guys and I got up to a lot of shenanigans: recklessly racing our cars down the highways, going on adventures in the woods, seeing how many of us we could stack on top of one another's shoulders (the record was four for a very brief second), jamming on instruments only one of us could play proficiently, attempting skateboard tricks in parking lots, yelling our lungs out to Queen songs in the car, being pseudo-intellectuals at the local coffee shop, picking books out for one another at used bookstores, and one of our favorites for a short time—declaring places No Pants Zones.

LATE NIGHTS WITH THE BC BIKERS.

It started with No Pants Coffee, but soon became No Pants Car, No Pants Rehearsal, and more. Sometimes No Pants would morph into Trade Pants, wherein four or five of us would go into a public bathroom together and come out having all switched pants.

This was 2007, when tight, skinny jeans had just come into main-stream style, so the No Pants game had just as much bearing in a prag-matic need to air out as it did in boundary-pushing whimsy. Whenever we traded clothes across gender lines, we called it "Rose Robert-ing," based on the gender-bending of Montreal song "Rose Robert."

Despite how it may sound, we were a group of rule-abiding virgins, and even most of the queers among us thought we were straight at the time. In other words, our inhibited teenage hormones were running absolutely fucking wild.

No Pants Coffee was just scratching the sur-face. For a period, everything we did became laced with sensuality. Truth or Dare, complete with mod-erate stripping and same-gender folks making out, was a weekly occurrence. We loved full-contact sparring with one another just as much as piling half a dozen of us on one twin bed for a nap. It was rare for us to walk through the hallways of school without at least one person on another's shoulders (a serious hazard if you wanted to use your study hall time to actually study, because you could liter-ally be picked up by a friend and taken to the Theater Department to goof off instead). For a while, one of the guys even tried to normalize European cheek-kissing as a standard form of greeting. And then there was our most libertine activity: skinny-dipping.

AFTER ONE INSTANCE OF CLOTHES-SWAPPING.

Growing up in suburban Texas meant that almost every single one of our houses had a built-in swimming pool that was warm enough for swimming most months of the year. I don't remember when we first skinny-dipped together, but I do remember that there was never anything sexual about it. It was usually just me and two or three of the

BC Biker guys—who to this day, despite all evidence to the contrary above, remain almost entirely straight. We were artsy faux intellectuals who genuinely just thought it felt good to be free and one with nature. We spent most of our skinny-dipping time floating on our backs and reciting poetry about the stars. Sure, our raging hormones made it a bit more exciting, but nothing ever happened between any of us.

When I explained this to my teammates on the Oral Interp. team in between semifinal rounds at a competition one Saturday, they looked at me like I was stupid.

"Wow," one of them said. "You are such a hipster."

(Actually, he didn't say "hipster," because that wasn't part of our personal lexicon yet in 2007. He said "indie," but today we would say "hipster" and it would mean the exact same thing.)

My teammates had to explain to me that there were actual teenagers out there who might be skinny-dipping together in order to have sex, like they did in porn and trashy movies. Or at least, if anyone heard that I had been skinny-dipping with a bunch of guys, that's exactly what they would assume we were doing.

The reason my teammates and I were even having this conversation was because someone had made that exact assumption. A very angry girlfriend-of-one-of-the-BC-Biker-guys-type someone.

A few days previously, on the first day of our senior year, she and I had been in line to buy chicken sandwiches in the cafeteria. While we waited, she started telling me about how mad she was at her boyfriend.

I always got uncomfortable when the girlfriends of the BC Biker guys talked to me about their problems with their boyfriends. I felt a loyalty to the guys, but the girls were my close friends too. I was usually torn in two directions, but that day she was so upset I knew I should be on her side.

She started telling me about how she found out we all went skinny-dipping together the previous weekend and how she couldn't believe her boyfriend would do that without her present when they're supposed to be in a relationship.

As she talked, her face got steadily redder and tears began dripping onto her T-shirt. Crying is usually my cue to exit stage right as quickly as possible, but I was the only one there for her, so I mentally flipped through my social etiquette book and remembered I should offer her a comforting hug.

As I reached my arms toward her, she pushed me away and started yelling. Turns out, she wasn't mad at her boyfriend. She was mad at *me* and in the process of confronting me for getting naked with her boyfriend.

Oh. Right.

I guess that made sense. But we didn't do anything! Why would she think we would do anything? Nothing would ever happen between him and me. We had just been a bunch of guys being dudes!

Reflecting on this incident many years later, I find it ironic, and terribly embarrassing, for a number of reasons. First, as evidence that I've always been awful at reading people's social cues when they're upset. And second, due to the fact that I genuinely never considered it would be wrong of me to get naked with guys who were in relationships because, in my head, no matter how feminine I presented at the time, I was "one of the guys." I might not have been consciously aware of my gender identity or look anything like it, but it seemed like my cognitive reasoning was solidly male identified.

Not that that was an excuse. I was still completely in the wrong, and I eventually realized that after seeing how upset my friend was. Our skinny-dipping escapades fizzled out shortly after that, but the dissonance of my internal sense of identity continued.

There was such a strange battle going on in my mind in those latter years of high school. I was playing the game so well as a girl and reaping the social benefits of being accepted and desired. I had completely convinced myself that there was no way I could ever be a guy, but I still daydreamed about it on occasion. I might have had a real-life outlet for my boyishness with my goofy dude friends, but even around them I needed it to be clear that I was a cute, desirable girl. I started repressing my true feelings so intensely that I began to overcompensate.

I was petrified that anyone would suspect something was off about me, so I amped up my skirt-wearing and makeup game. I became even more of a flirt than I had been. I lived in fear that the few people I still interacted with from elementary school would out me to my new friends as having once been a tomboy. The idea that anyone would know about my boyish past was mortifying for some reason. So mortifying that one weekend morning when organizing family photo albums with my mom, I tore up every photo I found from my childhood in which I looked too masculine.

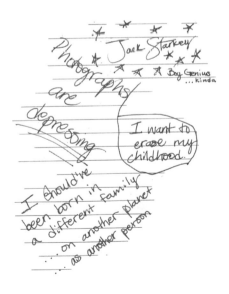

One morning when my then-boyfriend called me before I had fully woken up, I had a frog in my throat and answered the phone with an unexpectedly gravelly voice. He stumbled out nervously that he must have had the wrong number and, humiliated by my voice sounding so mannish, I let him think he had. I chugged a glass of water to clear my throat and answered his next call pretending I had no idea that he had first dialed "the wrong number."

I even stopped eating beef because my English teacher mentioned that Victorian women thought red meat was unladylike. I had careened to the complete opposite end of the spectrum from my childhood with incredible velocity and, despite flickers of Jack in my daydreams, I had no intention of turning back. This steamrolling of my true feelings, however, was not without consequences.

I had several breakdowns toward the end of my senior year and heading into college—acute moments where I'd flip a switch and have to excuse myself to go fall to the floor somewhere private, screaming and crying uncontrollably. I was never certain *what* I was crying about. Everything just felt like too much, and sometimes I couldn't take it anymore.

Senior year of high school.

Maybe it was the repression of my gender; maybe it was starting to see signs of my parents' marriage unraveling; maybe it was just the stress of ending high school and going away to college. I had, after all, unlike many LGBTQ+ people or indeed many people in general, loved high school. Despite everything I was going through, I made some true, lifelong friends and had more amazing, belly-laugh-filled moments than I can even remember.

Prom 2007.

But, after we had danced our butts off to "Apple Bottom Jeans" at prom and screened a compilation video I edited together of all the irreverent photos and videos we'd taken over the years, it was time to say good-bye to one another and to the only life we'd ever known.

CHAPTER NINE

it was the breast of times
It Was the Worst of Times

In August 2008, I matriculated at Southwestern University in the heart of Texas as an English/Religion double major. English because it was the one school subject in which I had always excelled and truly enjoyed. Religion because I had begun to doubt that institution and wanted to know more about everyone else's religions so I could best them in debates. I'm not joking. Thankfully, that angry skeptic period of my life was short-lived.

Despite having always been an honors student with grand dreams of the hallowed halls of university, when the time finally came to apply to college, I didn't put much thought into it.

Part of that stemmed from the realization of just how expensive it was. Even if by some miracle my grades got me into my dream schools (Stanford, Columbia, and Reed College), there was no way I would earn a merit-based scholarship substantial enough to afford them. Southwestern wasn't cheap, but it was at least in-state and I knew I could get a decent scholarship there. I applied for Early Decision, got accepted, and didn't have to worry about college applications for the rest of my senior year.

The other reason I became unenthused about college was because I'd had an existential crisis backstage at a play my junior year and realized that, apart from the stark financial realities of being an actor, I just didn't see the point of the craft anymore. So even though acting was about the only career I'd seriously considered my entire life, I did a one-eighty at the end of high school and thought maybe I'd be a college professor instead, unless something better came along.

So it was with a lost sense of purpose that I moved the three-hour drive south from my hometown to a cinder-block dorm room in Georgetown, Texas.

I may not have been certain about my academic and professional aspirations, but I was increasingly confident in my body. Finally satisfied with my sense of fashion, I still made faster friends with boys than with girls, which, combined with the confidence in my good looks, meant I was basically a one-stop-shop manic pixie dream girl for all the overly pretentious English-major boys smoking their tobacco pipes and quoting Jack Kerouac on the patio of the freshmen dormitory building.

Just as in my high school days of returning from a glitzed-up night at prom to write about the tux I would have worn had I been a boy, my gender dysphoria persisted in college despite my outward appearance and salacious behavior—and this time it manifested in a steady contemplation of my sexuality.

Just a year prior, I had been parroting my AP Psychology teacher's assertion that there are only two sexual orientations: gay and straight. Bisexuals have to choose one. This had been reassuring to me because even if I was sometimes interested in girls, I was also interested in boys. So I "chose" boys and got to tell myself I was a perfectly ordinary straight girl.

It's FASCINATING THAT I APPARENTLY TOOK NOTES ON GENDER IDENTITY DISORDER IN AP PSYCH CLASS BUT WASN'T ABLE TO MAKE THE CONNECTION THAT IT WAS THE SAME THING AS BEING TRANSGENDER OR THAT IT APPLIED TO ME. DID I JUST NOT UNDERSTAND? WAS I REPRESSING SO HARD THAT IT DIDN'T MATTER? WE'LL NEVER KNOW.

cont'd. lecture on human sexuality
Homosexuality:
enduring erotic response to one's own gender
not experimentation, ritualistic practice
DSM-I = disorder (1974- declassified)
Gender Identity Disorder - if het or hom
and is uncomfortable & seeks therapy
psychologists say bi need to pick something
1948 & '53 - took survey - most 8% men
3% women = homosexual
confounding variable - done in San Fran Bay

Between long-distance relationships, friends-with-benefits arrangements, and casual hookups, there was only ever one boy I got serious enough with in high school that we actually met each other's families and made it Myspace official. That boy was Joel, whose friends in the BC Biker Club I stole after I broke his heart. That's apparently how I treated the only guy who was willing to accept me as something more than his dirty little secret.

I don't know what it was that made a serious relationship with me seem unappealing to the general male populace at my high school. Some possibilities could have included the fact that my family didn't come from the strong Christian background many of my peers did, which was a no-go for a lot of boys who only wanted Good Christian Girlfriends; I was also a bit of a loose cannon, always saying the wrong thing and cracking inappropriate jokes just a bit too loudly, so I never made a great impression with parents. But maybe boys could just tell. Maybe there was an aura about me that said, "I'm really a man. Stay away!"

I did genuinely *want* to be in a real relationship, and whenever I wasn't dating someone, I collected make-out buddies like Pokémon cards. At one point, I was determined to make out with every single boy in the Choir Department that I found passably attractive—and even some that I didn't. It was just about the numbers.

Did I enjoy making out with boys? Sure. The ones who were good at it, anyway. It was high school after all. There was still a lot of slobber and overeager tongue action going on. While a lot of it felt like a game I simply wanted to win, I did genuinely enjoy gettin' physical with some boys.

The farthest I ever ventured with a girl in high school was making out with my best friends during games of Truth or Dare. It was always good for a laugh, but I never felt anything. Sometimes I even hoped for those fireworks old rom-coms tell you you're supposed to feel when you kiss the right person. Even if seeing fireworks with a girl wouldn't have been exactly the outcome I was hoping for, at least it would be *something* definitive. Something crystal clear to tell me who or what I was. As it happened, kissing those girls felt exactly the same as kissing boys I wasn't particularly attracted to.

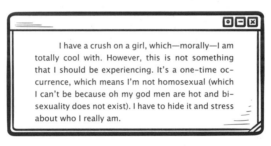

I have a crush on a girl, which—morally—I am totally cool with. However, this is not something that I should be experiencing. It's a one-time occurrence, which means I'm not homosexual (which I can't be because oh my god men are hot and bisexuality does not exist). I have to hide it and stress about who I really am.

AUGUST 23, 2006.

I didn't go into college expecting any sort of big revelation about my sexuality (and certainly not about my gender), but as for many young people, college was a brave new world of ideas and people I'd never known existed.

Compared to the LGBTQ+ desert of my high school, Southwestern was like a verdant oasis of gayness, an *ogaysis*, if you will. At the club fair during orientation there was a pride club, several feminist organizations, and some type of sex-positive group. Nearly every club was handing out free condoms, and even one of the fraternities had a little rainbow flag included in their display.

This might have been Texas and technically a Methodist school, but I would soon find out it was a gay haven for many of the queer kids from small Texas towns. I could imagine their school counselors recommending this one-thousand-student, closed-campus university located in the then #1 Retirement Town in America as a school where they could be themselves without experiencing the culture shock of going to a bigger city.

Compared to my high school, where I could never tell which you'd get in more trouble for, being gay or being a Democrat, Southwestern was staggeringly progressive. I once heard that a professor at the nearby Baptist school, Baylor University, referred to Southwestern as the Gomorrah to the University of Texas at Austin's Sodom.

Lɪᴏɴ ᴘʀɪᴅᴇ ɪɴ ᴛʜᴇ ᴅᴏʀᴍs! Aɴᴅ ᴍʏ ғʀɪᴇɴᴅ's ᴛʜᴜᴍʙ ᴏᴠᴇʀ ᴛʜᴇ ʟᴇɴs!

Even the professors represented diversity on a level I hadn't encountered from educators before. I had three (three!) Jewish professors. That was more Jewish people than I'd ever met in my life up to that point. My professors were proud socialists, pacifists, feminists, and openly gay. Gayer than gay, in some cases.

In the first month of school, a few of my classmates told me about their First Year Seminar professor who used "they/them" pronouns and told my classmates that they were pansexual and genderqueer.

I had heard the word *pansexual* before and *sort of* understood it to mean attraction to people regardless of gender (though I think at the time I might've been confusing it with *polyamory*, which is the practice of or desire for relationships involving more than two people), but I had never heard the word *genderqueer*.

It was described to me as being neither male nor female. This didn't entirely make sense to me. Yes, I'd heard about transgender kids from that one harrowing *Oprah* special, but those were people who lived entirely as an opposite gender—and I kept forgetting exactly the right word for them anyway.

Was it *transvestite*? No, that's what Dr. Frank-N-Furter and Eddie Izzard were. Men who dressed as women sometimes, but not for performance like drag queens. Eddie Izzard said it was like being "a male lesbian."

Was it *transsexual*? *Transgender*? One of those was definitely the one where the anatomy you're born with isn't quite male or female, right?

WRONG.

Terms to Avoid

I was pretty confused about what certain terms meant back in my freshman year of college. Even though some of these are covered at the front of this book, let's do a refresher, and also talk about terms you should try to avoid.

Transgender refers to someone whose gender does not match the sex they were assigned at birth.

Transsexual refers to someone whose gender does not match the sex they were assigned at birth, usually in reference to binary trans women and trans men who undergo some type of medical transition. The term has gone out of favor with most people in the current and upcoming generations, but remains an important identity marker—as distinct from *transgender*—for older generations.

Someone who was born with any number of conditions in which their sexual or reproductive anatomy does not adhere to the typical definitions of male or female is intersex—*not* transgender or transsexual, as I thought my freshman year. Some intersex people identify as transgender, but they are two very separate things.

Genderqueer refers to someone whose gender is beyond the binary of male and female. It can be used as an umbrella term or as one of many distinct nonbinary genders, alongside *agender*, *genderfluid*, *bigender*, and more. Some genderqueer people identify under the larger nonbinary umbrella and/or as transgender, but not all of them do.

Pansexual, or *panromantic*, refers to being attracted to people regardless of gender. It's a sexual/romantic orientation, not a gender identity. People of any gender can be pansexual and/or panromantic.

Now on to terms you should avoid:

"Transgendered," "a transgender," or "transgenders": The word *transgender* is an adjective and should not be used as a noun or a verb. You should say "Jack is a transgender person," not "Jack is transgendered" or "Jack is a transgender." Using it as a noun rather than an adjective implies it's the only thing we are, rather than just a part of who we are.

"Transvestite": This word may be used by individuals who identify with it (like Eddie Izzard, for example). However, it has fallen out of popularity, and many transgender people associate it with historically discriminatory and hurtful usage.

"He-she," "she-male," "it": Phrases like these are extremely hurtful and dehumanizing to the person you're referring to. Instead, you should use the person's correct name, pronouns, and gender label. If you are uncertain about any of these, listen to how other people are referring to the person or ask someone who knows them. As a last resort, you can ask the individual themself respectfully and privately—possibly by first introducing yourself and giving your pronouns.

"Hermaphrodite": This term is regarded by most people as a slur. It originally referred to intersex individuals, not to transgender people (see above). Unless you are intersex yourself, you should not use this word.

"Tranny": This word has become a slur in most people's books. You may hear some trans women using it in reference to themselves. They are the only ones with the right to reclaim the term, as they're the ones it has been predominantly weaponized against. If you're not trans, you should never use this word.

"Biologically male," "biologically female," "genetically male," "genetically female," "natal male," "natal female," "born a man," "born a woman": Sex and gender are far more complex than these terms imply. A better alternative is "assigned male at birth" or "assigned female at birth." Though you should also ask yourself why you need to bring up that part of a person's history anyway.

"Sex change," "sex-change operation," "the surgery," "preoperative," "postoperative," "pre-op," "post-op": The preferred term for transition-related surgery is *gender affirmation surgery*, but it's important to note that there is no one surgery that magically transforms a person into the other sex. Transition is a long journey that can take anywhere from a few months to several years and can include many different social and medical processes. Furthermore, not all transgender people undergo medical transition. Using these sorts of terms is inaccurate, fuels misconceptions, emphasizes a before-and-after transformation, and causes unnecessary fixation on a transgender person's anatomy and medical history.

It is never appropriate to ask a transgender person about their anatomy or medical history. Would you ask someone who isn't transgender about their genitals? We understand your curiosity, but please treat transgender people with the same respect you do all other humans. Googling takes the same amount of time and doesn't make your transgender friend feel uncomfortable, exploited, or dehumanized. You can learn more about the medical side of transition in the resources at the back of this book.

Trans terminology is constantly evolving. It's important to always be listening and learning. If you are not trans, do not correct other trans people on the words they use to describe themselves—even if you've heard that those words were wrong or outdated.

Overall, think about what the words you're saying actually mean, prioritize using everyone's correct name and pronouns, apologize if you mess up, and always let trans people know that you see and respect them as who they are. True effort and compassion will always be appreciated.

Despite being presented with a real, live gender-nonconforming person (who probably would have been happy to talk me through my feelings and provide me with resources), I didn't see myself in them at all. Maybe it was because the repression train was still rolling right along, but learning about a genderqueer person in my midst didn't ping my radar in the least.

Still, gender and sexuality were being discussed in all my classes in new ways——as perfectly normal, beautifully variant, and as a facet of all parts of life. Hearing sexuality discussed in this way by respected, qualified adults made me start reconsidering some of the stricter ideas about sexuality I had been taught in high school. And I say "taught" with a grain of salt. Our sex education growing up had mostly consisted of annual school assemblies about practicing abstinence and saving ourselves for marriage. They showed us gruesome close-ups of genital warts and made us carry around lifelike dolls that cried bloody murder every half hour until you stuck a key in their back—to show us how horrible teen pregnancy would be.

But none of the presentations ever mentioned being gay. The only two times I remember any part of the LGBTQ+ initialism being uttered by a teacher was in the aforementioned misled AP Psychology course, and when my Pre-AP Biology teacher warned us that bisexual people are more likely to contract the flu. It's possible I misheard her, but honestly I kind of doubt it.

So having been exposed to all these new people and new ideas about sexuality in college, I became pretty certain not only that there were more choices than just gay and straight, but that all sexual orientations were just a hoax invented by The Man. I was hesitant to slap an identity on myself, but philosophically I believed all humans were sexually fluid, so I must be too. We should just be who we are, man. What even are "labels"?

It turns out this is not the way you should answer the question "Are you bi?" to an inebriated girl at a party with whom you have no interest in making out. She'll take it as a yes and cut you off halfway through your Carl Jung quotes by sticking her tongue down your throat.

I learned that one the hard way. In front of a boy I desperately wanted to hook up with that night. We didn't end up hooking up, which could have been for any number of reasons, but at the time I was convinced he saw my making out with her (as nonconsensual as it was) to be evidence that I wasn't actually interested in him. College parties, man; what a trip.

The thing was, for all my philosophical espousing and evolving toward the idea that I maybe wasn't really entirely straight, I wasn't ready to tell people that or to act on it just yet. It was still easier to tell myself, and everyone else, that I was only attracted to men.

There's a moment in a deleted scene from *Miss Congeniality* when Sandra Bullock's character, a disheveled, mannish FBI agent who later has to go undercover as a beauty queen, is asked by her dad if she's a lesbian. She guffaws with her trademark snort and says, "I *wish*."

I completely understood what she meant. Falling masculine of center as a woman who's attracted to men was complicated. I didn't feel free to dress in the boyish ways I wanted because I didn't think any straight man would ever be attracted to me if I looked like that. Attraction or not, everyone would assume I was a lesbian. Like Sandra Bullock's character, I couldn't help feeling like life might have made more sense if I were wholly and exclusively attracted to women.

As it was, I continued only hooking up with men for my first year of college. I ended up falling into an unhealthy not-quite relationship and making a lot of bad decisions. The all-consuming and manipulative nature of the relationship made me emotionally volatile. I would have outbursts in public that made me too embarrassed to show my face in the dining hall or at campus events. I failed to make real friends on campus and burned bridges with the few classmates who tried to reach out. I also kept getting sick because, at my boyfriend's insistence, we weren't using protection.

When I mentioned that I had missed two periods in a row and was only using the pull-out method, an older classmate who was trying once again to drag me out of the mess I'd gotten myself into forced me to take a pregnancy test.

I *had* suspected I might be pregnant for a few weeks, but I hadn't taken a test because I didn't want it to be real—and I also didn't want to spend the money. Those little sticks are expensive!

It was all too much to think that I might've been ruining my future just a few months into my college career by having to drop out to raise a kid. Even if I decided to give the baby up for adoption, pregnancy would still require a lot of time and money—not to mention the humiliation of everyone knowing what I had done.

I considered abortion, but as I lay on my poppy-flower-print bedspread alone in my dorm room, running my hands along my stomach, imagining the beginnings of another human forming inside me, I felt an overpowering sense of love and protection for that maybe-not-real and definitely not-yet-sentient cluster of cells. It shocked me that I could already feel such deep warmth for something that might not even exist.

In the end, the two pregnancy tests I bought both came back negative. I was relieved, of course, but a small part of me was sad to lose the tiny human who might have been.

Trans Men and Pregnancy

When you begin hormone replacement therapy, you are told that you need to prepare yourself for the fact that you might be unable to bear children. There is certainly a chance this can happen (and if you took hormone blockers as a child, followed by hormone therapy, you will definitively be unable to conceive), but there have been countless transmasculine people over the years who have successfully conceived and delivered children after beginning hormone replacement treatment—some who went off testosterone with the intention of conceiving and some who were still taking it when they conceived by accident. For this reason, it's very important to continue practicing some form of birth control while on testosterone if you're engaging in sexytimes that could lead to baby making.

It might seem strange to some that a person who has ostensibly spent so much time and energy on being seen as a man or a masculine person in society would want to bear children. Certainly a few decades ago, such desires were seen as disqualifying for a gender dysphoria diagnosis in trans men (and likely still are by some less-informed therapists). But there are several reasons trans guys might physically bear children: they may not be aware of their identity yet, they may be actively trying to repress that identity, they might know they will probably transition one day but want to have children first, or they are comfortable enough in their identity to be a man who is pregnant.

Even for the last category of people, it can still be a tough period of dysphoria as your body goes through something traditionally so associated with femininity as you navigate the world as a pregnant man. J Wallace has a fantastic piece in the book *Gender Outlaws: The Next Generation* called "The Manly Art of Pregnancy," about how being pregnant made him feel *more* like a man, both due to certain masculinizing features pregnancy hormones can cause and because of the deep, fatherly sense of protecting and caring for his family.

To learn more about transmasculine people and childbirth, I recommend the 2006 documentary *Transparent*, directed by Jules Rosskam, and the podcast *Masculine Birth Ritual* by Grover Wehman-Brown.

After a trip to the campus health center, I found out I'd been missing periods because I was anemic. I had lost ten pounds in just a few months because I had stopped being able to stand people's looks of judgment when I went to the school's lone dining hall and honestly, I was so depressed I barely had an appetite.

I'd like to say I fixed my ways after all those wake-up calls, but I didn't. I was still so deep in that relationship and so consumed with self-revulsion because of it that my unhealthy and dangerous habits continued. Even after the pregnancy scare, we didn't start using condoms—

though I did start taking birth control. I didn't start eating better, even with the anemia scare, because I had always dreamt of being as thin as I finally was, my hips were the smallest they'd ever been, and I didn't like having periods anyway, so it seemed like a win-win to me.

My day-to-day life was spiraling out of control. Looking back, I'm still not sure how I got myself into that mess of a relationship. Maybe I just felt *that* negatively about myself. Maybe it had something to do with repressing my gender. Maybe I just fell into a bad situation by accident, like so many people do. Whatever the reason was, I paradoxically hated everything to do with the guy I was seeing, yet my every thought and action revolved around earning his love and attention. He'd drawn me in when I hadn't wanted him, groomed me to be what he wanted, and then tossed me to the side when I finally loved him back. There were several harrowing months when I tried to convince him to stop sleeping with other people and be in a real relationship with me, but he wouldn't budge. When he finally broke things off for good the night before Easter, I was a shivering shell of a person.

Spring semester of freshman year.

The following weekend, I drove home to have my mom nurse me through the breakup. When I met her for lunch at her office where she worked as the manager of a community-relief agency, she shared the news that she and my dad were divorcing.

So much for the breakup help.

CHAPTER TEN

down the rabbit hole

That spring semester of my freshman year was so harrowing that to this day I can't remember most of it. People who were there have told me things I did that I have absolutely no recollection of doing. In the years following, I occasionally got flashbacks of lost scenes in vivid detail—always at the most inopportune times, like while walking down the street or in the middle of class.

There was one moment, however, that I remember with complete clarity. It was an evening toward the end of the year when the expedition to uncovering my gender identity got an unexpected kick start.

I was in a dorm mate's room doing homework while he scrolled through Facebook. Suddenly he sat up straight and said, "Oh, wow."

When I asked him what was up, he scooted over so I could read off his monitor.

A classmate I knew as a guy had posted a Facebook status announcing her intention to begin living as a woman. Starting the very next day, she would be wearing women's clothing to classes, using female pronouns, and asking people to call her Luna.

I was floored. You could do that? Without any surgeries or anything, you could just tell people you were living as another gender? I had never heard of such a thing.

I tried to hide my shock from my friend.

Luna had just blown a hole in my entire worldview of what being transgender really consisted of, and I needed to know more. I had never clarified my confusion around the different words like *transgender* and *transsexual* back when I met that genderqueer professor, so I was still pretty fuzzy on the whole thing.

Back in my own room, I pulled out my laptop to begin my investigation. Even a quick scan of Wikipedia showed me that I had been laboring under some far-flung delusions about the correct meanings of various trans-related terminology. As I bookmarked page after page for further reading later, I couldn't help thinking I might finally be on the right path.

If there was so much more to the world of gender variance than I previously thought, then maybe, just maybe, there was a place for me there and an answer to my Big Dark Secret.

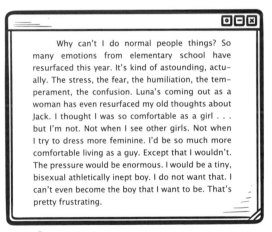

Why can't I do normal people things? So many emotions from elementary school have resurfaced this year. It's kind of astounding, actually. The stress, the fear, the humiliation, the temperament, the confusion. Luna's coming out as a woman has even resurfaced my old thoughts about Jack. I thought I was so comfortable as a girl . . . but I'm not. Not when I see other girls. Not when I try to dress more feminine. I'd be so much more comfortable living as a guy. Except that I wouldn't. The pressure would be enormous. I would be a tiny, bisexual athletically inept boy. I do not want that. I can't even become the boy that I want to be. That's pretty frustrating.

FEBRUARY 27, 2009: I BECAME A TINY, BISEXUAL, ATHLETICALLY INEPT BOY AFTER ALL, BUT I'M OKAY WITH IT.

I didn't spend much time with those bookmarked pages when I went home that summer. The trouble was that a lot of it didn't make sense to me yet. I was also fairly preoccupied with getting accustomed to life post-divorce and deciding if I should transfer schools the following year since I didn't think I could face going back to the scene of my horrific relationship.

In addition, I was considering a change in academic direction. Just three weeks into trying to be an English major with zero interest in the performing arts, I'd ended up falling back in. I had gotten permission to make a documentary for my final project in my First Year Seminar, instead of writing a paper. I'd been making goofy videos more or less my entire life and in high school had gotten particularly adept at getting out of assignments by editing together clever, on-topic videos with my classmates, so I thought I'd see if the trick still worked in college.

The short documentary I put together analyzing how the students in our class mirrored the political science concepts we'd been taught in the seminar impressed my professor so much that he ended up getting me a job as an on-campus videographer and convincing me I had real potential as some type of filmmaker. The problem was, our small university didn't offer film courses. If I wanted to pursue that career path in earnest, I'd need to transfer.

Add to all of that working nearly full-time as a barista and spending most evenings losing myself and my problems at parties, I had a lot on my plate that summer. So I didn't make much progress on my research mission until I was back on campus in the fall.

Pretty early into that fall semester, a fellow sophomore on the newspaper staff wrote an absolutely horrendous piece about why the Women's Studies Department was pointless. He claimed it was satire, which I believe was his intention because he wasn't a mean-spirited guy, but he also clearly had no clue what satire was. Or what the Women's Studies Department actually was, for that matter.

The school was rightfully up in arms. Within a few days, the writer had agreed to go on the campus radio and talk to some of the brightest folks in the Women's Studies Department. They were relatively decent toward him, and he was eager to learn. After a while, the Women's Studies majors diagnosed his main problem: a misunderstanding of the difference between sex and gender.

Listening from my on-campus apartment as I worked on my Mandarin penmanship homework, I scoffed. There isn't a difference between sex and gender, I thought to myself. They're synonyms!

But I kept listening and was soon opening tab after tab in my browser, Mandarin homework abandoned, to supplement the discussion they were having on the radio. I needed to see simple, clear definitions of these apparently different terms.

Sex vs. Gender

Part of why I was confused by the difference between sex and gender (apart from my prudish Texan insistence that gender was simply the polite way to refer to the sex of a person) was because the distinction *is* pretty complex, and can vary depending on whom you talk to.

An easy way it's often explained is that *sex* is your biological classification and *gender* is what you innately feel in your head and your heart. *Sex* is what you're assigned at birth, and *gender* is how you identify . . . but that's not exactly accurate either.

First of all, what does "biological classification" even mean? Does it refer to anatomy? Hormones? Chromosomes? All three? Despite what we're taught, not all of those line up so cleanly between the binary sexes of male and female. Babies are assigned a sex at birth based on their apparent anatomy, but one in two thousand babies is born with atypical genitalia and either classified as intersex or forcibly assigned a binary sex (often with nonconsensual surgeries performed on the infant). What we usually think of as "male hormones" and "female hormones" are both present in people of all sexes at varying levels and can change due to all sorts of environmental factors, from pregnancy to taking antidepressants to hormone replacement therapy. Chromosomes are not something most people have analyzed, and there are a number of intersex conditions that lead to a person having chromosomes that differ from the ones we typically associate with their assigned sex. Examples abound of biological sex characteristics not matching up along clearly divided lines, so it would seem the strict binary classification we've created for sex is a cultural belief in itself. Because of this, some trans advocates prefer to call everything described above *gender* and reserve the word *sex* only for the act of having sex.

But let's work here with the framework that sex is what you're assigned at birth based on some combination of your anatomy, hormones, and chromosomes. So what's gender? Gender is your innate sense of being male, female, both, neither, somewhere in between, or some combination thereof. It's also another way of classifying humans based on characteristics. Like sex, it's largely informed by cultural beliefs and societal norms. For trans people, their gender identity differs from the sex they were assigned at birth. Personally, I prefer to simply call gender identity "gender," as I feel "identity" implies it's more a choice and less a fact.

Beyond your gender identity, there is also gender expression, which is how you present yourself—how you do your hair, what clothes you wear, how you speak, etc. Someone's gender expression doesn't necessarily define their gender. A woman can wear masculine clothes and sport a crew cut and still be a woman. A man can wear makeup and paint his nails and still be a man. This applies to cis people as well as trans people. Just because a trans man chooses to wear more feminine clothing doesn't make him any less of a man.

Other concepts related to gender include roles and attribution. Gender roles are the cultural expectations of your gender; for example, we've all heard the one where women stay at home to raise the kids and men go to work. Gender roles are constantly changing with society, and, as with how you express yourself, gender roles do not define your gender. A woman who joins a male-dominated field does not become a man because of her job.

"Attribution" refers to the buckets we sort people into when we first meet them. It's natural for our brains to group people into various boxes at first glance—tall, black-haired, friendly, attractive—and sorting people into genders is the same, but that doesn't mean it's unproblematic or should be immutable. Just like you would accept it if someone you assumed at first glance was straight informed you they're gay, so should you respect someone who informs you that their gender is something other than what you initially assumed. What *other* people attribute a person's gender to be doesn't define what it actually is. The only person who can define a person's gender is that person.

And if we really want to complicate things, we can throw sexuality into the mix. Your sexual orientation is who you are sexually and/or romantically attracted to. Trans people can be any sexual or romantic orientation, just like cis people can. Many gay trans people are asked why they bothered to transition when they could've just "stayed straight." As the trans male character Coach Beiste astutely described it on *Glee*, being trans is not about who you want to go to bed *with*, it's who you want to go to bed *as*.

Sexual orientation is a whole other rabbit hole. If you want to learn more about the many variances of sexual and romantic attraction, I recommend *The ABC's of LGBT+* by Ash Hardell. For more on the differences between sex and gender, check out "The Gender Unicorn" by Trans Student Educational Resources.

It was starting to make sense, but I wasn't quite there yet. I could tell I was being shown more pieces of the puzzle to add to the ones I'd gathered after Luna's coming out, but I needed to figure out how they fit together.

For a few weeks thereafter, I spent several hours sitting alone in my bedroom just thinking. The nuances between the terms *sex* and *gender* had me considering the implications of all these revelations for my own life. If all these things—sex, gender, and sexual orientation—were disparate parts of a person's whole, could it be true that it was possible to be a person who was assigned female at birth, who was mostly attracted to guys, but who also felt more like a guy herself?

At the very least, these discoveries had led me to new terms I could try googling in conjunction with how I felt and a growing confidence that, whatever I was, there were probably a few other people like me out there in the world.

Finally, one day that fall semester when I had finished my homework and begun my favorite evening activity of searching online for clues to my identity, I stumbled on TransPulse (at the time called Laura's Playground), a resource hub and message board for transgender people of all stripes. I had fallen headfirst into a vortex of real stories, new vocabulary, and other people asking questions just like mine. It was more than I ever could have wished for.

Almost immediately, I noticed people who identified as trans talking about being gay. Just like that. Like it was no big deal. There were tons of them. Maybe even more than half of the trans people I came across on that message board were attracted to people of the same gender at least some of the time.

Had it seriously been that simple all along?! I was furious that I'd missed out on a whole teenage-hood of living as the gender I was meant to be because I'd been too stupid to realize that, of course, trans people are just people and can therefore be straight, gay, bi, pan, ace, or anything else just like cis people can be!

The big mistake I had made was assuming that there was only one way to be trans. This idea is pervasive both within and without the trans community—the idea that you must feel, act, dress, and believe a certain way in order to *really* be trans.

There's Not Just One Way to Be Trans

Across time and cultures, trans people have always been here. Exactly what being trans encompasses and how we describe it, however, has shifted throughout time and place. These shifts in language necessarily change how people have chosen to express and act on their feelings of incongruence with the gender they were assigned at birth. Some cultures embraced gender diversity to varying degrees, like the hijra in India and Pakistan, the māhū in Hawaiian culture, and two-spirit people in some indigenous American nations. Other cultures responded by doubling down on strict gender roles, often using their sacred texts and government policies to stigmatize and punish people who broke free of those roles or to mandate gender expression.

Throughout US history, we can look at instances of gender nonconformity and guess at who may have identified as transgender given modern definitions, but we can never know for certain, of course, since we can't ask them. For example, many people assigned female at birth served in the Civil War, but was that because they identified as male—or was it out of pride for their country and a desire to escape the limits on women's rights? A good indicator is whether they continued living as men after the war, like Albert Cashier did after the Civil War and Deborah

Sampson attempted to do after serving in the Revolutionary War—but again, we can only guess.

Even now, as labels like *nonbinary*, *genderfluid*, *agender*, and many more have gained popularity, the way we think about gender individually and collectively is shifting. Some trans people who in the past may have felt pressure to conform to a binary in their transition in order to protect their safety and reputation or to gain access to resources, might today feel freer to be true to themselves in a less rigid expression.

Knowing our history can give us a broader view of the possibilities out there to help us better understand ourselves as well as others. In the LGBTQ+ community, our history isn't taught to us by our families as we grow up. We have to discover it on our own—whether it's passed down by chosen family and community elders, uncovered in library books, or sometimes, sadly, never discovered at all. Learning about who came before us and what they fought for can help us appreciate what we have now. Even as we acknowledge that we have so much farther to go, we can be inspired to keep fighting by the resilience of those who came before us.

Here are just a few transcestors and gender-nonconforming icons I recommend learning more about:

Alonso Díaz Ramírez de Guzmán
Deborah Sampson
Albert Cashier
We'wha
Alan Hart
Lili Elbe
Louise Lawrence
Michael Dillon
Christine Jorgensen

Stormé DeLarverie
Reed Erickson
Marsha P. Johnson
Sylvia Rivera
Lou Sullivan

Flip to the Further Learning section at the back of this book for more print and digital recommendations to kick-start your journey through history.

There is no one way to be trans because no one trans person is the same, and because gender is a wibbly-wobbly mess that is ever-undulating with the ebbs and flows of society. Up until the mid-twentieth century, pink was seen as a strong, masculine color for boys. Women in the United States weren't completely free to wear pants as everyday wear until the 1960s. The idea of what men's and women's roles in the household should be have changed rapidly even just in my lifetime. What people of all genders are supposed to do or not do is always changing across time and across cultures.

Even for transgender people, the way we have defined ourselves and how we have lived our lives has varied drastically throughout history. While nowadays people seeking to transition from one binary gender to another, such as from female to male, probably share some common feelings and a common path, they have just as many differences among them based on other factors at play like their age, sexual orientation, race, religion, ability status, cultural heritage, and more. And when you consider all the people who aren't male or female, whose gender falls somewhere in between or on a different plane entirely, the variations are even more infinite.

It was a lot for me to digest at the time. I had discovered an entire world of people just like me, but I didn't know where exactly I was comfortable fitting in just yet, and I definitely had no idea what I wanted to do about it in the world beyond the message board. One thing I knew I wanted to do was try binding my chest. I was overjoyed to discover that binding was a common and effective practice among transmasculine people. All the guys on the message board regularly discussed their various methods and the best products. I quickly learned that binding with an Ace bandage was not a smart thing to do. It was painful, led to long-term rib, lung, and skin damage, and wasn't as effective as a real binder anyway.

So naturally, the first thing I did was go to the grocery store and buy an Ace bandage.

Alone in the en-suite bathroom of my on-campus apartment that evening, I took off my shirt and bra and wrapped the Ace bandage around my breasts. It flattened them better than anything I had ever tried before. Four layers of sports bras had nothing on this!

Standing in profile, I actually teared up gazing at the body in the mirror that I had so desperately wanted to see for so many years. It would be another year before I would buy a proper binder and another five and a half before I was sure enough in myself to tell other people who I was. But in that moment, it felt as though the world was exactly how it always should have been.

What Is Binding? (and How to Do It Safely)

Binding is the use of a compression device to flatten one's chest, usually with the purpose of relieving dysphoria in transmasculine and nonbinary individuals.

It's common for people to experiment with household items like duct tape or compression bandages for binding; however, these methods are extremely unsafe. They can lead to reduced breathing, skin irritation, bleeding, bruised ribs, fluid buildup in the lungs, and more.

To combat unsafe practices, many companies produce safe, nylon compression vests designed specifically for people who want to bind safely. A growing but still less common option for folks with smaller chests is to bind using K-Tape, or kinesiology tape. This elastic cotton adhesive tape is designed for athletic pain and injuries, which means it is relatively safe for skin. K-Tape isn't meant for taping around your whole chest; rather, you place one to three six-inch strips on either side of your torso to pull your chest back and flat. Individuals should still use caution and stop using it if they experience skin irritation, trouble breathing, or soreness in their ribs.

Even though binders are the safest method of binding, they still come with risks. To avoid rib damage or breathing complications, you should never wear a binder for more than eight hours a day, and never while sleeping. When breaking in a new binder, you should wear it even less. Take breaks throughout the day to remove it, take a few big breaths, and give your lungs a good cough.

Despite how tempting it might be, never buy a binder that's too small for you. The company you're buying from should have a size chart and measurement instructions alongside each product. Use them.

Similarly, don't double up on binders, tape your chest under or above the binder, or otherwise combine methods. This puts you at the same risks mentioned above.

You really shouldn't wear a binder to swim or to exercise, as the binder can compress your chest too tightly. In the case of swimming, chlorine can degrade the binder's material over time, making it more dangerous. Some companies like gc2b have designed binders specifically for swimming.

Extended binder use over many years can decrease your skin's elasticity and possibly affect any top surgery outcomes. If you can, I recommend rubbing cocoa butter or another lotion onto your skin each night to help keep it healthy.

CHAPTER ELEVEN

the great escape

I tried wearing the Ace bandage to class a couple of times, but apart from it nearly asphyxiating me, it usually slid down my chest within a few minutes of putting it on. Nothing is as distracting as feeling your boob slowly peek out of its cocoon beneath your shirt while your gentlemanly gray-haired professor intones on the social ramifications of *The Country Wife*.

Despite its complete inutility, I continued attempting to wear the Ace bandage here and there. I had discovered the absolute joy and reassuring comfort of an item that affirmed my gender identity. Even if I hadn't changed how I was dressing or presenting to people with my outer layers, I at least knew that my chest was wrapped tightly beneath my shirt and cardigan.

By then I had learned the term *gender dysphoria*, which refers to distress experienced when your gender doesn't match the one you were assigned at birth. This dissonance can be felt in your relationship to your body, in how society treats you, and more. In addition to being a useful term to explain that intense feeling, it's the current diagnosis for transgender and transsexual individuals in the *Diagnostic and Statistical Manual of Mental Disorders*. It's the diagnosis that usually has to be stamped on our medical records in order to receive treatment and to change our gender markers on legal documents.

Gender Dysphoria

In addition to being a useful term to describe deep unease and discomfort with one's assigned sex, gender dysphoria is currently the name of the diagnosis required to access transition-related services and legal gender-marker changes in many jurisdictions in the United States.

Gender Identity Disorder first appeared in the third edition of the *Diagnostic and Statistical Manual of Mental Disorders* (DSM-III) in 1980. By DSM-V in 2013, transgender activists had successfully assisted in changing Gender Identity Disorder to gender dysphoria. As explained by the World Professional Association for Transgender Health (WPATH), "A disorder is a description of something with which a person might struggle, not a description of the person or the person's identity. Thus, transsexual, transgender, and gender-nonconforming individuals are not inherently disordered. Rather, the distress of gender dysphoria, when present, is the concern that might be diagnosable and for which various treatment options are available." In other words, this classification implies gender dysphoria is a treatable condition, whereas the prior one, Gender Identity Disorder, pathologized a person's very identity.

Whether gender dysphoria should be removed entirely from the DSM (as homosexuality was partially in 1973 and fully in 1987) remains a matter of debate among trans people. On the one hand, many believe that its inclusion gives trans people a better chance of securing health insurance coverage for hormones and other medical services. Others, however, argue that it makes no sense for something with a physical treatment, rather than a mental one, to be classified as a mental condition. Further, including it in the DSM as a mental condition that is often required to be diagnosed before medical and legal steps toward transition can be taken is another layer of gatekeeping preventing trans people from accessing care.

One option that would retain the ability to access medical services and insurance coverage is something similar to what the World Health Organization (WHO) did in 2018. They removed what they called "gender incongruence" entirely from the mental health section of their International Classification of Diseases (ICD), stating that "evidence is now clear that it is not a mental disorder" and that classifying it as such can cause "enormous stigma" for transgender people. However, gender incongruence remains in the ICD, now housed under the sexual health category, because the WHO acknowledges that gender incongruence *can* come with significant health care needs, and medical and insurance providers therefore need a way to code it.

As we work toward the best solution, it's important to remember the history of how and why we got to where we currently are, as well as the effects various decisions have on all different stripes of trans people, especially those with additional barriers to access.

I was more than familiar with dysphoria. The curves of my hips and chest never looked like I thought they should in clothing, no matter what kind I tried on. Even when I was trying to be a "normal girl," I still felt frustrated by being treated like one. Nothing about how I moved through the world felt right. But when I started exploring solutions that would help me feel more at home in my body, I started experiencing a new sensation: intense happiness and contentment. Looking in the mirror and seeing my flat chest felt so innately right that it would flood me with a rush of endorphins.

After a time, I decided that this feeling of being affirmed in my authentic gender, so opposite yet still so related to the concept of gender dysphoria, could perhaps be properly described as gender *euphoria*. I used that term in my head for many years before I discovered that other trans people referred to that feeling with the same term. It's such a natural inverse to dysphoria that it's unsurprising so many people would coin the term independently of one another.

A few passing moments of euphoria when experimenting with items that affirmed my masculine gender didn't take away from the still-present crushing dysphoria, however. Dysphoria can be complicated. It's impacted by so many other factors in life. For my part, it's possible my chest dysphoria has always gone beyond my gender identity. Even during those periods of my life when I thought I might be content living out my life as a girl, I still wanted a flat chest. I could've settled for a very small chest, though I would've pined for the freedom to run around the beach in nothing but board shorts.

Perhaps those desires *are* wrapped up in my gender dysphoria. Or perhaps they're a result of the fat-shaming environment I grew up in, where rail-thin girls were praised and curvy girls tried to hide their bodies.

Whatever the cause, the curve of my hips and the relatively large size of my chest compared to my small frame were a constant ache of despondency in my daily life. So finding a solution to at least one of those things made my heart soar.

I wasn't ready to commit to buying a real binder just yet. I don't think I even really researched them for a while because, despite having read about them on TransPulse, the first time I ever saw one was in the docuseries *TransGeneration*. And I didn't like it.

One of the supporting characters is shown from the back putting on his white Underworks binder for one of the last times before his top surgery. The binder was discolored from use, a constricting, high-necked tank top. Its flimsy-looking material squeezed the guy's body in all sorts of unflattering ways. It was not sexy. I immediately understood why binding was so often portrayed with compression bandages in art and the media. Those real binders had zero aesthetic appeal.

Jack's Top Ten Favorite Trans Documentaries (in No Particular Order)

Paris Is Burning

You Don't Know Dick

A Year in Transition

True Trans with Laura Jane Grace

Free CeCe!

Kumu Hina

Growing Up Coy

Screaming Queens

Southern Comfort

My Prairie Home

This first impression put me off buying a binder for quite a while. I had also absorbed the common narrative that binders are expensive and assumed I couldn't invest in one just yet. In truth, they're about thirty bucks, which is definitely cost-prohibitive for many people out there, but it wasn't for me at the time. I had gotten it into my head that they were closer to a hundred dollars, something I definitely would've needed to save for.

And while I did spend countless hours a day reading and watching as many stories from trans people as I could find online, I had a lot going on in the rest of my life to distract me from making any tangible steps forward in transitioning.

• • •

I had decided that I definitely did need to transfer schools. I wanted to give the whole filmmaking thing a shot, and the breakdowns I had every time I ran into my ex on campus meant that Southwestern sadly was not a healthy environment for me anymore.

I wasn't going to just fade quietly away from the university, however. Even if it didn't work out for me, I loved Southwestern. I kept my departure a secret while I made as big of an impact as I could before leaving. In addition to being a videographer for the Admissions and Alumni departments, I had also started work as a campus tour guide and overnight host for prospective students. I joined student government, where I debated with other students on decisions affecting the future of the university. I even helped a group of students win a five-thousand-dollar grant to start a steel drum club that I was not going to be around to join.

Despite my love for the school, I knew I needed to get away from campus as soon as possible for my own mental health. The problem was, by the time I had made the decision to transfer, I had missed the application deadline to enroll in a new school for the spring semester.

Neither staying at Southwestern for one more semester nor taking a semester off to float between my newly divorced parents' houses and their accompanying drama appealed to me, so that left me with one final option: escaping to Amsterdam.

Studying abroad seemed like the best way to stay enrolled at Southwestern without having to actually *be* at Southwestern. I'd never had a particular desire to visit The Netherlands, but when I asked the study abroad counselor about a place where I could experience a new culture without needing to master a foreign language, Amsterdam was at the top of the list. When the counselor added that this particular university had a very strong gender and sexual studies program, my mind was made up.

I thought the semester abroad might additionally help me gain some clarity on my gender identity. I had recently realized that I had been dating or chasing after guys back-to-back for all my developmental years, and while I didn't completely change my personality based on who I was dating, I still didn't trust that my personality had been given the space to develop on its own, without outside romantic influences. So my first step was to stop dating people cold turkey. I reasoned that it was crucial to discover exactly who I was to figure out if transitioning would be the right step for me.

In addition to providing me with some distance from Southwestern, boys, my family, and the rest of my problems, studying abroad had one final perk: an opportunity to regrow my eyebrows.

Really. I started plucking my eyebrows in the early 2000s, when the height of fashion was having pencil-thin brows. Anything thicker than a horsehair worm was terribly uncool. I mean, if your eyebrows were visible without squinting, you might as well have had a bushy unibrow.

By 2010 the trend was dying and I'd gotten pretty fed up with it personally, but was too scared to grow my eyebrows back to their natural slightly furry caterpillar size because of that awful in-between period when it just looks like you neglected your plucking hygiene and have two millipedes shedding their legs above your eyeballs.

So, decision made, I called it off with all the guys I'd been stringing along, packed up my Ace bandage in an overlarge suitcase, and moved into 19 Funen Park in Amsterdam with a tattooed bisexual girl from Ithaca, New York, I had never met before.

She was a vegetarian Sociology major with an identical twin and a septum piercing who knew way more about the world than I did. Via pre-trip Facebook stalking, I had also discovered one very important thing about her: She had dated a trans guy.

This was perfect. I could confide in her and spend the whole semester figuring out who I was, maybe even start transitioning!

Unfortunately, that never happened. I'm slow to share personal things about myself on a good day, but divulging my Big Dark Secret for the first time was proving to be nearly impossible. Plus, I was pretty intimidated by my roommate.

While I had spent the last several months gobbling up as many accounts of trans people as I could find, there were still some glaring gaps in my expertise that had left me desperately behind on my street smarts.

To give you an idea: One evening, while my roommate and I sat quietly browsing the internet on our respective beds, I called out to her, "Hey, have you heard of"—I squinted back down at the web page I was reading from—"G . . . LBT?"

She stared at me. Probably trying to decide how to patiently respond to my utter lack of knowledge.

"Yes, but I usually call it LGBT."

As I said, desperately behind.

I *hmmed* in assent and returned to my computer. I knew I had sort of heard that initialism before, but that evening was the first time I was really trying to remember the correct order of the letters and what they meant.

I had gone a little backward in my self-taught learning about the LGBTQ+ community. While I could by that point explain to you step-by-step what would happen on hormone replacement therapy, I still hadn't spent much time around any actual LGBTQ+ people, so I didn't know very much about the culture and how to speak about their challenges or the realities of their lived experiences.

As an example: At orientation on one of our first days in Amsterdam, where we students from schools all across the United States were meeting for the first time, I saw more butch lesbians than I had ever seen before——and I thought they were all trans guys.

I *knew* what butch lesbian meant, but I had never met someone who identified that way before, especially not someone my age. I had a vague idea of the stereotypical middle-aged butch with a crew cut, wearing a white tank top and motorcycle boots—but these women at orientation had faux hawks and wore stylish sweaters and fitted jeans. I envied their wardrobes, their haircuts, and their effortless confidence in their masculine femininity.

I really didn't know that it was possible to be a woman and look like that. I think had I been exposed to more masculine-presenting women from an earlier age, I would've felt more freedom to experiment with my own presentation and maybe even not feel so much fear around possibly liking girls. But as it was, I was terribly naive in my exposure to and understanding of the LGBTQ+ community, and I think becoming aware of my own naivety added to my nerves in coming out to my roommate.

I did drop hints here and there, which I'm sure went unnoticed due to how positively feminine I still looked—despite how much I thought I was butching it up. I mean, I had reduced my makeup routine to only eyeliner, mascara, and concealer. I hardly wore jewelry and I had two shedding millipedes above my eyes!

Looking back, I'm not sure even people who knew me well back in Texas would've noticed these slight changes to my appearance, let alone people who were meeting me for the first time, but in my head I was taking very intentional and meaningful steps toward an outwardly masculine expression.

I was so in my head about those things that semester abroad that I didn't do a very good job of making friends. Or doing much of anything, really. As excited as I had been to live in a country where I, at age nine-

EATING CRÊPES ON A
WEEKEND TRIP TO PARIS. SEE
HOW GLARINGLY OBVIOUS MY
NEW MASCULINE LOOK WAS?

teen, was legally allowed to drink and where marijuana usage was also legal, I rarely went out to take advantage of these freedoms.

Late in the semester, as the icy winter finally thawed into spring, I too finally warmed up to a few folks in the study abroad program. After classes one night, I accompanied a friend to a coffee shop. We ordered some beers and settled into a pew-like bench against the basement wall, just across from a billiards table where a few guys were in the middle of a game.

I don't remember what we discussed, but at some point in the conversation I decided to come out to her. I had never told a single real-life person my Big Dark Secret, but I was about to burst with how many thoughts about my gender were filling my head and I guess I thought that telling this one person, who I was unlikely to ever see again after a few months, would be better than keeping it all in.

I had just started working up the nerve to say the words when *whoosh!*

A billiards ball throttled toward us. I ducked just in time for it to smash into the wooden wall where my head had been just a split second before.

One of the guys came over to retrieve the ball, apologizing profusely in Dutch. We laughed it off and told him it was fine. "*Geen probleem.*" It *was* fine, but I wondered if I should take it as a sign from the universe *not* to come out to my friend.

No. I'd been trying to pluck up the nerve all semester to tell my roommate. I was sick of keeping this inside of me. I was determined to make some type of tangible progress on my budding transition that semester. So I took a deep breath and told her that I wasn't really sure, but I felt like I was probably a trans guy. The first thing she said to me was, "But you wear makeup!"

That was true. I wore my long hair down, did my makeup, and wore form-fitting clothing (even if most of it did consist of T-shirts and jeans). While it was frustrating that she didn't immediately see the man inside and validate all the feelings I'd kept inside of me for twenty years, I understood. I still presented entirely like a woman.

Once I explained to her how I had been repressing my feelings for years and how I was just starting to figure things out, she was incredibly understanding and welcoming. She even told me that there was another not-out trans guy in our cohort and coaxed the two of us to talk to each other, which we did briefly and nervously on the rooftop of our apartment a few nights later. He and I never kept in close touch, but when all was said and done, I came out to two people, the very first two people, while I was abroad. I may not have taken any other steps toward my transition, but those were big ones I can be proud of in retrospect.

CHAPTER TWELVE

new mexico, new york, new me?

While I was abroad, my mom moved from Texas to New Mexico and it was decided I would join her when I returned. Living in New Mexico that summer was fantastic. We had a small house at 6,500 feet altitude nestled in the Sangre de Cristo Mountains, with a small creek flowing in the backyard. There was no dishwasher or laundry machine in the house, so we washed everything by hand. I spent the afternoons while my mom was at work washing our clothes in the bathtub and hanging them out to dry on a clothesline out back while the 2010 World Cup played on the TV in the background.

VISITING ABIQUIU LAKE
MY FIRST SUMMER IN
NEW MEXICO.

Since I wouldn't be able to continue the seasonal barista job I'd had in Texas, I decided to do an internship with the local radio station, KSFR News. After showing me how the equipment worked and giving me a few pointers on radio journalism, the station heads handed me some assignments and set me free to do as I liked. I researched, interviewed, wrote, recorded, and edited two stories that aired live that summer—one on the city's new poet laureate and one on a local pro-choice organization.

KSFR News didn't require me to be there too many hours each week, so I also filled my time by volunteering remotely for a nonprofit called the Harry Potter Alliance (HPA), which I had heard about here and there over the years.

My childhood love for Harry Potter had never dissipated after that failed Hermione Granger costume in fourth grade. I attended the mid-night release for every single book and movie, in costume, up until the final book came out the summer before my senior year of high school, which I felt, rather melodramatically, really closed the book on my childhood.

WITH MY FUTURE ROOMMATE AT THE MIDNIGHT RELEASE OF THE Harry Potter AND THE Half-Blood Prince MOVIE.

I USED TO SAVE EVERY NEWS CLIPPING THAT MENTIONED Harry Potter.

In middle school, I had started getting my fix in between book releases by frequenting fan sites, reading fan fiction, and listening to fan-created podcasts and wizard rock (songs written about the books, usually sung from the perspective of a certain character). The amount of content being generated by fans like me who had fallen in love with the books' world and were theorizing about what would happen next was staggering, and totally awesome.

Seeing as so many of my peers growing up in Texas weren't allowed to read Harry Potter because their parents didn't want them getting involved in witchcraft (yes, really), these online fan communities were my primary outlet for my enthusiasm and my source for Potter-related news.

It was through these fan sites that I first heard about the HPA and how they were bringing together Potter fans all around the world to achieve amazing things, like raising money to protect victims of genocide in Darfur and Myanmar, collecting tens of thousands of books for communities in need around the world, registering first-time voters at wizard rock shows, and more.

I'd had my eye on them for a while, so when I saw they were looking for a volunteer video editor, I applied and got the gig. They were in the midst of a big fund-raiser that summer, so while I had fun getting to know other volunteers via email and occasionally tweeting my support for the campaign, there wouldn't be much for me to work on until the fall.

Without friends or a demanding job, I spent a lot of that summer in New Mexico by myself. I took up running, read a ton of books, and frequently drove across town to Target to buy more and more men's clothing. Since I'd always had an eclectic sense of style, even when it was fully feminine, my mom didn't bat an eye at my new baggy cargo shorts or the board shorts I wore to Pilates class at the rec center. Still, I thought ordering a binder and starting to wear it would be too much under her watchful eye. While a part of me wanted to tell her my new revelations about my gender, I just wasn't ready yet. A proper binder would have to wait until I moved to New York City that fall to attend NYU.

I had spent my semester abroad sending transfer applications to eight different schools around the country, all with some type of film program I could at least take a few classes in even if I didn't have enough of a reel built up to apply to proper film programs outright. In the end, I settled on NYU, where I could use my existing credits to cobble together a major in Comparative Literature at their liberal arts school and also complete a cross-school minor in Documentary at the Tisch School of the Arts.

• • •

I saw my move to New York as a chance for a fresh start. The city has long been a haven for queer and gender-nonconforming folks. Sometimes these days I think of it as the Island of Misfit Toys, a place we've all flocked to where we can finally be ourselves. Fortunately for us misfits, the city has our back with numerous discrimination protections and government-funded awareness campaigns. There are tons of community-based organizations providing access to health care as well as legal, employment, and housing assistance to LGBTQ+ people. It's not perfect. The rate of violence against LGBTQ+ people, particularly trans women of color, is still far too high, and just because it's a blue state doesn't mean everyone there is progressive. But compared to Texas, I felt like I was moving to one of the best places in the world to be transgender.

Nonetheless, I wasn't making any major resolutions for my big move—like going by a new name or telling all my new classmates to use the pronouns "he" and "him." I had too much on my plate being a transfer student in the Big City to be able to devote brainpower to making pivotal changes right off the bat.

I did think I could at least start going to events and meetings at the campus LGBTQ Center. I didn't have to tell people I was trans. I could just say I was questioning my gender, or maybe claim to be bi. The idea of half-lying to a group I wanted to be a part of didn't sit well with me, but I knew I needed to start talking to real people about how I felt or I would never move forward.

I circled every LGBTQ mixer on the orientation schedule during move-in week . . . and chickened out on every single one. What would I have said? What would they have thought of me? Would they think I was some straight girl invading their ranks?

It was all too much. Every time that semester I told myself I would do something relating to my gender in the real world and interact with real people, I ended up staying home instead and writing about my lack of progress to my anonymous Tumblr followers on my secret blog.

The blog was a useful outlet for trying out new male names, writing openly about how I was feeling, and interacting with other trans people going through similar things, but I struggled to translate that online energy to the real world.

Even when one of my documentary courses screened *Prodigal Sons*, a film about the director Kimberly Reed's relationship with her brother since her transition, and Ms. Reed visited our class to talk to us—the very first grown-up trans person I had ever knowingly come face to face with in my life   I couldn't muster up the courage to say a single word to her. I didn't even ask technical questions about the documentary, as we were encouraged to do during these Q&A sessions with the filmmakers, because I was scared if I opened my mouth I would just start crying.

I am so frustrated by everything. I don't like disrespecting my professors by not putting effort into classes, but how can I keep interested & motivated when I am distracted every minute of every day by being in the wrong body. I hate being ugly & perceived as awkward. I'm neither of those, but I'm uncomfortable in my own skin--- in the outer skin we put on as clothes. I wish I could be that beautiful, fashionable head-turning girl I was when I was 17-19, but I'm not. I can't be. It makes me sick. It depresses me. That was a lie. A

wonderful, amazing lie. A lie that built up my confidence and then sent it crashing to a low so low I thought impossible. I thought I was cured, but I knew that whole time that I wasn't. If only I had been able to keep up the charade for the rest of my life, but I can't now. I wouldn't say I accept who I am, but I know now. I sort of almost comprehend and that's enough to make me unable to be comfortable living as that person any more . . . which I freaking hate. Sometimes I think I could do it. Be that person

I was making absolutely no progress toward coming out to another flesh-and-blood human, but early on in that first semester I did take one small step toward my transition: I ordered a binder.

I had had plenty of time over the summer to do my research on the brand and style that would be right for me. I settled on a white Underworks Tri-Top and used their website's measurement instructions to select the appropriate size for my chest.

There was a bit of a hiccup with my dorm's mailing address not coming up in their system, which led to the Underworks' shipping company actually having to *call me on the phone* to verify my address. I was mortified, thinking the person on the other end of the line might've known what I ordered and why. I had wanted so badly to avoid interaction with a real live human during this nerve-wracking solo mission and I'd been foiled by a single integer in my address.

But eventually the shipping issue got sorted out and, on September twenty-ninth, I retrieved the thin, unassuming envelope from my dorm's mail room on my way back from morning classes and headed straight for my suite's shared bathroom on the seventeenth floor.

As I tore open the packaging and let the nylon garment splay over my hands, I was reminded of the first time I held a cigarette. The object in my hands was so much lighter than I had expected it to be. Surely something with so much power should be heavier, more solid.

But being lightweight would be good for breathability in everyday wear, so I shrugged off my doubts and started tugging the binder on over my naked torso. I had been warned from other people on the internet that new binders are nearly impossible to take on and off, but that they stretch out in a few days.

They weren't kidding. I got elastic burns all over my neck, underarms, and collarbone as I maneuvered every which way to squeeze into entrapment.

Finally, I remembered a tip I had read to step *into* the binder and pull it up your body. Predictably, it got a bit stuck at my hips, but I stretched it over them and got it up around my chest. Then I nearly dislocated my shoulders trying to jockey my elbows through the armholes.

Heaving a sigh of accomplishment, I turned to the side and gasped. I was so flat! I quickly grabbed my T-shirt from the pile I'd discarded at my feet and pulled it back on, grinning at the way the cotton-poly blend slid sleekly over the nylon binder, leaving plenty of loose fabric where it would usually be stretched across.

This was the real money shot. Binders really aren't flattering on their own, but they work absolute magic with clothes on top of them. By the time I had pulled myself away from the mirror and my MacBook's Photo Booth app, it was time to head to my afternoon classes—and my first time wearing a proper binder out in public.

TRYING ON MY FIRST BINDER.

I crammed into the elevator with the other students leaving Lafayette Hall and wondered if anyone would be able to tell. Did I look unusually flat for a girl? Could they see the seams of an unusual garment through my T-shirt? Had I even made close enough acquaintance with anyone yet that they would be able to notice a change in the appearance of my chest?

While I was running through every possibility in my mind, black flecks appeared in the corners of my vision, painting the elevator doors like a Kandinsky. I stumbled back against the wall of the elevator and everyone turned to look at me quizzically.

Well, they would certainly notice me if I passed out in the elevator.

I took a few deep breaths, regained my full vision, and everyone turned back to their phones. As I exited the elevator, still a bit light-headed, I resolved to only wear the binder for short periods of time until it stretched out and I got used to it. I also made a mental note to make a game plan for the possibility of having some sort of medical emergency and getting taken to the ER while unconscious. They would probably have questions about the compression vest I was wearing. They would also probably cut it off of me, and then I'd be out thirty-eight bucks on top of hospital fees.

Trans People and Health Care

In addition to the headaches and injustices surrounding trans-related health care, there remain countless hurdles for trans people accessing care even unrelated to their transitions.

If you're visibly trans, you might face judgment or discrimination at doctors' offices from the get-go. If you're not, there's the question of whether to disclose your status when it really shouldn't be relevant (such as at the dentist). Or worse, you may be outed against your will: What happens if you lose consciousness and are taken to an emergency room before you can inform the staff about your trans status on your own terms?

So many medical providers are unfamiliar with our bodies and how to speak to us. There are regular stories, for example, about trans men who identified themselves as such on intake forms being asked about their prostates. Trans people who have gone to the emergency room for critical injuries and illnesses get misgendered by every new person who walks into the room, even when their name and pronouns are marked on their chart. It's a frightening thing to have your life in the hands of someone who doesn't have basic knowledge about trans people's bodies and the effects of medical transition, or who's making snide comments about who you are.

Insurance is a whole other issue. While coverage for transition-related care is ever-expanding, trans people are often still denied coverage for other procedures or medications because insurance companies try to claim that unrelated conditions like gallstones or broken bones are caused by hormone use. Many trans people also run into the issue of being denied coverage for procedures after they've changed their legal gender. A trans man whose legal gender is male, for example, might be denied coverage for a Pap smear.

When we talk about a need for greater trans awareness, how we're treated by medical and insurance providers is a big part of it. We shouldn't have to be educating doctors. We shouldn't have to fear discrimination when we go to the hospital. We shouldn't be denied coverage for the services for which cisgender people are covered. Greater cultural competency on trans issues means fewer instances of discrimination and more allies fighting for us in situations when we can't fight for ourselves.

After a few months of easing into the habit of wearing a binder, I was hooked. I could rarely go out in public without it. I started getting carded a lot more, because the combination of a flat chest and not wearing makeup anymore aged me back to prepubescent levels. A stand-out example: the time during my senior year of college when I got carded for a PG-13 adaptation of *Snow White*. Really.

When the few people in New York City who had known me from high school made comments about how I used to have an impressive rack, I made up excuses about fat redistribution from running and a newfound preference for sports bras.

Binder aside, figuring out my identity while also adapting to life in New York City turned out to be much more challenging than I was prepared for. The culture shock and unrelenting gender dysphoria turned me into a very sullen person.

For some of us, when we're in the depths of dysphoria, on the verge of transition, it can be very difficult to think of anything, or anyone, else. We're so consumed with figuring out our gender, worrying about interacting with the world, and making a plan for transitioning that little else sticks in our minds.

As the semester went on at NYU, I became an antisocial rage machine, alternating between perplexing and pissing off my professors and failing to make any friends.

In lieu of a social life, I found solace in the tiny transgender section of books in a far-off corner of the twelve-story NYU Bobst Library. I read all the books they had on offer about transgender people and gender theory. Sometimes, when I wasn't in the mood to read, I would just sit among the books, surrounding myself with the ghosts of my trans cousins and hiding from my real problems beyond the stacks.

IN MY FAVORITE AISLE OF THE NYU LIBRARY.

Jack's Top Ten Favorite Trans Books (in No Particular Order)

Despite my best efforts, I haven't read *every* trans book yet, and more awesome ones are being published all the time. More of my favorites are at the back of this book. To keep up with what I'm currently reading and to see more of my recommendations, follow me on Goodreads at jackisnotabird.

Amateur: A True Story about What Makes a Man by Thomas Page McBee

Revolutionary by Alex Myers

Darling Days by iO Tillet Wright

Stone Butch Blues by Leslie Feinberg

If I Was Your Girl by Meredith Russo

Tomorrow Will Be Different: Love, Loss, and the Fight for Trans Equality by Sarah McBride

Before I Had the Words by Skylar Kergil

Beautiful Music for Ugly Children by Kirstin Cronn-Mills

Becoming a Visible Man by Jamison Green

Whipping Girl: A Transsexual Woman on Sexism and the Scapegoating of Femininity by Julia Serano

My other coping mechanism was calling my mom. Every. Day. Sometimes we'd just talk about what we'd both been up to, often I expressed my fears that I had made a mistake in moving and freak out about not being able to afford living in New York City, but I never mentioned my gender.

I wanted to. Desperately. She was the closest person to me in my life at the time and had always been the one to whom I could tell almost anything. I felt bad keeping such a big thing from her and I knew she would still love me, even if there was a long, awkward period of adjustment, but I just couldn't bring myself to say the words.

The one bright light I had that first semester at NYU was my volunteer work for the Harry Potter Alliance. I was editing campaign videos for them, managing a team of other video production volunteers, and increasingly getting to attend events in the city and in Boston to film the event or run their merchandise booth.

Shooting a video for the HPA at the Quidditch World Cup.

The people I met in the Harry Potter fan community were incredible. They didn't judge people based on appearance, ability, or awkwardness. So long as you were a compassionate, respectful human with at least a passing interest in Harry Potter, you were in.

Since I only saw my new fandom friends in person every couple of months, it was easier befriending them than my NYU peers, with whom every time we hung out I would struggle to get dressed in something both affirming to my gender and appropriate to the outing. Picking one outfit a couple of weeks in advance was moderately easier than finding a new one for class every single day. The infrequency of the face-to-face fandom events was easier on my dysphoria at the time, and gave me at least one outlet to keep me going when everything else around me seemed so heavy and dour.

CHAPTER THIRTEEN

up in flames

It was mid-January, toward the end of my first winter break at NYU, and my mom and I were sitting on the couch in our Santa Fe home watching the Golden Globes. Not having much better going on, we decided to make a real event of the night, cracking open some Prosecco to sip while we watched the glitzy award ceremony.

Halfway through the show, Chris Colfer, who played Kurt on my then-favorite TV show, *Glee*, won for Best Actor in a Supporting Role. Completely shocked by his win, he managed to deliver an affecting acceptance speech, ending it by saying, "To all the amazing kids that watch our show and the kids that our show celebrates, who are constantly told 'no' by the people in their environments, by bullies at school, that they can't be who they are or have what they want because of who they are, well"—and here he thrust his new trophy in the air—"screw that, kids."

It could have been the Prosecco, but I got teary-eyed by his win and eff-the-haters speech. It made me feel proud to be a part of a community that had come so far, far enough that an openly gay young actor could win a Golden Globe for playing an openly gay character on a prime-time TV show. It also made me feel like I should listen to Chris Colfer and screw it. Screw my fears and my doubts. I needed to move forward and be who I really knew myself to be. So with plenty more

Prosecco building up my courage and loosening my lips, I started the conversation to come out to my mom.

We talked for a long time. I was massaging the discussion to lead it in the direction I needed it to go, without making a big deal out of it. We eventually got to how I used to be such a tomboy as a kid. I pushed myself to tell her that I had really wanted to be a boy back then.

"You don't still, though, right?" she asked me.

I looked at her, sitting mere inches from me on the couch. This was it. This was the moment I'd been imagining for years.

"No," I told her, immediately losing eye contact and looking back down at my drink.

The conversation moved on. Blood rushing in my ears drowned out what my mom was saying as I berated myself for my cowardice. Eventually she announced it was long past time for her to go to bed and stood up to go.

"Wait!" I reached toward her. "I want to say something."

She turned back and sat down again. I could feel my face going red as I gathered my words.

"Remember earlier when we were talking about me being a tomboy as a kid?"

"Yes," she said slowly.

"Sometimes . . ." I swallowed. The tears were starting to come now. I could barely get the words out, my throat was so thick with nerves. "Sometimes I do still wish I could be a boy, a man."

She reached across and hugged me as I let out a sob.

I imagine she told me she loved me. Maybe she told me she'd had suspicions. Probably she shared some anecdotes from my childhood.

All I can remember is that I told her. And that it was okay.

What Is Transitioning?

Physical transition doesn't happen overnight or over the course of a weekend. Some [cisgender people] assume that a female enters a hospital on a Friday night and emerges Monday morning a fully developed and fully functional adult male. I wish I knew where that hospital was.

—Matt Kailey, *Just Add Hormones*

Transitioning is the act of taking steps so that your physical, social, and/or legal expression aligns with your authentic gender. Transition can encompass a number of things, including coming out, using a new name and pronouns, wearing different clothing, adopting a new hairstyle, legally changing your name and gender marker, taking hormone replacement therapy, undergoing various gender affirmation procedures, and more.

As far as the medical elements of transition go, there isn't one all-encompassing surgery that changes us from one gender to another. Most trans people seeking medical transition start with hormone replacement therapy, which causes a change in secondary sex characteristics, putting us through a kind of second puberty.

Transfeminine people usually take a combination of testosterone blockers, estrogen, and progesterone. These can be taken in the form of pills, injections, patches, gels, creams, or sprays. From hormone therapy, transfeminine people can experience reduced strength, body fat redistribution, breast development, changed body odor, facial shape changes, slowed growth of body hair, and more.

Transmasculine people usually require only testosterone, which can be taken in the form of injections, gels, creams, or patches. It can cause increased strength, body fat redistribution, facial hair growth, facial shape changes, voice changes, acne, male pattern baldness, increased body hair, the cessation of menstruation, and more.

For those who choose to pursue gender-affirming surgeries, there are top surgeries for chests, bottom surgeries for genitals, facial feminization and masculinization surgeries, and more.

While some insurance companies in the United States are beginning to cover gender-affirming surgeries, the procedures still remain financially out of reach for many trans people. Others are unable to undergo procedures due to health conditions, and many more simply choose not to. How a trans person transitions— medically, socially, or legally—is entirely up to them and does not in any way negate their gender or trans status.

The next day, I woke up with one of the worst hangovers of my life. I'm not convinced it was entirely from the Prosecco because I wasn't nauseated, as I usually am when I imbibe a bit too much; I was just sore. Every muscle in my body felt stiff and heavy. It was like my body was having a physical reaction to the emotional exertion of the night before.

When I finally got out of bed late in the morning, my mom hugged me again and told me that it would take some getting used to, but that she loved me no matter what.

I went back to bed and slept for the rest of the day.

We talked a little bit more about my gender over that winter break. I explained that I might one day want to transition, but that I wasn't sure. She shared with me what she would've called me if I had been assigned male at birth: Harrison.

I had to laugh at that one. Harrison, so easily shortened to Harry, is not a great name for someone who's last name is Bird. Hairy Bird? Oof. I'd dodged a bullet there.

When I went back to school, we mostly avoided the topic on our phone calls, which began getting less frequent as things finally started looking up for me at NYU.

After a year of living in a triple dorm room with two girls who had ended up in a relationship with each other and weren't shy about getting physical when they thought I was sleeping, I was moving off-campus with one of my best friends from high school. She had been gone all year playing the lead role in the national touring company of a show, but was now back to finish her degree in Musical Theater at another university in the city.

Her understudy's husband happened to work as a broker and got us a great deal on a newly renovated fourth-floor walk-up in Queens with two decent-sized bedrooms and even a small dishwasher. It all felt *so* New York and *so* adult and *so* much better than where I had been living. It also just about bankrupted me. I saved up to take one taxi trip of suitcases from my dorm in Chinatown up to Queens, but otherwise spent a week moving handfuls of items via the subway.

Our official move-in date was on my new roommate's twenty-first birthday, just three days before mine. Since our sweet sixteen in high school, we had typically celebrated our birthdays together, and that year was no different. We sat on the empty hardwood floor of our new living room and exchanged gifts of margarita glasses and corkscrews. Life was good.

Putting together the most important furniture: bookshelves.

The next day she flew home for an extended vacation before she would start her summer job in the city a few weeks later. This was all right with me. After years of lottery-drawn roommates, I was stoked to have a whole apartment to myself for a little bit and was looking forward to returning from classes in the evenings to do and wear whatever I wanted without anyone watching.

Things started falling apart by the second day.

There had been some problem installing our internet that required the service provider to go back-and-forth with our building's management, and meanwhile I had three final papers due on my birthday that I was seriously behind on due to the distraction of the big move. Since the summer heat was picking up and we also didn't have an AC unit, I resigned myself to effectively living out of the school's library until I finished my papers.

The saga with the internet dragged on for weeks, all the way into the start of my summer semester. I had still yet to really enjoy the perks of having my own place since I was having to spend so much time at the library and at cafés to get my schoolwork done.

In the meantime, I'd started noticing little red bumps all over my body that itched way more than a normal mosquito bite. After some googling, a meticulous scan of our mattresses, and a frantic call to my roommate, it was official: We had bedbugs.

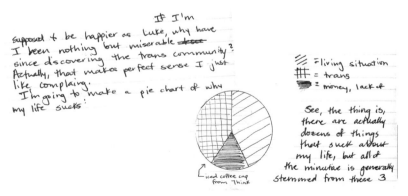

It was in the midst of this happy state of affairs that I found myself at Duane Reade one day after my Physics lecture. I was on the hunt for an anti-itch cream for the bedbug bites that were increasingly covering my body as well as a card for my dad's upcoming nuptials.

As I was pondering which card said "I'm happy for you, but not *too* happy," I got a text from a good friend from high school asking if I was in an okay place to receive bad news.

I lied and said yes, because my life was in such shambles that I didn't think there was any time in the near future when I'd be in any better place to receive bad news.

She texted back and said our friend Nathan had died by suicide the night before.

I froze. Nathan, who was Santa Claus in the fifth-grade play. Nathan, whose foot got run over by our school's float in the Christmas parade. Nathan, who, after I turned him down for a date junior year, gave me a burned CD of a song he wrote me, which I'd *never listened to.*

Suddenly the most important thing in the world was to go back to my apartment, find that CD in the box of high school mementos I had yet to unpack from the move, and listen to it.

I grabbed a random wedding card off the shelf and made my way to the checkout counter, rushing back to Queens as fast as the N train would take me.

The CD was there in the box of old journals and photos of friends. I don't even know why I'd hung on to it, but in that moment I was so grateful that I had. I shoved the CD into my computer and lay on the floor listening to the slow, electronic melody on loop for hours.

Still in shock, I boarded a plane to Alabama the next morning to attend my dad's wedding. No one in either the bride's or the groom's families has ever lived in Alabama, but they had decided to do a destination wedding on the beach, which also meant there were only a handful of us in attendance.

Ahead of the wedding, my dad had kindly offered to send me money to buy a new dress and swimsuit for the trip. It was legitimately nice of him, but it also meant that I was locked into wearing a dress for the ceremony. I hadn't had any reason to wear a dress for well over two years at that point and was wary about how it would make me feel.

Still, I had dutifully gone to the clearance racks in SoHo the week before to pick out a dress that I thought would look nice for a beach wedding, as well as a bikini I didn't hate—I got one patterned with fish skeletons to make me feel slightly badass.

I spent most of the first day on the beach wearing my boys' swim trunks and a T-shirt on top of my bikini, feeling reluctant to look so feminine even though I could feel the questioning stares of my dad's friends and our extended relatives, wondering why I was dressed so butch.

My wardrobe choices did not remain the center of attention for long, however. A forest fire had been steadily spreading on the other side of town and, by the morning of the wedding, half of the guests had been evacuated from their hotels, the whole town had lost power, and the caterers therefore didn't know if they'd be able to finish making the food for the reception.

For a few hours, it was complete chaos.

Luckily, the power came back on with an hour to spare before the wedding's start. My dad's levelheaded problem-solving skills smoothed over most of the issues, and the wedding went on just fine—though the photographer did have to be careful how to arrange us to avoid the backdrop of a raging forest fire.

For my part, wearing a dress wasn't the worst thing in the world. I discovered I could flip a switch in my brain and pretend to be the person I used to be back in high school, giggly and excited to show off my body. It wasn't foolproof and it only lasted a few hours before I had to change back into my denim shorts and punk band T-shirt, but it allowed me to save face with my dad's side of the family and not have to broach coming out to them just yet.

THE VIEW FROM THE WEDDING. A METAPHOR FOR MY LIFE THAT SUMMER?

CHAPTER FOURTEEN

daring, nerve, and chivalry

After three years without a single formal occasion, I suddenly had *two* within the span of a month. First my dad's wedding and next LeakyCon, the largest annual Harry Potter fan conference, which was being held at the Wizarding World theme park in Orlando to coordinate with the release of the final movie in the series. Attendees would get to enjoy a private after-hours experience at the theme park and then go see the movie a full six hours before the rest of the world. And for the first time, I got to be one of those attendees.

Through all the schoolwork and moving and bedbugs and the forest-fire-tinged wedding, I had remained committed to my volunteer work for the HPA. In addition to my behind-the-scenes video editing, they had recently selected me, alongside two other college-aged volunteers, to become the faces of their YouTube channel. Three times a week, one of us made a video updating HPA members on the organization's current campaigns or discussing a topic related to causes the HPA worked on.

I had been posting videos to YouTube on and off since 2007, but those videos were just inside jokes for me and my friends. The HPA's YouTube channel already had several thousand subscribers, and the organization's regular partners included all the internet-famous You-

Tube creators I had looked up to for years. There would be a lot more eyes on the videos I made for the HPA, so when they first asked me, I wasn't positive I wanted to do it.

Though I was still so far in the closet that I could see Mr. Tumnus, I was fairly certain transitioning was in my near future. On the off chance I gained any type of following from this endeavor, what would happen when I came out? Would viewers hate me? Would everyone reject me?

I had discovered the world of transgender YouTubers a few years prior, pioneering folks who created resources for the rest of us by documenting their transitions in videos. But that community was still fairly underground and most of those YouTubers had started their channels as openly transgender. Many of them stayed anonymous and kept their channels hidden from people in their real lives. In 2011, there weren't any previously established YouTubers who had come out as trans that I knew of. So I had no precedent for how the YouTube community might react to such a thing, but in the end, my ego again won out over my fear and I agreed to be a part of the channel.

I needn't have worried so much. Each of our videos received only about five hundred views. While that number did mean a bit more back in 2011, it still wasn't much at all.

Nevertheless, we had a small but loyal viewership of HPA members and, for the first time in my life, people I didn't know started following my social media accounts and seeming to care about what I had to say. I used that tiny influence to my advantage and started packing my HPA videos full of LGBTQ+ educational content. I had spent years reading up on gender theory and following the stories of transgender people in books, documentaries, and online, but I'd never had anyone to share that information with. Now, I had an audience eager to listen and an outlet for that pent-up closeted energy.

Even if our following was small, the videos were valuable to a scrappy nonprofit, so the HPA granted me a scholarship so I could fly out to Orlando and attend LeakyCon alongside the HPA's employees and several other volunteers.

I could hardly believe I'd be going to one of the fan conferences I had heard so much about! I was going to see the last Harry Potter movie *early*, with a crowd of dedicated fans, and even get to go to *Hogwarts*. Well, the theme park re-creation, anyway.

There was just one problem: The conference ended with big formal dance, and I'd have to decide whether to be uncomfortable wearing a dress or show my true self to the community and wear a suit.

Tomorrow ▮▮▮▮▮ ⬥ I will film it at Central Park and I'm going to dress like I did in 2009 so people will find me attractive, current, confident, enviable, powerful. I just want to be a sexy, goofy, confident, fashionable man, but I can't be any of those yet so I'm having trouble achieving those adj's while living between genders. Might go back to presenting as completely female, but it is confusing me b/c I have to pick one for Leaky Con.

JUNE 14, 2011.

I ended up packing a huge suitcase full of two wardrobe options for every occasion—swim trunks *and* a bikini, baggy khaki shorts *and* skinny jeans, a suit *and* a dress for the ball.

Well, not a whole suit. I'd found suit pants and a matching vest on sale at H&M that I planned on wearing with an old button-down, a Gryffindor tie I'd ordered online, and Converse shoes since I didn't own any dress shoes. At least, that was the plan if I didn't chicken out.

There was so much to do before the ball, though. The HPA had about half a dozen different programs and press events I had to shoot footage of, I lent a hand selling merch in the vendor hall, and each evening we all let loose by scream-singing and jump-dancing at the raucous wizard rock shows.

I also had an unexpected new experience to contend with: people recognizing me from my videos.

You don't really expect to get noticed when you're barely scraping five hundred views a video, but if there's one thing I've learned over the years it's that it takes very little attention online for someone to reap the consequences, positive or negative.

I didn't have a Sharpie on me when the first person asked me to sign an autograph and all they had, oddly, was a thick whiteboard marker. I sloppily tried to sign my name and a quick, encouraging message with the cumbersome utensil. I'm pretty sure it was illegible. I might've even misspelled my name.

Overall, probably fewer than ten people recognized me, but that didn't make it any less weird or humbling. There was one person in particular who really took me aback. They pulled me to the side after one of the evening's wizard rock concerts and told me that they had recently come out. They said they had shown the educational videos I'd made on LGBTQ+ topics to their parents and that it had helped their parents understand what they were going through.

I was floored. I had felt like such a fraud making those videos when I didn't even have the guts to be out yet myself. Knowing they had helped at least one person, and *meeting* that person in the flesh, was astounding. It made me feel like I needed to continue making more videos on less-talked-about LGBTQ+ topics and work harder to make them even better.

Even with that boost of confidence and inspiration from a queer person who wasn't afraid to be themself, I still didn't have the guts to wear my suit to the ball. I dug out the same dress I'd worn to my dad's wedding from the bottom of my suitcase, flipped that switch in my brain, and tried to forget about what I was wearing so I could enjoy the dance with the two thousand other sweaty nerds.

DANCING OFF THE DYSPHORIA WITH MY FRIEND SAM.

The Esther Earl Rocking Charity Ball @ LeakyCon 2011

Despite how much fun LeakyCon had been, I still wasn't in the best place mental-health-wise, and being thrown immediately back into another session of summer classes didn't help. The stresses kept piling up onto years of untreated gender dysphoria, and unhealed sorrow had left my defense mechanisms depleted. After a routine meeting with my advisor to plan for the following semester, I ended up being counseled to drop out of my summer classes and encouraged to not even take a job. Just take some time off, they told me, or else you might have to take a leave of absence during a full semester.

It was a bit of a reality check to be told I was too fragile to finish a few summer classes, but with scholarship money and savings giving me enough to survive on for a month and a half, I took it as a much-needed staycation.

I spent the rest of the summer finally unpacking the last boxes from the move, hanging out with my roommate, watching TV, and spending *a lot* of time on my secret Tumblr account dreaming of a future I didn't dare to live just yet.

That was the summer when J. K. Rowling launched a mysterious online platform called Pottermore. No one knew exactly what it was going to be, but as the day of its release got closer we learned that one feature would be a Sorting Hat quiz.

For the uninitiated, the Sorting Hat is an enchanted wizard's hat in the Harry Potter books that sorts all Hogwarts students into one of four houses, kind of like teams, for the duration of their education. The houses—Gryffindor, Slytherin, Ravenclaw, and Hufflepuff—each have their own personality trademarks. The Sorting Hat looks deep into each student's core values and attributes to determine where they would be best suited.

For the Potter generation, these houses have become as much a facet of our personality markers as our zodiac signs and Myers-Briggs profiles. It's not at all unusual to see a millennial's social media profile description read something along the lines of "Scorpio. ENFP. Hufflepuff."

There are countless quizzes online to help you find which House you belong to, but, unlike all of those, the quiz that was to be included in Pottermore was actually developed by J. K. Rowling herself. She designed it and wrote each multiple-choice question using her extensive knowledge of the universe she had created. This was the *ultimate* sorting quiz.

In the lead-up to Pottermore, people were freaking out about whether they would get sorted into the House they had identified with for years. Whether through those unofficial online quizzes or personal reflection, people had self-sorted into Houses for years before this new platform came along. House pride was especially huge in fan communities, where people bought ties, scarves, T-shirts, Hogwarts robes, and even got tattoos of their house. The notion that Pottermore's ruling could contradict what you had self-identified as for years was sending people into a frenzy.

After my early years of claiming to be a Ravenclaw in middle school because Gryffindor seemed too mainstream, I came around to the fact that my boldness, impulsiveness, and stubbornness were all hallmark traits of a Gryffindor. I've been pigheadedly proud of that fact since then, and, while some people were freaking out that the quiz was about to upend their identities, I remained cool as a cucumber.

"I've gotten Gryffindor on every quiz I've ever taken. It won't be an issue," I arrogantly told people.

Probably because I had laid it on so thick, I was a bit nervous when Pottermore finally launched and I got access to the Sorting Quiz. I tried to answer all the questions as honestly as possible and bit my tongue as the page loaded with my results.

GRYFFINDOR!

Thank God. In talking with friends, we discovered that the questions changed slightly every time you took the quiz, no matter what your answers were. So just to be extra safe, I used all my email accounts to create multiple profiles and take the quiz again and again and again. I was sorted into Gryffindor every single time.

At the end of the day, should I have cared so much into which House the official Pottermore quiz sorted me? I seem to be in the minority here, but I say no. It annoys me to no end when I hear people these days say that they don't know what House they are because they haven't taken the Pottermore quiz yet or that they used to be one House, but now they're another because Pottermore said so.

What did we do before Pottermore? We self-sorted! You might have gleaned some insight from one online quiz or another, but for the most part, you just chose the one that seemed the most right for you—just like Harry essentially did in the books. The Sorting Hat considered putting him in Slytherin, but Harry asked to be in Gryffindor. What you want and what feels right to you is perhaps the most important factor in sorting.

I suppose it shouldn't be surprising that I'm an advocate of self-sorting Hogwarts houses, seeing as I believe in self-sorting ourselves when it comes to gender too, and just about everything else for that matter. I didn't stick to the gender I was sorted as at birth and, if one day some quiz does come along and says I'm not a Gryffindor, I won't believe it either.

CHAPTER FIFTEEN

he, him, his

After my inadvertent sabbatical, I started my senior year at NYU with refreshed vigor and motivation. I had a new job working at the front desk of the Comparative Literature Department, I was sticking to a gym routine, and I *finally* started going to the on-campus LGBTQ Center.

Twice a month there was a meeting called the T Party, specifically for transgender or questioning students. There were only two regular attendees other than myself and they were both trans guys. It was the first time I had spent substantial time around other trans guys in person, and the first time I got to try out using masculine pronouns.

What to Do When You Mess Up Someone's Pronouns

Before we tackle messing up, let's begin with what to do if you don't *know* someone's pronouns. Start by listening to how other people are referring to the person in question. If that doesn't work, you can politely ask them. A good way to do this is by introducing yourself and sharing your own pronouns. For example, you could say, "I'm (insert your name) and I use (insert your pronouns). What pronouns do you use?" If you're in a larger group, it's never a bad idea to suggest everyone go around and say their pronouns. If you're facilitating a meeting, adding pronouns to the list of things people say when they introduce themselves also helps prevent awkwardness and misgendering.

But once you know someone's pronouns, you might mess up. Maybe you've known this person for years and they recently changed their pronouns. Maybe you're new to using gender-neutral pronouns. Whatever the case, just quickly correct yourself and move on. Don't make it a bigger deal than you would for misspeaking in any other instance. If you make a big show of how bad you feel and how sorry you are, you're just going to make everyone uncomfortable. Plus, if some people in the room don't know that the person you're talking to is trans, your big apology might out them against their will. That's not only disrespectful but could also put them in danger if there's a transphobic person around.

Instead of apologizing loudly in the moment, try a smaller, private apology later. Pull them aside one-on-one and let them know that you're sorry, that you'll do better in the future, and that you see and respect them as their affirmed gender. Actually mean what you say, and don't make the apology about you.

One more note on pronouns: You should start referring to someone by whatever name and pronouns they affirm when they ask you to do so, not when *you* decide to. You don't need to wait until a certain procedure has happened to begin calling someone by their chosen name and pronouns. Respect their choices and let them tell you how they identify. Don't force an identity on them or act like it's such hard work or a favor you're doing for them. If we can change the pronouns we use for people's pets as soon as we're corrected or memorize all the different names of Pokémon when they evolve, I think we can make the same effort for the people in our lives.

The weird thing about pronouns is that they're always used in reference to you, so it's actually not *that* often that you hear them in your presence. It was several months before this ever happened at the T Party. We were all lining up to take a photo with a guest lecturer, and someone told one of the other guys that he needed to stand in front of me to be seen.

"But I'm taller than him!" he protested, referring to me. He wasn't actually taller than me, but I couldn't care less. I'd been called "him" intentionally and genuinely for the first time in my life and it felt . . . weird? I think I liked it, but it was definitely a strange feeling.

Pronouns are absolutely affirming, but in the early days of being referred to by a new pronoun it can take some getting used to. You've probably only ever been referred to with one set of pronouns your whole life. Even if you didn't like it, you're used to it, so a new one can be jarring—especially if you're not using the new pronoun full-time yet, as was the case for me. Apart from twice a month at the campus LGBTQ Center and whenever my mom and I got over our awkwardness to talk about it on the phone, I still wasn't out to anybody in my life.

So despite having once dreamt of coming out and starting testosterone before my college graduation, that day came with my feet still firmly in the closet.

Nonetheless, I was determined that I *would* transition one day and I wanted to be able to look back on photos from my college graduation with pride. It had, after all, turned out to be so much harder to get to graduation day and earn my degree than I had ever imagined as a high school senior. If I was living as a man in the future, I didn't want to look back on my college graduation photos and see a girl in a dress. So I picked out some skinny-cut khakis and a button-down that I wore over my binder with my hair pulled back in a low ponytail, all of which looked androgynous enough to not set off red flags to my visiting family—I hoped.

I was probably more obvious than I realized, but they didn't say anything, and I successfully graduated from NYU with all the pomp and circumstance one can muster when "graduating" means briefly standing up with five thousand other people at the same time in the stands of Yankee Stadium while the president of the university calls out "and the College of Arts and Sciences!"

And so began the first summer of my real adult life. I didn't have a job right away. I had saved up so I could take the summer off to rest and take my time with my job search. I thought I might get a job as a video editor, or working in social media, or maybe in a publishing house. Honestly, anywhere that would pay me.

That summer there was another LeakyCon where I had slightly more HPA responsibilities, was recognized slightly more by followers, and was slightly more uncomfortable with the dress I inevitably wore to the ball.

The one significant event from the conference was that I left with a job. In the haphazard way that sleeping assignments can sometimes be doled out at fan conferences when people are trying to save money on hotel rooms, I last minute ended up sharing a bed with a woman I had never met before who was there to shoot footage for a documentary she was codirecting.

When she noticed I was editing video for an upcoming YouTube video on my laptop before bed, she asked me where I lived and if I was looking for work. Turns out she was also based in New York City and in the market for an editor for the documentary.

And just like that, I got my first job out of college by sleeping with someone at a Harry Potter conference!

●   ●   ●

As I started work on the documentary, I was also getting to know some of the other YouTube creators in New York City. Two of them had reached out to me, asking to use the HPA's platform to promote an upcoming meet-up they were having in Central Park. It used to be something of an annual thing in the earlier days of YouTube and they were trying to bring it back.

I promoted it as they asked, helped with a few other minor logistics, and then showed up for the big event. It had a decent turnout and was a fun way to spend a couple of sunny hours on a hot New York summer's day. When it was over, one of the hosts, myself, and a few others went out for drinks at a local beer garden.

I had seen a few videos from the host before, but had never given him much thought. He was one of those YouTubers who had made it big in the early days when he was still in high school, but he had grown and changed a lot over the years and his audience didn't necessarily go with him. These days, he still made YouTube videos, but his day job was working for a television network.

As we all chatted at the beer garden, I realized he and I had a lot in common and were really enjoying talking to each other. Before I knew it, all the others had left, and just the two of us remained. He bought us another round, and we kept talking far too late into the evening. Before we finally parted ways at the subway station, he asked for my phone number.

Despite all the signs, I couldn't believe he was interested in me. I had shown up to the meet-up wearing some horrendous salmon-colored knee-length shorts and a graphic tee—not to mention my usual binder and low ponytail. I hadn't even worn any makeup. Not that any of these things should be requirements or deal-breakers for attracting the interest of another person, but I was the product of hyper gender stereotypes and repressed gender dysphoria. I saw the world in black and white: Women have to be conventionally attractive to be liked, and there is a direct correlation between being pretty and how successful you will be in all spheres of life. More pertinently, I *felt* so self-conscious and unattractive in my androgynous state that it didn't make any sense to me how someone could see past that.

But as text messages turned into drinks turned into dates, it was clear he was indeed interested in me.

It was the most supported and happy I'd felt with a guy in years, but it was also awkward. Apart from the massive guilt I felt in keeping a huge part of me secret from him, there were some practical considerations. In addition to my androgynous outer wardrobe, I hadn't left my house without a binder on for nearly two years and had taken to wearing boxer briefs on most days. Anytime we hung out, especially if I thought I'd be spending the night, I had to find a way to balance my dysphoria with wanting to appear like a normal woman with normal women's undergarments. He ended up seeing my binder once or twice, because I just couldn't stand being out and about all day without it on. I lied and said it helped my bad back (it actually made my bad back *worse*, but he didn't need to know that).

> So I'm dating ████████, which is weird
> for a million reasons (most of which unrelated
> to who he is), but it's also oddly nice so
> far. If I don't think about it. If I
> don't think about me.
> Sigh.

Once when we were on a subway escalator commuting to our respective offices for the day, I was a step above him and thus on eye level with him for once. I got an overwhelming urge to pull him close to me and peck him on the lips. Before I did, he caught me looking at him and asked what was up. I got nervous, afraid I would sound cheesy or too clingy if I told him I had wanted to kiss him, so I panicked and said I was sizing him up to determine if I could take him in a fistfight.

Who *says* that?

I could tell it was a stupid thing to say as soon as it was out of my mouth. He gave me a weird look and we spent the rest of the commute in an uncomfortable silence.

That incident *might* have had to do with some lingering issues from the bad relationship I'd been in back in my freshman year of college, of constantly being told everything I did was clingy and pathetic, but the excuse I covered it with, that weird show of aggression, certainly wasn't doing me any favors in the making-him-believe-I-was-a-normal-girl department.

In the end, he broke it off after a couple of months. After taking me out to dinner, he led us on a walk across the Williamsburg Bridge. As we entered the pedestrian walking path, he told me that he wanted to end things. I accepted his decision more quickly than he had anticipated, and we ended up stranded on the bridge with twenty more minutes of walking to do and all the breaking up done with.

Tips for Dating a Trans Person

If you're a cis person who finds yourself dating a trans person, here are a few things to keep in mind:

- *We're not that different from you.* Really. Most of us just want to be treated like normal people and not like a special "other" category. Talk to us like you would any other person you're going on a date with.

- *Do your own research.* Nothing ruins the mood more than having to educate your date on something that's easily found on Google. You should especially focus on terminology, what questions are too invasive to ask (like medical history), and some basic information about transitioning.

- *Ask them about their boundaries.* Some trans people might have parts of their bodies that are off-limits, or they may prefer to use different words for parts of their bodies. Like with any partner, you should have an open line of communication with clear, affirmative consent on both sides.

- *Dating them doesn't change your sexual orientation.* If you're a straight man dating a trans woman, congratulations! You're still a straight man because you're dating a woman. The same goes for lesbians dating trans women (still lesbians), straight women dating trans men (still straight), and gay men dating trans men (still gay).

- *Be prepared for backlash.* By dating a trans person, you will become intimately familiar with the discrimination and prejudice they face on a regular basis. You might even become the object of that prejudice from people in your life or from strangers. Consider using those moments and your relative privilege as teaching opportunities when you can. Trans people get exhausted always having to educate and stand up for ourselves. Taking the weight off our shoulders on behalf of someone you care about can make a big difference.

- *Know that their bodies might change.* Many trans people choose to medically transition and, depending on when you've met them, they might undergo various procedures while you're together. Don't try to talk them out of it or make it about you. This is something they need to do for themselves. If you don't think you'll love them as much when a part of their body is different, you may have larger problems you need to evaluate in your relationship.

Even though I accepted the breakup easily to his face, inside I was crumbling. As soon as I got home, I called one of my best friends from high school in tears. While recounting the whole relationship to her and freaking out about everything else going on in my life (though carefully not mentioning anything to do with gender), something gray and furry darted out from under my bed, past my feet, and into the living room out of sight.

I screamed.

My friend was terrified on the other end of the line. "What happened?!"

"I think there's a *mouse* in my apartment."

I leaped up on my bed to get to higher ground and searched around for signs of the mouse or more of his friends.

I've never done well with rodents. Even friends' hamsters used to freak me out. But having a wild one in your *house*? I felt like I had lost control of the last thing in my life I had any marginal control over.

"That's it," my friend said. "I'm buying you a plane ticket. You're coming to stay with me for the weekend."

Not sure I was going to survive even one night knowing there was a mouse lurking somewhere, I agreed—so long as she let me pay at least half. She earned way more money than me working in Silicon Valley, but I couldn't just accept a whole plane ticket for free.

While I stayed with my friend in California, we analyzed the whole relationship from every possible angle so I could feel some closure on what might have gone wrong. It became clear pretty quickly in our analysis that he had probably gotten spooked by some of my more boyish behaviors and style of dress.

I struggled to explain why I had become so masculine in the years since my friend and I had seen each other every day at high school, when I was one of the girlier ones in our friend group. While I would have loved to come out to her then and there, I had recently overheard her and my roommate talking on the phone about how they were worried that I was "turning into a man." Ever since hearing that, I had started noticing how they both used positive reinforcement anytime I did something feminine. Posted a photo with my hair down? They'd leave effusive comments. Actually wore makeup? They would tell me I looked like myself again. It was like getting fed Scooby Snacks for being a girl.

I got this from a lot of women in my life during that time period. They'd try to get me to go for manicures, citing it as a stress reliever, or encourage me to buy more feminine clothing, just to treat myself. Maybe they thought that my masculine appearance was some type of side effect of the depressive state they'd noticed in me, a lack of self-care and self-confidence in my appearance—and not the purposeful choices of someone trying to reflect on the outside how they felt on the inside.

By the time my friend and I had dissected every nook and cranny of my life—other than what I hadn't admitted to her, about my probably being trans—I had come around to believing that maybe I *was* just depressed and confused. I wasn't transgender. I'd just lost my way, and now I was ready to find it again. I mean, after all, hadn't it been since first discovering the possibility of transition my sophomore year of college that I'd turned into this dark, sullen person? Maybe if I put it all behind me, I could go back to being the happy, content-with-her-gender person I had been in high school.

WE EVEN STAGED A PHOTO SHOOT TO MARK MY REINTEGRATION INTO THE WORLD OF WOMEN.

I know, *I know*. It was all bull crap, but I was distraught and embarrassed by being spurned for my gender expression. Even when I had been trying to be more of a girl, I was still too masculine for straight men to like me anymore. The shock of it sent me back to the repression zone.

The facts of the matter were that I *hadn't* been entirely content with my gender in high school and I *had* started struggling emotionally even before my big trans discovery sophomore year. But even besides the revisionist history I was feeding myself, it's completely normal for transgender people to feel *worse* before they feel better.

In my case, I was working through a lifetime of entrenched gender stereotyping and several periods of repression of my affirmed gender. I had put so much value on the social capital gained by being conventionally attractive and fitting in with mainstream society. That apparent loss—by appearing more androgynous—had been a painful, morose process. Even though I've never wanted to fit in as far as my personality and interests go, I have *always* felt a strong desire to pass as ordinary. So as someone who, for better or worse (mostly worse), cared so much about what people thought, it made sense that I would be dispirited when I could no longer dazzle and impress.

I'm dying looking at all the men in the city pulling out their full fashions with the cold front.

Everyday I tell myself I can do this. Wear skinny jeans and form fitting tops and be fashionable. The looks I get from friends and strangers that clearly tell me I've been accepted into normal society, if with a bit of blundering under-whelm —— that feeling converts me.

But everyday I end up in the t-shirt and jeans unsure of how to try new female styles, feeling uncomfortable and

like I'm suffocating in a rubber unitard that hugs in all the wrong places.

I look at the fashionable men & the city and see the body shapes I want, the hair I could have, the clothes that I know would feel right – that I could be excited to wear and the only barrier would be having enough money to buy everything I wanted and only being able to wear one outfit at a time.

But, despite all that, I'm not entirely unhappy living as female, I don't think.

OCTOBER 9, 2012.

But I didn't see all of that at the time. Instead, I convinced myself that I should give being a girl a go again. Even as I told myself that, I struggled with the effort. I tried wearing my hair down again, donning clear mascara, and digging out my girl jeans. I started convincing myself that I wasn't really trans; I was just a socially awkward girl who had fallen off track.

This false reasoning faded pretty quickly. Within a few weeks, I had come to my senses, but I maintained the slightly more femme appearance. It helped me find that equilibrium of passing as ordinary, instead of feeling the judgment of strangers' stares as I had before with my more masculine look.

Outside of my head, life kept going on and the bills had to be paid—which had become a bit of a problem, actually. Working on a documentary crew doesn't produce the steadiest of paychecks. For months, I'd been bouncing between feast and famine as checks came in whenever the director was able to secure more funding, often requiring me to pay rent and bills on my credit card. Realizing that this lifestyle wouldn't be sustainable for someone just out of college without any savings, I resolved to leave the film industry behind for now and find some type of job with a salary.

Fortunately, the HPA had been looking to bring on a full-time social media manager and, as the person who had been running their YouTube channel and other social media platforms as a volunteer for several years, I was a shoe-in for the position. After an informal interview, a salary negotiation, and a backyard initiation ceremony that included a number of whelks and quahogs, I had my first full-time job.

* * *

The HPA position included a role as one of the organization's spokespeople, which made sense because my presence on their YouTube channel had already led to several invitations to speak at various events on the organization's behalf even before I was an employee. It would require a lot of travel, however. So much so that when my roommate announced in April that she was moving in with her boyfriend, I decided that, rather than find a new roommate or a new apartment, it would be easier to rent out a storage unit and couch-surf all summer in between trips.

Halfway through the summer, the couch-surfing was going well. I'd run my first ever 5K race out in Portland at LeakyCon, where I also got to speak on a panel with Hank Green, one of my favorite YouTube creators, and Anthony Rapp, who had played my favorite character in *RENT* in the original Broadway cast. I hosted a candy-topped pizza party at VidCon, the annual online video conference, I'd taken an eighteen-hour train journey from Los Angeles to Santa Fe to visit my mom, and I was getting ready to travel to London for a bonus international edition of LeakyCon.

I was just leaving my storage unit in Manhattan, having dug out my old power adapters to pack for London, when I got a call from my old roommate. We didn't often *call* each other, usually opting to text, so even before I heard the quiver in her voice, I knew something was wrong.

Joel, the one boy I had ever been in an extended, exclusive, meet-the-parents, Myspace official relationship with, had died by suicide the night before.

Head spinning, I got the logistical details about funeral arrangements from my roommate, thanked her for doing the incredibly hard task of telling me, assured her I would be okay, and then hung up and fell to the sidewalk in tears, the hot concrete permeating my jeans. Crying in public is something of a rite of passage in New York City, and one that I had long before passed, but this was on a whole other level. I was crouched against the wall of a building, wailing uncontrollably as people crossed to the other side of the street to avoid me. I couldn't believe Joel was gone. We had *just* started to message each other for the first time since high school. We had plans to get pizza together when I returned home to Texas later that year. There would be no pizza now. Not ever.

I immediately adapted my travel plans so I could fly home for the funeral. While I had never gone home for previous friends' deaths, not being sure if I could afford the plane ticket or take the time off, this time it wasn't even a question. A lot of people on the peripheries of my life had died, far too many from my own age group, but this was the closest person to me yet and I needed to be there to say good-bye.

I had a little black dress I had bought for the Tribeca preview of the documentary I'd worked on that was probably a bit too short for a funeral, but I put a black cardigan over it and tried not to think too hard about how uncomfortable I felt. This ended up being fairly easy to do because the second I rounded the corner into the main room of the funeral home and saw his casket, I broke out in stunned tears and had to be led to a seat by an old friend from high school.

His grandfather conducted the service, being sure to point out how wrong it is for a grandfather to have to speak at his grandchild's funeral. The high school choir reunited to sing one of his favorite songs. I got up to speak at one point, legs shaking as I recounted stories and, in my nerves, lapsed into clichés that weren't even true about the guy I had known—that he was always smiling and it was such a shock—but felt like what his parents, sitting in the front row looking right at me, needed to hear.

Every now and then, I think about how long it took me to finally come out and transition after learning about the possibility of it, and how badly I had wanted to do so in college. Joel's funeral is one of the few reasons I'm grateful that I didn't transition earlier. I *needed* to say good-bye to him properly at his funeral, and I'm not sure I would have been able to attend the ceremony as a guy. I don't know that I would've thought it appropriate to show up, recently out, in front of so many people who might not have accepted my transition, including his parents, distracting from the somber occasion.

I have since felt the pain of not getting to attend the funeral of someone I loved very much because not everyone there knew I had transitioned and it was agreed that my presence wouldn't have helped matters. It hurts, a lot, to have that taken away simply because of who you are. So I'm glad I at least got to say good-bye to Joel.

CHAPTER SIXTEEN

the first cut is the deepest

After the funeral, I finished up the last of my summer travels and moved into a new apartment with a friend. She and I had been friends for only about a year, meeting through a mutual friend from NYU, but the timing of us both needing a place worked out and we decided we had similar enough temperaments, interests, and cleanliness standards to make a go of it.

Even though I was so broke by the end of my travels that I couldn't afford a bed for six months while I paid off my debts, having my own place, a consistent salary, and a great roommate improved my mental health by leaps and bounds. I was feeling stronger and happier than I ever had, finally feeling like I had a base of stability to work from when minor stressors came my way.

Shortly after we moved in together, my new roommate cut off her long hair into a pixie-style quiff to give herself a more mature look after her college graduation. It looked awesome. She had this natural wave to her hair that made it look perfectly coiffed without her doing anything to it.

Despite many of my women friends talking about getting short haircuts over the years whenever they undulated back into style, this was the first time any friend of mine had actually done it. I had spent years being scared to cut my hair short, in part because I didn't know how people would react, but with her having done it first, maybe our friends wouldn't think it was a big deal.

The opinions of friends wasn't the only thing keeping me from getting the boy cut I'd wanted my whole life. There was a lot going on in my head, under my scalp.

Once I had given up on my mom ever letting me get a crew cut as a kid and had grown my hair long enough to wear a ponytail, I actually started being scared of having short hair. Unlike many transmasculine people, when I watched the scene in *Mulan* in which she swiftly chops her hair off with a sword, I wasn't envious. I was uneasy.

Numerous times throughout elementary school, my mom had threatened to shave my head if I didn't start washing and brushing my hair properly (most likely an empty threat, looking back on it). In seventh grade, one of the boys in my class thought it was hilarious to chase me around the room with scissors every single day, threatening to cut my long blond hair before English class.

These threats frightened me, in part, because I had spent so long growing my hair out and I didn't want to have to start all over again. But on a deeper level, I was fearful that having short hair would somehow reveal to people the boy inside of me that I was trying so hard to keep secret.

After discovering the possibility of transitioning my sophomore year of college and wanting to experiment with different styles, my apprehension at cutting my hair became more nuanced. For starters, I was simply worried that I would look awful with short hair. I've always had a round face with slightly chubby cheeks and dimples. I thought a pixie cut might emphasize those features in ways I didn't want. I also have very fine hair, which I knew from watching my brother over the years is very difficult to style into anything when it's so short.

But more than that, I had gotten it into my head that this would be something I couldn't go back from. It felt permanent somehow. It's true that it would be the most drastic visible change other people would see of my transition—but they didn't need to know I was cutting my hair because of my gender. Logically, I knew that I could make up any excuse about why I had cut my hair. But not having grown up around any women under the age of seventy with short hair, I knew it would be a big deal that warranted explanation.

I mean, when I showed up to a family Christmas with thick-framed glasses, all my cousins asked if I was a lesbian, and my uncles all told me I'd never get a man with glasses like that. I hadn't even changed anything about my appearance at that point. I just got glasses, the kind that, by the way, were totally in style in New York City at the time. But that was enough for them to accuse me of being too masculine and unappealing. I dreaded hearing their responses if I did something even more drastic.

I was so apprehensive about other people's reactions that I started thinking perhaps I would get top surgery before cutting my hair. No one had to know I'd had an outpatient procedure to remove my breasts unless I took my shirt off. If I could keep the surgery secret from most people in my life, they'd never need to know. I could relieve one huge source of my dysphoria without having to come out to a single soul. I was far more dysphoric about my chest than my hair at that point. It seemed like a perfect solution. Until I pulled myself back to reality.

In addition to the realization via my roommate that this was a perfectly normal thing for a young woman to do, what really pushed me to finally go for it was the thought that maybe with an "alternative" haircut people would start seeing my androgynous clothing as a style choice, rather than a reflection of the self-conscious unfashionable dope I always feared I appeared to be. When someone has a cool haircut, you just assume they know what they're doing with their clothing choices, even if you don't get it.

Actually getting the haircut turned out to be a challenge unto itself. Having grown up with a hairdresser for a mother and not needing more than twice-a-year trims when my hair went down to my mid-back, I had never in my life been to a salon or barber. No one had ever cut my hair except my mom. I didn't have a regular hairdresser I could go to in my neighborhood who was familiar with my hair and my style. I would have to start from scratch.

I heard horror stories from women, nonbinary, and transmasculine people alike about hairdressers refusing to cut their long hair because they didn't want to be responsible for any regrets. Even when asked explicitly for a particular short haircut, the stylist would only cut it to about the ears, if that. Worse still, for transmasculine people especially, was going to a hairdresser to get a solidly masculine short haircut and leaving looking like a soccer mom who just asked to speak to the manager.

Fearing any of this happening to me, I armed myself with a mood board of short hairstyles I'd be okay with—all using people with a similar face shape and hair texture as mine. I mixed it up so there were photos of people of all genders to keep the hairdresser from getting suspicious, but I was also ready to say, "If you have to choose between making me look like an older woman or a young boy, err toward young boy." I practiced this line in private countless times so I'd get it right.

The problem still remained of where to go. My roommate had yet to find a hairdresser she was happy with, so she didn't have any recommendations. I decided to reach out to one of the few other women I knew with short hair, a friend of mine from the Harry Potter fan community.

Lauren had an adorable pixie cut, having steadily cut her hair shorter and shorter over the course of several years. When I reached out to her, she told me the only reason she didn't cut it that short to begin with was because none of the hairdressers she went to would do it. They all thought she'd regret it or not look feminine enough, so they just gave her the haircut they thought she should have.

When she finally got the cut she wanted, it was from a fantastic hairdresser at a salon near where she lived in Rhode Island. She still went to see him every month and he was always eager to experiment with her on new styles. He was encouraging and talented, and always gave you exactly what you wanted, or better.

I was sold. I asked if I could come stay with her and her husband, Matt, who just so happened to be one of my coworkers at the HPA, for a few days and if she would go with me to get my hair cut—I'd need someone to film, after all. Even if I wasn't out yet and would end up lying about *why* I cut my hair, I wasn't letting this big moment go unreported on my YouTube channel. As a fellow YouTube creator herself, Lauren more than understood—and also had the skills to get some good action shots.

As the day got closer, I was more excited than nervous. I kept reminding myself of why I was doing it—I'd never know if I didn't try. I wanted how I felt on the inside to reflect my outside. If I only ever wore my hair in a low ponytail anyway, what was the point of keeping it long?

I kept telling myself that it was my body and I didn't have to make excuses to anyone about the changes I made to it. Telling myself that it was just hair. It could grow back, even if there would be some awkward stages in the middle while it did.

Going to Providence to get my hair cut, as extravagant as it might have been, was the right decision. Matt and Lauren were calm, compassionate friends who I had always felt I could be myself around. They were exactly the kind of people I needed surrounding me while I took such a big step in my not-quite-yet transition, even if they weren't explicitly aware of the full gravity behind the occasion.

Lauren's hairdresser was exactly as she'd promised. He was enthusiastic and artful, honored and overjoyed to be a part of my first big haircut. I showed him the photos I'd gathered on my phone and repeated the line I'd been practicing, "If you have to choose between making me look like an older woman or a young boy, err toward young boy." He smiled and said he knew just what to do.

After he combed the bulk of my hair back into a ponytail, Lauren got the camera ready for a close-up shot as he made the first big cut.

There was no going back now.

He took a while snipping and shaping, as the three of us chatted and I snuck peeks in the mirror. Toward the end, he pulled out some styling wax and taught me a few methods for applying it and styling my hair. Then he whipped the cape off of me and it was done. I put on my glasses and looked in the mirror at my new haircut. It didn't look too feminine at all. It framed my face just fine. It was *short*, kind of chunky on top, and most importantly, *mine*. I had done it.

My NEW HAIRCUT WAS
OUTTA THIS WORLD!
(I'll SEE MYSELF OUT...)

As we walked to lunch afterward, the chilly December wind blew through my newly short hair. My head definitely felt cold, but I didn't want to cover it with a beanie just yet. I was too excited.

For a brief moment the next morning, I wondered what I had done to myself, but it passed after a few minutes, and I've never regretted it since.

CHAPTER SEVENTEEN

i must not tell lies

The haircut had done its job. If it had been a test to determine whether transitioning would be right for me, I was feeling fairly certain I was on the right path.

At the very least, I was excited to try out different ways of styling it and dyeing it fun colors, things I'd hardly ever been excited to do with long hair. I could finally wear all the cool hats I'd collected over the years that didn't fit over a ponytail, and if the new haircut did emphasize the roundness of my face, I hardly noticed and couldn't care less.

Matt would even tell me a few weeks later, when I nervously revealed to him that I was questioning my gender over post-work drinks at a conference in Philadelphia, that he and Lauren thought there was a new energy around me after the haircut, like I had broken free from chains that had been weighing me down.

With the short haircut and my wardrobe veering between androgynous and full-on men's attire, there were a few instances where, for the first time since that fateful funnel cake purchase in fourth grade, I was actually mistaken for a guy. At least until I opened my mouth and my high voice ruined the effect.

My favorite instance of this was when President Jimmy Carter was on my flight to South Carolina to attend the Quidditch World Cup. *I* was attending the Quidditch World Cup, that is. I never saw President

Carter at the Potter-inspired sports event, but he *was* on my flight, so who knows? I thought this was odd at the time, but I've since learned that he was instrumental in deregulating the airlines and continues to fly commercial to support the industry. What a gem!

Before we took off, President Carter, flanked by half a dozen security guards, walked down the aisle to shake the hands of every single passenger. When he got to my row, he shook my hand and said, "Nice to meet you, young man," then leaned a hand on my shoulder to reach over me and shake the hands of the two women sitting in the middle and window seats of my row. As he walked away, he ruffled my hair with a chuckle.

JIMMY CARTER GENDERED ME CORRECTLY!

What's even wilder is that a few years later, a trans woman friend of mine who wasn't totally out yet happened to meet President Carter at an event and he gendered *her* correctly too! Man's got a sixth sense for correctly gendering trans people.

INTERVIEWING PEOPLE IN CHARACTER AS HARRY POTTER AT THE QUIDDITCH WORLD CUP—FOR MY ACTUAL JOB!

If I'm being honest, I was never mistaken for a guy per se, but rather for a young boy. Probably fifteen at the very oldest, due to my lack of facial hair and tiny frame. Even when people read me as a woman, I still looked several years younger than I actually was. This frustrated me at times. I was twenty-four. I had a bachelor's degree and a 401(k). I had employees, for Pete's sake! It was bizarre to be treated like a child while encountering all the challenges and joys of being an independent adult.

Part of that frustration, though, was that for all the realities of adulthood I faced and enjoyed, I felt stunted in my growth. I *did* feel younger than my peers, especially the women in my life. I didn't feel like one of them at all.

While at eighteen, I felt like I had cracked the code and fit in with newly adult women, at twenty-four I saw the women around me changing and maturing in ways that I, definitively, wasn't. The interests they were adopting, their modes of dress, their ways of interacting with the world—it all felt like a foreign language, one I had been supposed to learn, but skipped out on the classes for.

It was becoming more and more apparent to me that this mask of girlhood was expiring. I had to grow up. And considering I couldn't even make my mouth form the word *woman* in reference to myself, it was clear what the path forward needed to be.

But I just couldn't bring myself to come out as a man and start transitioning yet. I still hadn't *really* accepted that I was transgender, that all my desperate attempts to live a normal, successful life would now be marred by this stigma. I had fully internalized the world's shame surrounding trans people and was embarrassed by the thought of people knowing this part of me I had kept so deeply hidden for so long.

As a sort of compromise, I had started divulging to people who were queer themselves or familiar with nonbinary genders that I was maybe not quite female. I would tell them, "If I could take a magic pill and wake up completely male with no one ever noticing or caring, I would, but as it exists in our reality, I'm not sure."

I, of course, wish I could wake up tomorrow morning biologically male (or at least post several years of T and top surgery). I feel like I'll have trouble entirely showing myself as male & making others believe it until the looking glass stops betraying me.

OCTOBER 4, 2011.

If they pushed further, I would allow them to use the gender-neutral pronouns "they" and "them" in reference to me, but only around other people who were in the know about my gender confusion. This was a good experiment to see if, perhaps, I was not a man or a woman, but perhaps nonbinary. I did, after all, have quite a few feminine qualities that had always made me doubt I could really be a man. Like sometimes preferring conversation to sports, or having an interest in fashion, or crying when I got overwhelmed. But were those true, core qualities about me or qualities that had been allowed to flourish because I had grown up free of the restrictions put on boys? And did certain character qualities or interests make a man, anyway? Why couldn't I be a man who likes rom-coms?

As far as I've been able to tell, the only thing that really defines a gender at the end of the day is the innate sense you have deep down inside. When I thought about a life lived in between the lines, using "they" and "them" pronouns, always subject to strangers' confusion and judgment, I knew it wasn't who I was.

Gender-Neutral Pronouns

Pronouns are an important part of one's gender expression and can play a big role in someone's transition. The pronouns we hear most often are *he/him/his* and *she/her/hers*, but some people also use gender-neutral pronouns, like *they/them/theirs*. A person might use the singular *they/them/theirs* because they're nonbinary or otherwise outside of the gender binary, or simply because they don't like the gendered implications of *he/him/his* and *she/her/hers* pronouns.

Sometimes people get nervous about conjugating *they/them/theirs* pronouns for singular usage, but you probably already do it without a second thought. If you find an abandoned phone at a cafe, you might tell the barista, "Someone left *their* phone here." If someone cuts you off on the highway, you might say, "Wow, *they're* a terrible driver" (with perhaps a bit more colorful language added in). *They/them/theirs* pronouns are used the same way when done so intentionally.

While it might seem like this is a new development people are trying to force into existence, using *they* as a singular pronoun has been a part of the English language since at least the sixteenth century, according to the *Oxford English Dictionary*. I like to think of it as being similar to *thou* as a singular, informal version of *you* in the Elizabethan era. We don't usually say it anymore, but it has a historical basis and is grammatically correct. And even if *they/them/their* pronouns *were* brand new, language is always evolving to fit the times. It's never been a completely static thing.

As we work to make our everyday language more gender inclusive, it's also important to consider other phrases you might say that erase certain people, such as "you guys," "yes ma'am," "hey, ladies," and more. A call for using gender-neutral versions of terms like these goes beyond trans awareness. People have been trying to break down the patriarchal connotations of terms like *fireman*, *mankind*, and *mailman* for generations. When I was growing up, I was told that any instance of *man* in documents like the Constitution should be assumed to include women, but why did women have to be an invisible afterthought? Why couldn't it just say *person?*

Here are few alternatives for more inclusive language options:

You guys ➡ Y'all, folks, everyone

Yes ma'am/sir ➡ use the person's title, name, or nothing at all

Hey, ladies ➡ Hey there; hi, all; hi, folks

Man-made ➡ Synthetic, artificial, handcrafted

Fireman ➜ Firefighter
Mankind ➜ Humankind
Mailman ➜ Mail person, postal worker
Ladies and gentleman ➜ Distinguished guests
Son/daughter ➜ Child
Mom/dad ➜ Parent
Brother/sister ➜ Sibling

These are not just useful for being gender inclusive, but also helpful for not assuming the genders of all the people you're speaking to. If you're ever referring to someone whose gender you don't know, you can avoid saying something like "the man in the second row" by saying "the person in the yellow shirt in the second row."

It's also important to know that some people, nonbinary and otherwise, use the *Mx.* honorific (pronounced "mix"), instead of *Mr.*, *Mrs.*, or *Ms.*

In addition to *they/them/theirs*, some people might use other gender-neutral pronouns such as *ze*, *xe*, *hir*, *ey*, or others. To learn more gender-neutral pronouns and how to conjugate them, visit minus18.org.au/pronouns-app.

One last note about gender-neutral pronouns: While gender neutrality is *often* the best way to be gender inclusive, sometimes it can be a real bummer for binary trans people. For trans men and women who have worked so hard to be seen as who they are, getting referred to as "they" can be really distressing and disrespectful. Eradicating gender entirely shouldn't be the aim, but rather creating spaces where people feel welcome to be and express whatever gender they are.

Yet there still remained just enough doubt in my maleness for me to fear coming out and physically transitioning. I was always belaboring the possibility that I could be unhappy with transitioning and decide to live as a woman again. No matter how small a probability there was of this happening, I was frightened of living as a woman with the facial hair, deepened voice, and squared jaw that testosterone would eventually cause. It all goes back to my internalized stereotypes of what women should look like. In more lucid moments, I acknowledged how telling it was that I could only stomach being a woman if I could be the societally perfect image of one. On the other hand, I felt I would be happy being any kind of man.

•   •   •

The breaking point came at LeakyCon that summer after my big haircut. On the final night of the annual Harry Potter conference, it was once again time for the Esther Earl Charity Ball, but unlike previous years, this time I had only packed a dress. There was no suit backup.

Since wearing a dress once or twice a year hadn't been bothering me too much ever since I discovered that mental switch I could flip on and off, I had decided to just go for it. I didn't want to make a big deal out of my gender by showing up in a suit, and only packing the dress would save space in my luggage.

That was a mistake. From the second I put on my standard little black dress alone in my hotel room, something felt off. I couldn't flip the switch.

I was looking in the mirror and all I could see was an ugly, mannish person in a dress. No doubt the short hair was helping that image. With my long hair, I'd been able to wear it down, style it a tiny bit, and create a feminine mystique. With my short hair, I couldn't see that transformation anymore.

This is not to say that people with short hair can't look attractive or cool or feminine in dresses. Indeed, a spectator might have thought I looked like any one of those things. But for me, staring at myself in the mirror, all I could see was wrong, wrong, wrong. I hadn't felt this prickling full-body discomfort, inside and out, since I was a little kid clawing at my parents in desperation as they pulled a dress over my head.

Despite the sickly feeling rising from my stomach, I went down to the ball to meet my friends. The ball, for all the grief it had caused me over the years, was always one of my favorite parts of the conference. I loved getting to dance around and let loose with all my friends after a stressful several days of presenting programs and managing vendor booths.

If I had thought my discomfort was bad when I was alone, it got much worse when other people could see me too. The friends I was meeting up with weren't downstairs yet and, as I stood off to the side texting them, some folks spotted me and asked for photos. I squeezed my discomfort into a pained smile for a handful of selfie requests, but the pain was mounting inside me. I didn't want these people to see me upset, so I excused myself and found an empty programming room to hide out in until my friends arrived.

Once I got the text that said everyone had finally made it to the cavernous exhibition hall where the ball was being held, I took a deep breath and tensely emerged back out among the LeakyCon-goers.

My friends were huddled around one of the white-cloth-covered tables lining the perimeter of the hall near the pop-up bar. They were all in good spirits, admiring one another's interpretations of ball wear.

While I'd always felt pressure to wear a simple dress, the wardrobes at the annual ball vary widely. Some go the whole ten yards in glittery gowns and three-piece suits, pretending it's the prom they wish they'd had as teenagers. Others cosplay, wearing wizard robes and Hogwarts house ties. Still others don their usual jeans and sneakers. Despite our desires to impress and delight at one another's creative choices, it truly is a judgment-free zone.

I wanted to join in on the fun. I wanted to flip the switch in my head that allowed me to relax, but I couldn't. I felt intensely uncomfortable, and the feeling of everyone's eyes on me only added to my stress. My whole body was seething with nerves, wrapped in annoyance, and topped with disappointment in myself.

When one of my friends held up his phone to take a picture of me, thinking the peeved-off scowl on my face was funny, I'd had enough. I shoved his hand down, inadvertently throwing his phone down to the hard concrete of the exhibition hall floor.

His phone was unharmed, but he'd gotten the idea. No more pictures. Perhaps understanding that my irritation went deeper than a slight annoyance at the night's affairs, he went to get a round of drinks and pointedly handed the first one to me. I downed it in one gulp and then decided I needed to leave. Dancing with my friends until the early hours of the morning was usually my favorite part of the conference, but I couldn't stand the eyes on me while I felt so miserable, and it was clear I was going to bring down everyone's good vibes with my churlish mood.

I shuffled back up to my hotel room with my head down, not responding to anyone's hellos as I went. When I got to my room, I tore off the dress and wrapped myself in my familiar hoodie and Levi's before screaming into a pillow for a solid ten minutes.

After a good while of listening to emo songs while sobbing, I went into the en-suite bathroom to clean up and took a hard look at my blotchy, snot-streaked face in the mirror.

That was the moment I realized I couldn't keep lying to myself. I'd been making excuses for years, but they were all played out. Transitioning was no longer a choice. It was a necessity. I couldn't keep living the path of someone I wasn't.

There was no time for major life revelations, however. Dress or no dress, I had to be back down in the exhibition hall by midnight to participate in a surprise for the conference attendees. I had hosted and helped produce a video to celebrate the life of Esther Earl, the young woman the ball was named after, who had been a LeakyCon attendee before passing away from cancer a few years prior. The video was going to start at 11:55 P.M., ending in a coordinated blast of music and confetti cannons exactly at midnight to ring in the start of Esther Day—a holiday in Esther's honor that is celebrated on August third every year by telling the people in your life that you love them.

Even with all the emotions I was battling, I wasn't going to miss something I had worked so hard on. So I swallowed my tears and headed back to the ball in my jeans and hoodie.

BACK AT THE BALL IN MY HOODIE AND JEANS.

The video and confetti drop went off flawlessly. There weren't many dry eyes in the hall as we all reflected on the impact Esther had had on our community and the incredible work her friends and family continue to do for other families battling cancer.

Duties done, I went back up to my hotel room exhausted. When I flew home the next day, I made a call to start seeing a gender therapist to begin the slow but certain journey of physically transitioning.

CHAPTER EIGHTEEN

you don't know jack

Finding a gender therapist is a surprisingly opaque process. There are plenty of directories online listing therapists specializing in gender dysphoria, categorized by city and state. But will they accept your insurance? What will the co-pay be if they do? Has the therapist actually worked with transgender people before or are they just saying "LGBTQ+ friendly" to attract more clients?

Some local LGBTQ+ centers offer temporary, often free, counseling for LGBTQ+ people in urgent need and will work to match you with a long-term therapist afterward. This was the route I tried to take all the way back in college when I first recognized I could do with some professional help. But the two times I tried calling back then, they were disorganized and unhelpful. They said the person I needed to talk to wasn't there, and kept giving me the runaround.

It had taken me months to work up the courage just to make those calls, let alone find out the resource even existed. I wasn't sure where else to turn and just gave up for a while. Similar results happened with other resources I found over the years. Local LGBTQ+ community organizations are often understaffed and underfunded, so it's pretty common to have to really push them and ask for exactly what you need; but when you don't know what you need, when you're struggling with your mental health so intensely that just getting out of bed each day takes a colossal effort, the idea of being so proactive is laughable.

Fortunately, shortly before the disaster at the LeakyCon ball, I had started going to an LGBTQ+ clinic in New York City for my primary care needs. Thanks to the Affordable Care Act, I finally had health insurance, and I knew I wanted to see a physician who would understand my needs as a transgender person when I probably, inevitably, transitioned. It had taken a lot to make *that* call too, but it wasn't as hard as the previous ones had been. I had come a long way in a few years. I wasn't the lonely, frightened college student anymore. I had a support system of friends, a fantastic living situation, and a stable income. Even if I was still nervous as crap about talking to people about my gender, I was stronger mentally and emotionally than I had been in years. Small (or not-so-small) tasks weren't as daunting anymore.

At the health center I was going to, every patient was assigned a social worker to help with things like building a medical plan for their needs, finding specialists outside of the health center, and figuring out how to afford it all. So when I returned from LeakyCon knowing I needed to see a therapist, I gave my social worker a call and we set up a time to meet. After calling around, we found a place that looked like it took my insurance and whose sliding scale would be within my budget if it didn't.

When I started seeing my new therapist, at first I was still saying I was genderqueer and using they/them pronouns even though I *knew* that didn't feel right. I was just too nervous to outright tell someone I was a man. I knew I didn't look like one and probably didn't talk or act manly enough either. I thought everyone would just laugh at me if I said I was really a man. I thought maybe they wouldn't believe me and would try to convince me not to transition.

As our weekly sessions continued, however, and I began to trust my therapist more, I opened up about how I really felt. When we could talk about the *real* issues—about my fears of coming out to people and transitioning—as opposed to simply being gender confused (which was hardly the case anymore), I began to make real progress.

At my therapist's nudging, I spent time imagining my future and thinking about how I saw myself. When I imagined my future as a man, I was flooded by scenes of myself at different ages—on set as a director being visited for lunch by my partner, chasing kids around a backyard, reading in my at-home library at a ripe old age. When I tried to imagine myself as a woman, my mind couldn't conjure a single image.

> I have this image of myself in a home library, ensconced in the dark wood, but w/ sunlight peeking in from a window behind my stately and much worn arm chair. Slight in stature, I have messy light brown hair, a shadow of stubble from neglect. I wear perfectly circular tortoise shell glasses. A sweater vest, sleeves rolled to my elbows, slacks and loafers all in intellectual earth tones. I smoke out of an elegant tobacco pipe, my other hand holding a book.
> I roam the library like a stag. Settling down contentedly.

I thought about what would happen if I kept going without transitioning. Even if I could somehow convince myself to live as a woman for a while, what would happen when that facade crumbled once again? My whole life had been a cycle of repressing my masculinity until I couldn't take it anymore. What if I tried that again, got as far as getting married and having kids, and then snapped? Then I'd have a whole family I would have to pull into my transition with me.

It's something that happens a lot with people who transition later in life and many families come out of it stronger and more loving than before, but not all of them—and I couldn't bear doing that to people I loved when I knew there was another option. It was bad enough having to bring my parents and brother into it.

With my therapist's help, I thought about every possible outcome and consequence of every possible decision. It was something I thought I'd been doing for years, but I was astounded to realize how much more productive that process can be when there's someone there to break your self-defeating spirals.

And so by December, I was finally ready to move forward. I wanted to start taking testosterone. I wanted to start living my life the way I had always been meant to. With my therapist there as a coach and a sounding board, I knew I'd be able to face whatever kind of reactions I got from people or other challenges that might arise in the process.

The first step would be updating my mom. Fortunately, I had to go to Tucson in January to convene on an academic journal I'd been invited to pen a chapter for, a case study of the HPA and its role in youth social movements using digital media.

Tucson is an eight-hour drive from my mom's house in Santa Fe. Not the easiest trip in the world, but given how expensive flights in and out of New Mexico are and therefore how rarely we got to see each other, my mom was more than up for the challenge.

So in between long days working on group revisions with a bunch of much-more-qualified-than-me professors, I went back to our shared hotel room and filled my mom in on my plans to begin transitioning in a few months.

We hadn't talked a ton about my gender over the years, so I wasn't sure how she would react to my saying I was finally really doing it.

When I told her, she said she was nervous for me, nervous about how other people in my life might react and how it would affect my job. But overall she was supportive. She'd seen how depressed I had been for years and was one of the few people aware of the reasons behind that depression. She thought this would help me finally be at peace, even suggesting that my lifelong struggles with indigestion might clear up when I wasn't as distressed by living as the wrong gender. Pretty sure there are actually *fewer* foods I can digest now that I've transitioned, but hey, it was a decent hypothesis.

Apart from informing her of my plans, I did have one more request before we parted ways: I needed a name.

Ever since I had vetoed her top pick of Harrison, I had privately tried out lots of other names, but none of them felt as intrinsically *right* as having one picked out by my mom.

Apart from the unfortunate Hairy Bird pairing, Harrison's quick shortening to Harry had begun to be even more problematic as my profile in Harry Potter fandom grew. At the time when I was preparing to come out, I had started performing as Harry Potter himself for the HPA's YouTube channel and live events. I couldn't bear the thought of coming out as a guy and saying my new name was Harry. People would think I had lost it!

When I had first started brainstorming names, I thought back to the name of the alter ego I'd created in high school: Jack. I don't know how I had come up with the name then. It had just seemed right. But as years went on and the daydreams about Jack became more fantastical, he seemed farther and farther removed from who I was. He had become a character unto himself—a character who was taller, tanner, more confident, less awkward, and better at singing than I was. I couldn't live up to that character, so I had written Jack off as an option from the start.

Tips on Picking a Name

Not all trans people change their names, but for those who do, it can be a long, nerve-wracking process. I went through so many different possibilities before I settled on Jackson.

At first I tried sticking to the same initial as my birth name. This can be really useful while you're transitioning or only out to a few people because you can just write your initial instead of your first name on informal documents. For example, I could have written my return address on mail as "J. Bird."

Some people like to find a name that sounds a little bit like their birth name, whether it starts with the same letter or not. This can feel a bit more familiar both for the person transitioning and for the people in their lives.

Others choose a name that their parents would have named them had they been assigned their affirmed gender at birth, like I ultimately did. Or they let their parents choose their new name when they transition. I've also known several people who have picked their new first name themselves but let a parent pick their middle name.

If living stealth is important to you, some people suggest sticking to names that were popular the year you were born as opposed to names that are popular when you're transitioning. This way you have a name that fits in with your generation instead of having to turn your head every time a parent calls after their toddler with your same name at the grocery store.

One problem with finding a name that was popular around the time you were born, however, is that you probably know people with most of the popular names and have strong associations with them. It can feel weird to pick a name shared by your best friend's sister or the guy who picked on you in sixth grade.

That's one reason a lot of people opt for more current names. There's also been a larger trend toward gender-neutral names with millennial parents. Even if a trans person identifies as a binary man or woman, they might opt for a gender-neutral name to make the transition easier, both for themselves and for the people close to them. Remember, we have to adapt to calling ourselves a new name too, and it can be weird at first!

When you're trying to decide on a name, don't feel like you need to have some chorus-of-angels, decree-from-on-high kind of moment. Names start to feel like us as we grow into them. In fact, if you *are* totally obsessed and excited right away, that might be a sign that you're picking a name associated with a passing fad of yours. Give it some time to try it out, ask people you trust if it seems like the right fit, and use it in anonymous spaces online. I recommend trying new names out at coffee shops or restaurants where they ask for a name with your order.

As you're making a final decision, pay attention to possible jokes or nicknames people might create and what your initials will spell. A half-kidding tip I've heard for expecting parents is to try out their baby's name with a group of middle schoolers. You'll find out all the worst, most inappropriate jokes that can be made from the name in a few seconds flat.

When you've finally decided on a name, just own it—and remember that you can still change it again later. There can be a lot of pressure with choosing your own name. You feel like everyone is going to judge your choice every time you introduce yourself, if they know that you're trans. You might feel like it's a burden to ask people to remember a new name. Usually, we trans people are making a bigger deal out of those concerns than they actually are. If you *do* encounter anyone who feels that way, remember that they're the exception, not the rule. And if you're feeling especially sassy that day, you might even say to them, "Yeah, what about your name? Did your *mom* pick it out for you?"

For resources on legally changing your name, see the Transgender Legal Defense and Education Fund's Name Change Project at TLDEF.org.

But in the months leading up to the conversation in Tucson with my mom, I had started going back to the name Jack. There was just something about it I still liked, much more than any of the other names I had ever tried on. It didn't have to matter that I had once named a character Jack. No one would have to know that (until now; whoops). And hey, maybe I could think of it as an aspirational thing. Maybe one day I *would* be as cool and confident as the fictional Jack.

Still, I wanted to give my mom one last chance. She had said way back during our first conversation after I came out to her that there were a few names she'd been considering for me if I had been assigned male at birth. Harrison was the top choice, but there had been others. She just hadn't remembered them off the top of her head back in 2011. I mean, I suppose your kid coming out to you as transgender *is* a little distracting.

So while I still had her in person in Tucson, I asked her if she could remember any of the other names she had considered for me.

"Oh, yes!" she exclaimed. "I remembered one the other day. I almost texted you. It was Jackson."

Jackson.

Huh. Now, *that* I could work with. It could be shortened to Jack, if I wanted, but it wasn't *just* Jack, so it gave me some distance from the fictional character. Plus, *Jackson* had a bit a Southern ring to it that I liked. A little bit of Texas to always carry with me even when I didn't live there anymore.

It was settled. I had a name (well, a first name at least). My mom was on board. All systems go.

It's weird to think that now I'm going to grow old as Jackson. Whenever I think of that, I keep imagining my headstone saying Jackson Bird and trying to figure out if that feels right. It still feels foreign. It's weird that I think of my gravestone more than anything else, isn't it? I guess I feel like that's the most permanent and final defining part of my identity. Like, that's who I'll be forever more until stones disintegrate on the earth so I'd better like that name and feel like that was being my genuine self. And is it? Will it be? I have no fucking clue.

April 2, 2015.

a coming-out spreadsheet

> For me, the process of coming out as trans was less like opening a closet door and more like slowly lighting a series of candles in a dark cave.
>
> —Jamison Green, *Becoming a Visible Man*

Maybe some people decide they're going to come out and do it right then and there. Just post a Facebook status and be done with it. But I have always been a planner and an overthinker. So my coming-out plan was to take place over the course of four months, with a precise timeline of whon I would tell people close to me, when I would start hormones, and when I would post a video to tell everyone else.

I had a spreadsheet listing each person who deserved to hear the news straight from me before the YouTube video was public, denoting how, when, and where I would be telling them. I also put together a ten-page resource document with explanations of transgender terminology and concepts, recommended further reading, some suggested songs and videos, and a personal letter from me. I would send this to people after I came out to them so I wouldn't have to answer all the same basic questions over and over again.

That was a thing that had always bothered me about coming out as transgender. It's not like coming out as gay or lesbian. People pretty much get what it means when you come out as gay, even if they might not approve or might still be working with a few outdated stereotypes. But coming out as transgender? There are still a lot of gaps in people's understanding of what exactly that means. And even if someone *is* familiar with transgender people, there are still a lot of questions. *What pronouns are you using now? What name should I call you? Are you going to physically transition? Can I have that dress now if you're never going to wear it again?*

The other thing that bothered me about coming out as transgender was feeling like I would be upending some people's lives, leaving a storm of shame and confusion in my midst. My family, mostly. I worried about my parents having to decide what to tell their friends who've always known them as having a daughter. There would be countless times they'd have to come out on my behalf.

I thought about ex-boyfriends having an identity crisis over thinking that the "woman" they were attracted to is "now" a man. I thought about the people who told me they hoped their daughters would grow up to be strong, independent women like me and how I felt like I had failed them and feminism altogether by not being a woman at all.

Most of these concerns were melodramatic, caused by my internalized shame about being transgender, but some do have a hint of truth to them. Coming out as trans can make people you know reexamine their own lives. They might think about how they too relate to gender and their identity. Many people I came out to responded by coming out to me in turn—as bisexual, as questioning their gender, or with some other revelation entirely. Seriously, I am *filled* with other people's secrets now. I'm surprised my hair isn't as big as Regina George's.

One of the first people I told after confirming my plans to transition with my mom was my roommate. Even though we were very good friends, we never really talked about personal stuff. Dating, emotions,

Big Dark Secrets. None of that ever came up in our conversations about craft beer and superhero movies.

But more than the awkwardness about having to talk about something so intimate to someone I'd never even discussed farting with was the very real concern that she wouldn't want to live with me anymore. Being roommates with her, and living in that apartment, was an integral component of the stability in my life that was enabling me to come out at all. If I lost that . . . I didn't know what I was going to do.

The thing is, at least in my head, she would've been well within her rights to kick me out. Even though nothing was going to change about my cleanliness or personal habits, she hadn't signed up to live with a man.

It's a delicate line to tread and varies depending on each person's situation, but I generally believe that most trans men can't have their cake and eat it too when it comes to women's spaces. If you're a part of a gym, a social club, or an office group that's implicitly or explicitly for women only, once you're out as a man, you shouldn't be a part of that group anymore. It's more complicated and situational for nonbinary people, but for binary trans men, as comfortable as *we* might feel in women's spaces as compared to all-men's ones, especially early on in our transitions, the women in those spaces may not be comfortable around us as men and it's their rights that matter in those cases. Of course, my apartment was not a declared women's-only space, but if my roommate said she wasn't comfortable living with a man, I was prepared to leave. Well, theoretically, anyway.

To help offset her potential discomfort with me being a man, I claimed something when I came out to her that I did with pretty much everyone I came out to at first: I said I was gay, that I was only attracted to men.

It wasn't completely a lie at the time. I was still trying to sort out my sexuality, which had been put on the back burner while I dealt with my gender. Even though it was clear to me that I wasn't *completely* gay, saying that I was comforted me for a few reasons during the coming-out process.

First, not understanding that trans people could be gay had been such a *huge* hang-up for me when I was first learning about trans people that I thought it might be difficult to grasp for other people too. I wanted to use it as a teaching opportunity.

I also didn't want people to think *so* much about me was changing. I didn't want it to be like, yes, I'm a man and, surprise, I'm also attracted to a different gender than you thought this whole time!

A key point I tried to hammer home when I came out to people was that I wasn't really changing. I'd be going by a new name and pronouns and there would be some slight changes to my appearance from testosterone, but personality-wise I'd be the same person I always had been—with a slight upgrade to my happiness index.

Beyond those considerations, I was also clinging to the gay identity because it helped me accept the feminine parts of my personality. I had spent a long time thinking I couldn't *really* be a man because I genuinely love *The Princess Diaries* and sometimes think floral patterns are nice. Telling myself I was gay made me feel like I had permission to express the feminine parts of my personality I couldn't otherwise reconcile with my male identity.

Of course, the truth is that your interests and personality traits have nothing to do with your gender or your sexuality. Would a cisgender man be told he's not a man just because he enjoys knitting? I mean, maybe he would by some rude people, but they wouldn't mean it *literally* the way a trans man might be told he's *literally* not a man for the same reason. Things like that don't define who we are. I knew that rationally, but I had trouble accepting it about myself.

Nowadays, I'm way more comfortable being a guy who happens to enjoy a tidy home, a solid skin-care regimen, and rewatching every episode of *Downton Abbey* on loop. Whether I choose to share those activities with a partner who's a man, a woman, or nonbinary is completely unrelated to my interests and personality.

But back when I was first coming out to people, I was a barrel of self-conscious explanations and apologies. "I'm not changing that much." "I still *only* like men, just like you've always known about me." "No, I'm not the manliest man ever, but that's okay because I'm gay!"

My roommate ended up taking it amazingly well and did *not* kick me out of the apartment. So that was a relief.

She was very matter-of-fact about the whole thing. She asked me a couple of logistical questions and then started calling me Jackson and using masculine pronouns right away. To this day, she has never messed up once.

She also started helping me plan how I would tell our friends. I wanted to knock out our whole friend group in one swing to save time and emotional energy, but needed a way to make sure they would all show up to something without anyone bailing. I also wanted it to be at a private residence so we could discuss my personal news without strangers overhearing, and I figured it should probably be at our place so there wouldn't be any awkwardness if the host was disgusted with me and wanted me to leave immediately.

We settled on hosting a pasta dinner at our place and, when people started showing signs of flaking, we ended up divulging that it wasn't *just* an evening to eat ungodly amounts of fettuccine. I also had some big news to share. That started the rumor train running. Guesses ranged from me being a lesbian to having a terminal illness.

When all the pasta had been devoured and I still hadn't told them anything, my roommate quieted everyone down and gave me a pointed look. I started trying to get the words out, but was overwhelmed by having all their eyes on me and told them as much.

"How about we all cover our eyes?" one of them suggested, enthusiastically.

So they all obediently put their hands over their eyes and kept them there for a whole minute as I went through the speech I was starting to get used to reciting. When I finished, there was silence at first. Then one of them asked if they could look now. I said yes, and there was tension-breaking laughter as everyone uncovered their eyes.

I got some of the usual questions. *When should we start calling you Jackson? Will the testosterone make you taller?* But no one was disgusted or angry.

Even though actually saying the words "I'm transgender" never got easier, it turned out that most people in my life were pretty chill about the whole thing. As I kept checking coffee dates and video calls off of the spreadsheet, not a single person rejected me. There was one friend who thought I was playing a prank on her, but in her defense I had unknowingly texted her while she was on a mountain of painkillers following a Super-Soaker-on-an-icy-roof-related incident.

Overall, I was starting to realize that I had maybe been overthinking their reactions and my plans. Maybe they didn't need as much hand-holding and adjustment time as I had anticipated.

How to React When Someone Comes Out to You

Listen to them. They've likely been practicing what they were going to say to you countless times. Give them space to say everything they have to say before you react or ask questions.

Let them know you support them. If they're a loved one, it's a good time to remind them that you love them unconditionally.

If they're a coworker, let them know you'll have their back at work.

Remember that it's not about you. This one is harder for families and loved ones, but even more important. Nothing you did or didn't do caused this person to be trans; they simply are. It might take a while for you to adjust. You might feel like they're moving too quickly in coming out to people or transitioning. Remember that they've likely been grappling with their gender for a very long time, and while it's new to you, it's not to them. If you're really struggling, talk to other people in your life (whom the trans person in your life has already told or explicitly approved of your telling) or seek out a support group or professional to talk to. PFLAG, a national organization for LGBTQ+ allies, has chapters across the nation for parents, families, and loved ones to learn and process together. There might be some conversations that are appropriate to have with the trans person in your life, but remember that they are not responsible for your emotions—especially not on top of all their own emotional and logistical challenges.

Respect their name and pronouns. They may or may not have a new name and pronouns for you to use. Ask when, where, and around whom they want you to use which name and pronouns. Especially if you're one of the first people they're coming out to, they might not want you to use their new name in most or any spaces just yet.

Don't tell other people without their permission. Every person reserves the right to come out on their own terms. This applies both when people are coming out early on with intent to transition and later on when they might be living as their affirmed gender without everyone in their life being aware of their trans status.

Ask a few questions, but mostly do your own research after. Questions about their new name and pronouns as well as plans for telling other mutual people in your life and how you can be supportive are great. Details about how transition works should be reserved for independent research later. This person has to come out to every person in their life and will have to answer a lot of the same questions over and over again. Save them at least one repeated conversation by taking the initiative and learning on your own.

Teach and defend when they're not around. Once you've done your research and processed the news, it's time to step up as an ally. Correct people who use the wrong name and pronouns (if the person is out to them). Speak up if people are disparaging them. Debunk trans myths you hear. Think about ways to make spaces you walk through safer for all trans people, not just the one you know. Navigating the world as a trans person can be awkward and exhausting. Whenever allies have done a little work on our behalf, it's a huge relief.

Celebrate with them! While difficult, for many trans people this can also be an exciting time. Sharing in that excitement shows that you support them. Maybe even give them a little gift that affirms their gender—like makeup, a tie, a T-shirt with a gender binary–smashing phrase on it, or one of those miniature license plates featuring their name. When I came out, a friend gave me a set of cuff links with my new initials engraved on them, and I loved it to bits. Depending on your relationship and the person's sense of humor, you can play into gender stereotypes a little bit. Greeting cards saying "It's a girl!" or "It's a boy!" can be funny and supportive. Nowadays greeting card companies are even making cards expressly for the purpose of congratulating people on coming out or starting their transitions. Heck, you could even throw them a gender-reveal party. Those become especially fun if the person is nonbinary. Pop balloons to reveal the gender. Whoops, they're filled with water. They're genderfluid! Time for a water balloon fight!

• • •

High on this revelation and starting to get exhausted by the sheer number of heart-to-heart conversations I was having every week, I decided to change my plans for coming out to my brother from a phone call to a simple email.

My older brother was a musician and had always hung around artsy queer and gender-bending folks. He was the one who had introduced *me* to *The Rocky Horror Picture Show* and the transgender comedian Eddie Izzard. I figured he must've had plenty of acquaintances who had transitioned by this point. So I drafted my email to him assuming that level of knowledge.

Big mistake.

He saw the email on his phone on the day he was making a big move from Fort Worth to Dallas (in hindsight, I should've known this and planned better), so he had only skimmed the message and came away from it thinking I was coming out as intersex and that our parents had kept this information a secret from him our whole lives.

I clarified the situation, but he was still concerned and, before I could convince him otherwise, he had booked a plane ticket to come see me in New York. I freaked out that he was freaking out so hard, but his visit ended up being exactly what we both needed. We talked more that weekend than we probably ever had.

He told me that he was having the most trouble with the fact that I would be changing my name. I told him I was surprised he didn't remember many of my gender transgressions from childhood. As we talked it out and started to get on the same page, I realized one smaller reason that my coming out was tough for him.

Being such a big fan of glam rock and androgynous icons like Marc Bolan and David Bowie, he didn't understand why I couldn't just do something like that. Be a man part-time, as a costume. Why did I have to change my name? Change my body?

I explained the difference between someone being open to or curious about living as the other gender part-time and what I felt. For me, part-time wasn't enough. I was a guy full-time in my head already. I just needed the rest of the world to see that.

Sometimes people who are familiar and comfortable with gender nonconformity can have the most trouble understanding trans people, binary or not, who want to transition. I've known a few butch lesbians, drag queens, and androgynous-presenting cis people, for example, who are comfortable in their assigned genders and struggle at first to understand why others might need to transition—why they can't be comfortable just wearing different clothes or being that gender part-time. No one is wrong here. It's just that there are so many ways to be so many different genders, and it can be difficult to understand something you haven't experienced.

After we talked it out, I think my brother understood. Even if he didn't quite yet, our relationship was stronger than it had ever been, and I was grateful for that.

Shortly after our Big Long Talk.

Having gotten a reality check after coming out to my brother, I was more apprehensive as I set out to check the final name off of my list: my dad.

Jamison Green, a writer and pioneering trans activist, noted shrewdly in his memoir *Becoming a Visible Man*:

> Some transpeople will unnecessarily cut themselves off from their families because they are fearful of confronting them . . . Family members may be the most difficult to approach because losing them would be the greatest loss so we impose that loss on ourselves rather than have it visited upon us.

That was *exactly* how I felt about coming out to my dad. I feared his rejection so much that I had begun to distance myself from him, whether there was a basis for my fear or not.

When I finally called him one evening that spring and talked through everything I had been feeling for years, he said, "Well, you've got to give me some credit. I had a hunch *something* was going on."

He had a few concerns about my physically transitioning and the consequences it might have on my career—which I partially assuaged by explaining that once I passed as a man, I would have far better career opportunities than I ever had as a woman. (Thanks, patriarchy. Even if I benefit from it now, I still hate it.)

Other than that, he couldn't have been more accepting and supportive. I do remember that at one point, he mentioned understanding why transitioning is so important to trans people because there had been an uptick in stories in the media recently. In fact, Caitlyn Jenner's exclusive interview with Diane Sawyer was airing *as we were having our conversation*. I hung up to a barrage of text messages from people I had already come out to asking my thoughts on the interview. I ignored them all until the next morning, because I'd had enough coming out for the day.

The fact that a former Olympian and current reality show star was discussing her transition on prime-time television right as I was coming out to my dad wasn't lost on me, though. Just three years ago when I'd been daydreaming about coming out to my family, I couldn't have imagined trans people would ever have been as visible in my lifetime as they already were by 2015. From Caitlyn Jenner to Laverne Cox on the cover of *TIME* magazine to the *two* trans characters on *Glee*, trans people were suddenly everywhere, and that visibility made my coming out significantly easier than it would've been in years prior. When I came out to people, they had a cultural reference point to help them understand.

Yes, I had worked myself up a bit too much imagining my friends and family would hate me for being transgender. But more than overthinking my own relationships, I had failed to notice how normalized trans people had suddenly become in America. We still have a long way to go, and with visibility always comes negative attention too, but I owe a lot to every trans person who publicly shared their story before me.

CHAPTER TWENTY

gettin' jacked

It's nice to finally feel like maybe my body is adapting to me instead of me trying to adapt to my body.

—Skylar Kergil

When some people transition, they choose to take people along for the ride from the very start. They might share with friends that they're questioning their gender long before they've figured out what their gender is and if they're going to take any steps toward transition—like I did with my mom, and as I especially recommend young people do with their parents. If you think your parents will be decently accepting (in other words, *not* try to kick you out or send you to a conversion therapist) but might struggle with the news, it can help to bring them into your journey earlier on so they can be there with you and have more time to process the information. There is one thing it's always important to keep in mind when you're coming out to people: Even though you've been mulling over your gender for years, it's brand-new information to most people you're coming out to. They need time to process and get used to the news. That doesn't necessarily mean they're not accepting or don't love you. It can just take time.

Even though I took that route with my mom, I didn't want to tell anyone else until I was absolutely certain that I really did want to transition. I was so embarrassed by the (albeit unlikely) possibility that I would tell everyone in my life about my Big Dark Secret and then decide that actually I just wanted to live as a woman. I couldn't bear the thought of living as a woman when people knew that I had, at least at one point, seriously harbored a desire to live as a man. It's not an overly rational thought and I would *never* judge others for their gender, sexuality, or any doubts or phases they went through in figuring it out, but we're always our own harshest critics. One day I might learn to treat myself with the generosity and compassion I afford other humans, but that day is still a ways off.

Instead, I decided to start hormone replacement therapy a full month before I was planning to post my coming-out video. I had read that some trans people don't feel absolutely certain that transition is right for them until they have that first dose of hormones coursing through their body. As someone who has often been unaware of his true emotions until they start manifesting with physical symptoms, I thought this might be true for me.

The thing about being trans is that you don't get a letter on your eleventh birthday from Dumbledore welcoming you to the Hogwarts School of Queerness and Transsexuality. Hagrid doesn't knock down your front door at midnight to confirm all the strange things that have always happened in your life and tell you, "Yer transgender, Harry."

People *say* they were absolutely sure about their gender and need to transition because that helps underscore the point that being trans isn't a choice, which it *isn't*, but that doesn't mean it's not a difficult thing to parse out and accept about yourself.

Maybe there are a few people out there who truly were absolutely certain that they were Grade A Certifiably 100 Percent Transgender and needed to physically transition right away, but I think most of us have a fair amount of doubt. We feel like we're not man enough. Not woman enough. Even not trans enough. It takes an incredible amount of soul-searching and self-reflection to figure out the best way forward, and then to face having to defend that path over and over again to every person in your life. The process can be so daunting, so all-consuming, and the reactions from people so severe that it's no wonder over 40 percent of transgender people attempt suicide.* It has nothing to do with transition being a mistake, but rather—in part—because of the prejudice and stigma still attached to being transgender and the emotional toll it takes to be yourself in a world that pushes you down at every turn.

Life is so strange. I've been really struggling with that feeling of "this happens to other people. I'm not trans. I'm not going through with changing my name and identity and body and everything about me. That's not what my life plan was." Then I keep remembering that woman in True Trans who says "surely these other girls got a note telling them they're trans." So it's like yeah all trans people feel this way. No one got a note telling us we are or that this is the right path for us. You just have to trust it's the best decision. Every list or chart I could possibly make would objectively tell me it's the right decision, but that still makes me unsure. Charts and lists are just short representations of what we want to think is true, they can't account for the complexities and blurs and nuances of brain soup and lived experiences.

April 2, 2015.

So before I let other people's opinions steer my life too much, I wanted to be as certain as I could be, and on April 14, 2015, my primary care physician gave me my first dose of testosterone.

Because the health clinic I went to specialized in transgender health care and I had identified myself as trans when I filled out my intake form, they had been asking me for over a year if I wanted to start hormones. The clinic in question practices informed consent when it comes to hormone replacement therapy, which means you don't need an official diagnosis of gender dysphoria from a licensed psychiatrist in order to get prescribed hormones. All you have to do is be read a list of potential risks and side effects, sign your name, hand over some cash, and voilà: vitamin T.

*Injustice at Every Turn: A Report of the National Transgender Discrimination Survey, National Center for Transgender Equality, 2015.

Inf•rmed C•nsent

Informed consent is simply the process of granting a doctor permission to provide you with treatment or to perform a medical procedure. However, it was seen as revolutionary when first used for trans patients at the Tom Waddell Urban Health Clinic in San Francisco, due to the history of gatekeeping in trans health care (see chapter four). After being used successfully at a number of LGBTQ+ health centers across the nation, the WPATH revised their Standards of Care to include informed consent. Instead of mandating strict requirements for mental health professionals to observe trans clients before approving them for medical transition, WPATH's Standards of Care now instruct mental health professionals to simply guide trans clients through the process, presenting them with accurate information as relevant to their individual experience. Not all medical institutions practice informed consent for trans health care, but with the revised WPATH Standards of Care and the work of unrelenting activists, more and more places are adopting it.

I actually *had* received a gender dysphoria diagnosis from the clinic's psychiatrist long before I committed to starting hormone replacement therapy, but knowing I had control over my own decisions about my own body and didn't actually need that approval was empowering. After all, you don't have to get a letter from a psychiatrist to receive treatment from your doctor for the flu or even for cosmetic surgery. So when I told them I was finally ready, they did some blood work to make sure I was healthy enough and to determine my dosage, and then we set a date for the first shot.

A lot of trans guys these days like to film their first shot and post it on social media to celebrate the milestone. I had always assumed I would do this too, even if I couldn't post it until I came out a month later. But in the days leading up to my appointment, I was told I couldn't film anything inside the doctor's office. Despite my initial disappointment, I managed to find a silver lining.

I knew that if this was the right path for me, I would end up sharing *a lot* of my transition online. Without the pressure to film and upload a video of it, without a friend joining me to help film, this could just be *my* moment.

For so many years, my gender dysphoria had been an independent internal struggle. While it had been thanks in part to the help of others that I finally turned a leaf, it had mostly been me. It had been my own strength and resilience that pulled me back up each time and I had made it. I'd survived, and I was moving forward with what I had wanted so badly for so long. I had been so stressed about the logistics of sharing the experience with other people and balancing everything else in my life that I hadn't really stopped to savor what was going on. I was going to be sharing so much that it seemed appropriate that this very sacred moment would be just for me, not for anyone else.

When I left the doctor's office with an extra 0.25 mL of testosterone cypionate simmering inside me and walked to meet friends for celebratory drinks at a nearby bar, I tried to sense if anything felt different yet.

RIGHT BEFORE GETTING MY FIRST T SHOT.

More about Testosterone

Testosterone can be taken via injection, patch, cream, or gel. Most people do injections, either subcutaneously (under the skin) or intramuscularly (into the muscle) and either every couple of weeks (more common in the United States) or every couple of months (more common in Europe).

Dosages vary from person to person. It's important to be prescribed testosterone by a doctor and have your levels checked on a regular basis. If your testosterone levels get too high (either naturally or by taking more than your prescribed dose), the excess testosterone will be converted to estrogen—the exact opposite of what you're trying to achieve.

Hormone treatment is not temporary. It must be kept up for the rest of your life to remain effective. That said, if you wish to stop at any point, you can (so long as you have not yet had a hysterectomy and discuss the change with your doctor first). Some side effects will reverse, while others are permanent.

Permanent changes from testosterone include a deeper voice and male pattern baldness. You'll also experience an increase in body hair, facial hair growth, and clitoral growth—all of which may decrease if you stop taking hormones but will not go away completely.

Reversible changes from testosterone include body fat redistribution, oilier skin and increased acne, increased muscle mass, and the cessation of menstruation.

You cannot pick and choose what changes will occur. The exact timeline and intensity of changes varies from person to person depending on their age, genetics, other health conditions they may have, or any medication they may be taking. While some people—some nonbinary people in particular—might elect to temporarily go on testosterone to get a deeper voice and then stop before more drastic changes occur, it's not an exact science, and people should do their research and talk to their doctor extensively before embarking on an atypical regimen. Generally speaking, you get the good with the bad. You might grow some facial hair and extra muscles right away, but they'll probably be joined by a face full of acne and a hairy butt. Did I mention hormone replacement therapy is basically puberty 2.0? It's a blast.

It's important to have realistic expectations going into hormone replacement therapy and be patient as you wait for changes. Many people are hopeful that starting hormones and medical transition will fix all their problems. It's true that, if it's the right step for you, you will likely be happier, maybe more at ease, and eventually may feel more at home in your body. However, it's important not to view medical transition as a cure-all. It won't fix relationships in your life. For the most part, it won't solve your anxiety or depression. It might even awaken other types of dysphoria you weren't aware of before: Perhaps when you're correctly read as your gender more often thanks to your new beard, you'll become more aware of the size of your hips. Hormone replacement therapy is a wonderful, life-changing thing for many people, but it's not the be-all and end-all.

It takes a few weeks on testosterone for any visible changes to occur and up to several years for some more noticeable effects, like thick, substantial facial hair and body fat redistribution. It's not an instantaneous transformation like the serum that turned Captain America into a super soldier. But you might notice a few new sensations in the hours and days following your first shot. It's not uncommon for your throat to feel sore almost immediately as your vocal cords begin to thicken, or to feel hungrier and have more energy in the first few days. I, like many other people, felt more clear-headed. Everything—my mind, my body, my perception of the world—just felt more balanced.

How much of this is really happening and how much of it is a placebo effect is difficult to tell. Apart from the obvious changes like your deeper voice and increased muscle mass, there's *a lot* about changes from testosterone that remains up for debate.

One example is the stereotype that taking testosterone makes transmasculine people more prone to anger. Thomas Page McBee investigated this in his treatise on masculinity, *Amateur: A True Story about What Makes a Man*. McBee talked to neuroscientist Robert Sapolsky about the misconception that testosterone increases aggression. Sapolsky says that research has shown "remarkably little evidence" indicating an ability to detect which men have higher testosterone levels based on which of them are more aggressive. Testosterone *can* cause the desire to defend one's status, he said, but at least in humans that doesn't always manifest as aggression. Instead, Sapolsky said, "If our world is riddled with male violence, the core problem isn't that testosterone can often increase levels of aggression. The problem is the frequency with which we reward aggression."

I didn't notice myself being more aggressive in the months following that first and subsequent injections. If anything, I was less hotheaded than I had been when I was in the closet and often at my wit's end with dysphoria. I did notice, however, that I was being more assertive. I was speaking up more for what I wanted, something I had always struggled with in the past. But I have trouble believing that was caused by new amounts of a specific androgen in my body and not due to some of the social and emotional changes in my life that happened at the same time.

I had gained quite a bit of confidence after working through so many of my thorniest issues and was better able to recognize the importance of advocating for my needs than I had been before therapy.

There's also the sad fact that people respect your opinion more when you're treated as a man by society. Even if I didn't get read as male all the time, just *knowing* I was a man made people listen to me more than they had in the exact same situations when I had been pre-senting as a woman. Whereas we had long ago had to take my phone number off my HPA business cards because men kept thinking I was flirtatiously giving them my number when I handed them my card at networking events, post-coming-out those same types of encounters generated a barrage of job offers.

So maybe testosterone can make people more assertive or a little bit quicker to anger, but I tend to think it has more to do with the other upheavals usually happening in your life at the time and the ways that people interact with you differently as a man.

But before those changes had occurred, when I was still riding the high of my first testosterone shot, I had to make the decision of whether I was still going to move forward with fully coming out. Starting testos-terone had been the final test to verify this was the right path, and my hunch had been correct—like other trans people had said before me, as soon as I got the shot, I knew. This was what was always meant to be.

•   •   •

The problem was that I still had several weeks before I could post the video that would tell everyone else in my life who I was. I couldn't just film and upload the video whenever I wanted to because I had told people in my professional life when it would be going up, when the day would come to switch over my name on public-facing documents at the HPA and start using my Jackson email address with partners.

I had already come out to my coworkers and our entire volunteer staff over the course of the preceding months, and they were all per-fectly accepting and happy for me. I wasn't surprised in the least, be-cause the HPA had been working on issues of LGBTQ+ equality since they opened their doors in 2005. During the 2012 general election, their members even broke phone-banking records in two states where mar-riage equality went on to pass in November.

I always said that if there had been a way to just tell my Harry Potter fandom family and my YouTube followers, I would have done so. I never had any doubt that they would be supportive. The problem was that, apart from people I knew personally like my coworkers at the HPA, telling the online fan community and my followers meant posting something publicly online. Even if I had only a small regular following, when something is on the internet, it's forever. Anyone can find it. Cousins, elementary school teachers, former coworkers. In order to tell my YouTube followers, I had to be prepared for everyone I had ever met to potentially find out.

So I planned it out carefully and worked closely with the HPA on my public coming-out schedule, my gender rollout, if you will. As the organization's spokesperson with partners to meet with, a campaign schedule to uphold, and public appearances on the calendar, there were a lot of logistics, and the image of the entire company, to keep in mind.

And in those intervening weeks, when I had started testosterone but could not yet be publicly out, life had started getting even more complicated. With the certainty I now felt in my decision to transition, the extra testosterone fueling my body, and so many people close to me treating me like a guy, it was extremely difficult to show up at events as a woman.

I had a few final speaking engagements and events promoting the HPA's annual literacy campaign that I had to attend during that time period. At one event, a punk rock show where my friends were performing, I was running a book donation drop-off for the HPA's campaign. I was particularly perturbed by all the people there who recognized me and greeted me by my old name and feminine pronouns. I understood that they didn't know any different, but it was a shock to my system after having abandoned that name and those pronouns in my day-to-day life several weeks before.

After the show, when the bands, the crew, and I were packing up the merchandise (or in my case, book donations), there were a few followers of mine who had been lingering a bit too long and a bit too closely. I didn't want to be rude by asking them to leave, but I was starting to get a little uncomfortable. Fortunately, without my knowledge, a friend of mine had spotted this and went to get a security guard to clear the area of anyone without a backstage pass. The folks talking to me tried to resist at first, but eventually acquiesced, and I bid them what I hoped was a cheerful good night.

Once all the audience members had left, I overheard the guard say to my friend, "I thought you had called me down for one of the guys," as he looked at me with skepticism.

I was embarrassed that he didn't read me as a guy, and by the whole situation, but it made me slightly happy to think that I had what this security guard thought was a "guy problem." Even if there was no basis in gendering what had happened, I had been so dejected by being misgendered all night that it weirdly made me feel better to have stumbled into an awkward situation that was erroneously defined by a stranger as something that would happen to a guy.

During this same time period, I attended the Quidditch World Cup in South Carolina again, and that weekend a preteen boy named Jack came up to me with his dad and asked me to sign his baseball hat. The year before, I had started a comedy series on my YouTube channel called *Will It Waffle?* in which I threw random foods on a waffle iron and hoped my kitchen didn't explode. Its stupid, messy humor had attracted a new legion of young viewers, especially boys.

As Jack handed me his hat to sign, I told him that I liked his name, and I silently wondered what he would think in a few weeks when I posted my coming-out video, revealing my name. What would all my young fans who were there for the silly waffle videos think about me discussing this side of my life? Would his dad be so enthusiastic about me and my videos after I came out as transgender?

Fortunately, soon after that trip, I got one reprieve from the stress of living a double life when my roommate and I took a weekend trip to Providence to visit my coworker Matt and his spouse Lauren, the couple who had hosted me when I went to get my haircut a little over a year before.

While the point of the trip was going to go to a special Neutral Milk Hotel show, Lauren and I also set aside time to film a couple of videos together for our YouTube channels. These were planned to be released as the first videos after my coming out, an intentional move to show I had the support of my fellow creators.

The whole weekend, with flowers blooming in the first sunny days of the spring and the respite of just being Jack to all three of them, was exactly what I needed. As we walked through downtown Providence, the sun's warmth soaking into my face, I could sense that this would be the last calm before a very big storm.

My roommate and me in Providence.

CHAPTER TWENTY-ONE

letting everyone in

HERE'S THE TRUTH ABOUT COMING OUT: WE ARE NOT
COMING OUT—WE ARE LETTING YOU IN.

—Jose Antonio Vargas

Everyone on the spreadsheet had been told. I'd had my first couple of T shots and was feeling great. It was time to go public.

I want to take a moment here to emphasize something: I am *not*, and certainly was not then, famous. The majority of you holding this book probably never heard of me before you picked it up. If you have, it's because I am, if anything, a nano-celebrity. Journalist Laurie Penny describes a "nano-celebrity" as the level of niche stardom in which "you get recognized on the bus, but you still have to take the bus."

In my case, at the time in my life when I was preparing to come out, I got recognized out in public maybe five times a year, tops. I was recognized more when I was at specifically nerdy events where many of my followers congregated, like fan conferences and wizard rock shows, but even then it wasn't much.

Getting recognized is always a wonderful feeling and never a burden. I love meeting people and hearing their stories. If they like my videos, we probably share some common interests, so there's always something to talk about. But the knowledge that you may be recognized out in public does make you aware that someone *could* recognize you at any time——when you're picking at your teeth while walking down the street, when you've had one too many beers at a show, when you're on a date, maybe even when you're attending a support group.

That was a big fear of mine before coming out—that someone in one of the support groups I frequented would recognize me and find out prematurely that I was transgender. It nearly happened once too. One woman in a group I was attending mentioned watching the videos of a friend of mine, whose videos I had appeared in before, but fortunately she had no idea who I was.

I liked to think that no one in my small community of viewers at the time would have been ill-spirited enough to spread my secret out of malice, but people can get excited about secrets and it only takes a few loose lips to ignite the fire.

I've always been more guarded about my privacy than my level of influence has required. When I was getting started, many of my friends were people who had been famous in niche communities for years and had the horror stories to go with it——fans showing up at their houses uninvited, storms of outrage after fans found out they broke up with another public figure, threatening items being sent to them in the mail. More than one of my friends has had to get the FBI involved over violent brushes with stalkers. Especially as I prepared to come out as one of the most reviled identities in our country, I was well aware of the potential for dangerous backlash.

My friends taught me how to be proactive with my privacy from the start. I never showed the outside of my house or surrounding block in photos or videos. I kept my address and other personal details on lockdown. I made decisions about firm boundaries early on—I wouldn't talk about personal relationships publicly. I'd keep my family out of the spotlight for the most part. And I would avoid talking about anything "below the belt."

All these checks weren't just about my personal safety, however; they were also about being a role model. As someone whose audience originated from my role as the spokesperson for a nonprofit organization with a substantial youth membership, anything I put online, whether I liked it or not, reflected back on the organization.

The thing is, it takes very little attention on the internet to gain both fans and detractors. Somebody once told me that there's no fifteen minutes of fame anymore. Now, everyone is famous to fifteen people. I've always been of the opinion that, for anyone in any position of influence, you should conduct yourself with the humility of not being famous at all, but with the integrity and responsibility of a megastar.

• • •

So that's why I had an intricate plan for coming out, why the date was on the books months in advance and cleared with several people in my life. I wanted to do it right—in a way that would honor the reputation and the privacy not just of me, but of everyone connected to me.

It was a formidable undertaking, though. In 2015, there was only one other YouTube creator I was aware of who'd had a substantial following prior to coming out as transgender—and she had over a million subscribers, so it wasn't like I could just call her up to ask for advice. Most trans YouTubers had started their channels openly as trans to document their transitions. I didn't have a road map for how to handle coming out and transitioning in the public eye as someone less than famous.

Not going public about being trans wasn't really an option. You can keep your sexual orientation under wraps when you're a public figure. It might suck to hide a part of yourself, but it *is* possible to hide it even while being proud and open in your private life.

When you're a transgender person who medically transitions, you can't just keep it a secret from your audience, especially on a video platform. Testosterone was going to deepen my voice, change my face shape, and make me grow facial hair. People were going to notice. Plus, you don't usually change your name or pronouns when you come out as gay, bisexual, or asexual. In addition to wanting to be referred to with the name and pronouns that affirmed my gender, I would have to change all my usernames.

For years, I had tried to stick to usernames that didn't incorporate my first name, knowing that this might be a challenge if I transitioned one day. But as the internet landscape evolved from punny pseudonyms to real names, I eventually followed suit and was now faced with the task of coming up with a *new* username based on my *new* name and handling the branding transition for all my social media profiles.

My only choice for *not* transitioning in the public eye was to quit making videos, abandon all my social media accounts, quit working as the HPA's spokesperson, and probably move to another town to start a new life.

That used to be the typical path for transgender people when they transitioned, whether by choice or as strongly suggested by their psychiatrists. It was kind of assumed that your friends and family would abandon you, that your employer would fire you. Even if those things didn't happen, many trans people would choose to leave to start anew where no one would know their past. It was just easier that way.

Some trans people do still choose that path to one extent or another, but it's not always necessary anymore. People are more accepting than they used to be. While it's still legal to fire someone for being transgender in thirty states, many individual workplaces have anti-discrimination policies that protect employees on the basis of gender identity and systems in place to support their trans employees when they transition.

States' Trans Rights

At the time of writing, transgender people can legally be:

- fired from their jobs in thirty states
- refused or removed from housing in thirty states
- discriminated against in public places such as restaurants, movie theaters, and government entities in thirty-one states
- unprotected from hate crimes in thirty-two states
- discriminated against in public schools in thirty-six states

For an up-to-date breakdown of trans rights by state, visit lgbtmap.org.

Knowing how supportive my work and online communities were, it seemed silly to abandon it all so I could live in stealth—as tempting as it may have been to do so. Ultimately, it was the lack of representation I had felt growing up that affirmed my decision to come out publicly. How the sum of my transgender male education had been that one *Oprah* episode and an Adam Sandler movie. How many years of loneliness and confusion that lack of representation had caused me. I had been given a platform, however small, on which to share my story and *be* that representation for people who might need it. I would have felt guilty *not* using my platform and privilege.

So it was with that motivation that I wrote the final script for my coming-out video—one I had written and rewritten for years as I imagined this day coming. I shot the video in my bedroom one afternoon, in the same place where I shot all my video blogs, adding in a few extra lines as I worked through my nerves on camera. I took a few days to edit the video and on Wednesday, May thirteenth, I hit upload, and waited.

The video was twelve minutes long, so the initial comments were guesses based off the title, "Coming Out"—most thought I was coming out as a lesbian; some were closer, guessing I was genderqueer.

When the early viewers finally got to the point in the video when I nervously said, "I'm transgender," and then ripped open a bag of gummy bears to decompress from the big moment, comments of support starting pouring in.

There was one denigrator, someone who had been leaving rude comments on my videos for a while, but other commenters quickly put that person in their place.

The Daily Dot

AJA ROMANO

Loved Harry Potter community leader comes out as trans in moving vlog post

'It didn't feel like me—it felt like a game. A game I was winning... but I wasn't playing the game as me.'

I breathed a tentative sigh of relief and closed my computer. I had intentionally scheduled a therapy appointment for right after posting the video so I could get my thoughts together and take at least an hour's break from being glued to my screen.

When I got out of my session, having updated my therapist on the news and discussed my fears and excitements with him, I turned my phone back on and was floored. My video was blowing up. Several of my internet heroes had shared the video and their congratulations— including Hank Green, his brother and young adult author John Green, author Maureen Johnson, and even YouTube royalty Tyler Oakley.

With the attention of all their audiences, the video was gaining traction. It broke ten thousand views in a matter of hours, something very few of my videos had done before that point.

People were sending me screenshots of them changing my name in their phones. I had requests for interviews with a few midsize media outlets in my in-box. Southwestern University even reached out and asked if they could update my alumni contact info to reflect my new name and gender.

I was absolutely floored by the response. There were hardly any negative comments. No one who mattered to me disapproved. I could hardly comprehend how I had gotten so lucky.

Now that everyone in my life knew, it was time to party.

In the whirlwind of coming out, I had failed to celebrate my twenty-fifth birthday. A friend offered to throw me a birthday/coming-out/starting-testosterone party on her rooftop in Brooklyn. We made it a T-themed party. There were flavored teas, T-rex decorations, shot glasses with the letter "T" written on them to become "T shots," and some custom gender-bending cocktails—a Trans Ginger and some Tom Colleens.

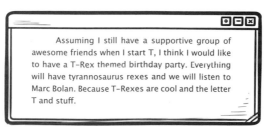

> Assuming I still have a supportive group of awesome friends when I start T, I think I would like to have a T-Rex themed birthday party. Everything will have tyrannosaurus rexes and we will listen to Marc Bolan. Because T-Rexes are cool and the letter T and stuff.

MARCH 29, 2011.

As I blew out the candles on my cake, surrounded by so many friends celebrating me as Jack, I couldn't believe how far I had come from channeling my agony into anonymous blog posts in my lonely dorm room—and it was just the beginning.

Blowing out the candles on my cake at my T Party.

CHAPTER TWENTY-TWO

life after the closet

Coming out was such an all-consuming, stressful experience that anytime someone tells me they're in the process of coming out as transgender, I start getting contact hives. I remember the constant racing of my heart, and I think how much I never, ever want to go back to those days.

While I was in the midst of it, I kept my eye on an ambiguous time several months in the future when I imagined things would be back to normal, or at least a new normal. I couldn't wait until the idea of me being a guy was no longer a spectacle to people in my life. I couldn't wait until testosterone had done its job enough that I was being read as male by most people I encountered. I couldn't wait for all the eyes to stop being on me.

Even though I kept my coming-out video and the resource document I'd compiled in my email signature for several months after coming out, some people still somehow missed the memo. I was once on a video call with my coworker Matt and a partner we had started talking to several months before I came out. At the start of the call, the partner said, "I saw your email changed to Jackson, but you're not Jackson."

He was so forward about his insistence that that wasn't who I was that I hesitated, unsure of how to respond. Luckily, some higher power intervened and my internet cut out at that exact moment. By the time

I had reset my router and logged back into the call, Matt had explained everything on my behalf and the partner apologized. Saved by unreliable Wi-Fi!

Especially after that encounter, I could never be certain who in my life had seen the coming-out video. One evening when I was walking around my neighborhood with some new friends who had only ever known me as Jack, I spotted a guy I had met at a party several months prior walking toward us from the opposite direction. I thought there was a pretty good chance he hadn't heard the news and I was worried he would greet me by my old name, effectively outing me to these new friends by whom I desperately wanted to be seen as just a normal guy.

As the distance between us closed, I kept my head down and prayed that he flat-out wouldn't recognize me. My ardent wishing was interrupted by a shout of, "Jackson!"

He held out his arms for a hug and I obliged, smiling a sigh of relief. Crisis averted.

There were still plenty more awkward moments to be had in those first couple of months after coming out, however. One thing I was trying very hard to avoid was going to the restroom at the same time as my cis guy friends. I had assumed this wouldn't be an issue because guys don't go to the restroom together like women do, right? Wrong!

I mean, we don't go as a buddy system to chat about things, to wait in line together, or any of the other legitimate reasons that women go to the restroom in pairs, but it does happen with surprising frequency. Like during intermission at a show or half-time at a game or before a ridiculously long superhero movie, when everyone's trying to empty their bladders before it starts.

I avoided it as much as I could, especially around guys who had known me before coming out, because it felt strange to be in this space with them that I hadn't previously been allowed into. I was scared that if I did anything to break etiquette in there, like talking too much while we washed our hands, they would no longer see me as a guy. Plus, I wasn't wild about having to walk into a stall while they headed to the urinals and knowing they were probably thinking about what I lacked in that department.

Lower Surgery

There are several types of lower surgery,* also called bottom surgery, available to transgender men, some of which might enable you to pee standing up and some of which won't. Some will enable you to have penetrative sex, some guarantee more erotic sensation, some include testicular implants, and on and on. There's a ton you can customize, but the main procedures fall into two camps: metoidioplasty and phalloplasty.

Metoidioplasty is the relatively cheaper and less invasive of the two options, which uses existing clitoral growth from testosterone treatment, instead of grafting tissue from other parts of the body, to form a phallus. Some people may also opt for a urethral lengthening through the phallus so they can stand to pee, or for testicular implants and a vaginectomy. Full sensation is retained and, in some cases, people can still get a phalloplasty down the line.

Phalloplasty is six to ten times more expensive and requires multiple procedures. It uses skin tissue from the forearm or thigh to form a phallus and usually also includes urethral lengthening and testicular implants. There is also the option of implanting a rod or pump in order to achieve an erection.

*Lower surgery can also sometimes include hysterectomy, which can be performed as part of these other procedures or on its own.

There have long been myths in the transmasculine community that lower surgery is too inaccessible, not advanced enough, or not worth it. While it is certainly an expensive procedure with many of the risks associated with a surgery of its caliber, it has come a long way in recent years. Thanks to expanded insurance coverage for gender-affirming procedures, many more surgeons in the United States have begun to be trained and innovate on metoidioplasty and phalloplasty.

There *are* tools that enable transmasculine people to pee standing up prior to having lower surgery, some of which are realistic enough for undetected use at public urinals. I've tried a few with varying success. They come in handy for camping, and one time when a fellow trans guy and I were drunkenly hanging out on the steps of some Wall Street building after last call, I used one to pee on a statue. But Occu-pee Wall Street aside, I generally prefer not to have to carry equipment on me all day.

So it's stall life for me, which can really stink sometimes. I mean, literally. The vast majority of cisgender men only ever use the stall to take a dump. I spend so much of my time outside occupied restroom stalls that I've considered penning an essay series entitled, "Waiting for the Cis Men to Stop Pooping: The Life and Times of a Trans Man."

Besides the wait times and my nerves about using the Wiz Palace alongside my friends, there is also the issue of safety. I'm well aware that my use of the stall and risk of not being read as male puts me in danger of getting harassed by a fellow restroom-goer, or even reported by one to nearby authorities.

So many US states keep yo-yoing on whether transgender people are allowed to use the restroom that matches their gender that I literally have to google my pee rights anytime I travel to another state or simply have a layover.

Of course, the reality is that I, a white generally straight-cis-passing guy, am at very low risk of being harassed by someone in the men's room. For transgender people that aren't consistently read as the gender of the restroom they're entering, it's much riskier—especially for trans women and nonbinary people. Most of the laws, after all, claim a transphobic "save our wives and children from predatory 'men in dresses'" argument. This is messed up for so many reasons. First, it perpetuates the myth that trans women are just cross-dressing men and not the real women that they are, and further, that they dress as women with the sole purpose of tricking cisgender people so they can assault them. It's absolute crap.

Even if some people want to claim that they're not worried about actual trans people, they're just worried about someone taking advantage of being able to pretend to be trans in order to assault someone in the restroom . . . since when would a law stop someone who's already intent on breaking it? We shouldn't have to remove protections from an already marginalized class based on the hypothetical idea that someone outside of that class might abuse the system.

The whole "save our wives and children" line of defense also usually fails to recognize that transgender men exist too. The same law that's trying to keep trans women out of women's rooms is forcing trans men, some of whom are burly dudes with impressive beards, *into* women's rooms.

Shockingly, for a law based in ignorance and hate, it's filled with more holes than a fine Swiss cheese. As many protestors of color have sagely pointed out, "It wasn't about the water fountains then and it's not about the bathrooms now."

The fact remains that trans people experience far higher incidences of harassment and assault than the general population. It's also worth noting that no states with protections on the books for trans people have reported seeing an increase in sexual assaults in bathrooms. There are, however, a number of US congressmen who have been arrested for sexual misconduct in bathrooms, so maybe we should be focusing on them instead?

But as it stands now, when you aren't read as one of the binary bathroom genders, every time nature calls in public you have to make a choice of which option feels safer on that day: getting yelled at or getting beat up.

I remember this feeling earlier on in my transition. Before I started testosterone, I was rarely read as male, so I continued using the women's restroom even after I had come out to some people as a man. However, after several instances in a row of women entering the restroom while I was washing my hands, stepping back out to check the sign, and then reentering furtively, narrowing their eyes at me, I decided it was time to switch to the men's room. I was petrified of being found out and beat up in there, but I'd rather face my own fears than make other people uncomfortable. And it turned out to be fine. Men don't look at one another in the restroom, and if one does, you can glare at him as if to ask why the heck is he looking at you. I generally try to avoid playing into homophobic toxic masculinity, but I'll do it to stay safe in such a tense, vulnerable space.

Another way trans men generally have it easier than trans women in early transition is with clothing choices. For whatever reason, society still shames men and people it assumes to be men for wearing skirts, dresses, makeup, certain types of jewelry, and basically anything too feminine. Women and people society assumes to be women, on the other hand, are allowed to wear pants, go without makeup, and generally pick from a vast array of gender-neutral wardrobe options.

Every trans person has a different style and different priorities for how important being read as their gender is, so how their wardrobe changes before and after coming out in certain spaces can vary greatly. In general, however, transfeminine people have a lot more obvious things to play with. They might don makeup in public for the first time, wear heels, or get their ears pierced—all of which can be just as nerve-wracking to show off for the first time as it is exciting.

Wardrobe changes are often more subtle for transmasculine people. In my case, I wore the exact same thing the day I came out as I did the day after. Probably literally, in fact. Since I work from home, I don't really care about repeating outfits a couple of days in a row. But the point is that I didn't have to change my day-to-day wardrobe when I came out as a man. I was already wearing masculine clothing and sporting a short, masculine haircut. The only difference was that there would be no more uncertainty about what to wear at formal events. I would be *expected* to wear a suit now. I can't begin to explain the relief I felt to have that certainty and to *want* to conform to the social custom being imposed on me.

CHANGING MY PRONOUNS AT PUBLIC
EVENTS WAS A HUGE MILESTONE.

One of the first places I got to conform after coming out in May was, of course, LeakyCon's Esther Earl Charity Ball. Like the year prior, I packed only one wardrobe option for the ball, but this time it was a suit. Or rather, black slacks, a black vest, a white button-down, and a purple tie with a neon-pink lightning bolt on it.

LᴇᴀᴋᴜCᴏɴ 2015. Fɪɴᴀʟʟᴜ ᴡᴇᴀʀɪɴɢ ᴀ ꜱᴜɪᴛ ᴛᴏ ᴛʜᴇ ʙᴀʟʟ.

I wasn't the only one with a new ball outfit that year. I noticed an uptick in trans, nonbinary, and gender-nonconforming attendees trying out new looks at the ball. I felt so proud to be a part of a community where people felt safe and encouraged to be themselves, even if they didn't know who "themselves" were yet.

Many of those folks came up to me and shared their journeys. It wasn't just because I had come out myself a few months prior, but also because I had begun making more and more videos on transgender topics.

At first when I came out, I had been adamant that my channel wouldn't become *just* a trans channel. That's not why people had subscribed and I had to honor that, even if I had a million things I wanted to say from my own perspective now that I could. I reined it in. I started a second channel where I posted videos documenting my transition to keep them separate and rationed out LGBTQ+-related videos on my main channel to just one a month. But steadily I started noticing that the LGBTQ+ videos were getting a much better reception than my other videos. *Will It Waffle?* still reigned as king of my channel, but the trans videos were coming for its throne. I was getting comments from trans people, questioning people, and cis people alike saying how much they were learning or how represented they felt by my videos.

It crossed my mind that I should start considering a more cohesive content strategy, but I still mostly considered my personal YouTube channel a hobby and a place to experiment with new ideas. I didn't need to take myself so seriously. Especially in those first months after coming out when I was enjoying just being me, without second-guessing everything.

And I really was. I felt like I had entered a new era of my life. Testosterone had added about ten pounds of muscle to my arms and shoulders without my having to lift a finger. I had gone up a shirt size in a matter of months, was sprouting pimples in places I didn't even know could get acne, and temporarily lost my higher register (aka my ability to "Woo!" while cheering at shows). Between the physical changes and finally having conquered the one thing I'd been frightened of for years, I was feeling more myself than I ever had. With this newfound confidence and sense of freedom, I started making friends left and right. Some from transgender support groups I was more comfortable attending now that I was out, some at parties that I actually *went to* and where I *talked to people*, and some I don't even know where they came from. I was having *that* good a time being out and being social.

WORKING ON THOSE T GAINS.

It helped that it was summer, my favorite season by far. No matter how old I get or what work I have going on, the middle months of the year will always feel like summer vacation to me. It's time for swimming at the beach, wearing tank tops, chasing fireflies, drinking shandies, and getting chewed up by mosquitos while you roast s'mores around a campfire.

The only problem this year was that, now that I was out as a guy, it felt significantly more awkward that I couldn't whip my shirt off at the beach than it had when *I* was the only one who knew I was guy.

My love for swimming and summertime mostly outweighed my discomfort, so I didn't skip any pool or beach outings due to having to wear a shirt and binder in the water, but I certainly didn't enjoy the experience as much as before.

Swimming aside, it's not fun wearing a binder when it's hot and humid out. It sticks to your sweaty body, it constricts your lungs, and it adds a thick layer over most of your torso that really isn't helping the ninety-degree heat.

A few weeks of being smothered in a binder in the veritable armpit of the New York City subway stations had me convinced: I refused to go another summer in a binder. I needed to get top surgery ASAP.

TRYING NOT TO LET SWIMMING WITH A BINDER GET ME DOWN.

CHAPTER TWENTY-THREE

nippolean complex

Not every transmasculine person wants to have top surgery. Not every trans person has to have any sort of surgery. Not every trans person has to go on hormones. Not every trans person has to dress a certain way, act a certain way, or do anything to make them trans enough. Each person's relationship to their gender is different and each person's relationship to their gender is valid.

But for me, top surgery was always what I wanted.

So toward the end of that hot and sticky summer, I took the bus to the annual Philadelphia Trans Wellness Conference—the largest free trans-specific conference in the world. I had heard about it long ago through trans people I followed online and had wanted to go for years. Now that I was finally out, I felt ready to attend, even if I ended up only going for a day and a half of programming because I couldn't afford to take off work or pay for a hotel room all on my own.

A big reason I was going was so I could do research on top surgery. The conference boasted presentations from surgeons, show-and-tells from people who'd had top surgery, and most of all, thousands of other trans attendees to meet and learn from.

From the first moment I walked through the glass doors of the Mazzoni Center, I felt an overwhelming sense of belonging. I had never seen so many trans people, of so many different identities, ages, and backgrounds, in one place before. There were people in all different phases of transition, families with young gender-variant children, older trans people with their partners, veterans handing out pamphlets about trans people in the military, attendees dressed like they were going straight to a Pride march after this, and others like they were headed to the bank to get a loan. Everyone was happily walking around, perusing the vendor booths, making new friends, and being themselves—as loudly and proudly as they wanted to (or didn't). Some of the vendors from health insurance companies and local bookstores might have been cisgender, as well as many of the partners and families there, but for once, for those three days, *we* got to be the majority. *Our* needs were first priority. *Our* voices were the ones being heard.

While I loved getting to spend time with so many trans women and nonbinary people, the best moments were when I was in trans men-only spaces. There's some kind of power in convening with people who have been through the same unique experience. Unlike when I'm around cisgender guys or trans people of other genders, I didn't have to make any explanations or provide context. We were all on the same page. We could skip over the basics and get to the meatier discussions at hand, such as how to navigate privilege and toxic masculinity, what it means to be a man when you're a man of color or visibly queer, where our place is in the larger trans and LGBTQ+ community, how we've tackled dating and marriage, what paths some have pursued for having children, what health issues we've faced and whether they're related to our medical transitions or not, and how all of that makes us feel.

On one evening of the conference, I went to a concert featuring a few transmasculine musicians. It was the first bar show I've ever been to in which I could actually *see* the performers because the audience of transmasculine people in front of me were all just as short as I am. For once, the line for the men's room was much longer than the one for the women's room, and I beamed overhearing casual, open conversations about binders and testosterone in between sets.

But my main objective that weekend was learning more about top surgery. I circled every top-surgery-related program in the conference guidebook and did my best to make it to all of them. The first one of the weekend was a presentation by locally based Dr. Kathy Rumer.

I sat on the floor in the corner of the overcrowded conference room, notebook perched on my knees, as Dr. Rumer introduced her practice and presented a slideshow of some of her past patients' results.

Kathy Rumer is a sharp, kindhearted doctor with a background in both art and science. She spoke sincerely about redirecting her career to serve transgender patients because she's passionate about being able to help other people love their bodies. I liked her immediately, but one part of her presentation especially caught my ear.

From her slides, it looked like she performed the less-invasive peri-areolar surgery on patients with larger chests than most doctors I had researched so far. Thrill shivered through my body. For the first time, I thought I might actually be a candidate for peri-areolar.

To understand why this was significant, it'll be helpful for me to give a brief overview of the types of top surgery. Lots of techniques continue to emerge, but most types of procedures fall under two main categories:

Double Incision:

- Incisions made at the base of each breast for tissue and excess skin to be removed
- Scars remain, running horizontally most of the length of the chest
- Nipples and areolas removed, resized, and grafted back into new position

- Erotic nipple sensation most likely lost; nonerotic sensation usually returns in a few months or years
- Available for chests of any size

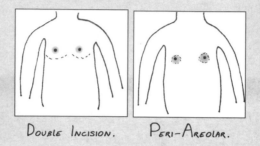

Double Incision.   Peri-Areolar.

Peri-Areolar:

- Some versions of this procedure are also called "keyhole"
- Incisions made around the borders of the areolas for tissue to be removed
- Minimal scarring, just around the areola
- Erotic nipple sensation preserved
- Shorter healing and recovery time, but sometimes requires revisions for optimal results
- Available only for smaller chests (B cup and below) with good skin elasticity

People tend to align into two camps about which procedure they prefer. Double incision leaves big scars that take years to fade, but otherwise provides a more dependable and masculine aesthetic. Plus, some people *only* qualify for double incision, based on the size of their breasts, elasticity of their skin, and other factors.

Meanwhile, peri-areolar leaves few scars, but also provides fewer options for nipple placement. It often requires revisions, and some people experience sagging or other complications throughout subsequent years. For those reasons, there are a decent number of people who qualify for peri-areolar but still opt for double incision.

I wasn't one of them. I dreamed wildly of being small-chested enough to qualify for peri-areolar and how indistinguishable my scar-free chest would be from that of a cis guy's. I was a realist, however, and had spent years trying to content myself with the scars I would gain from double incision, knowing that my chest was probably too large for peri-areolar.

Seeing the before and after photos Dr. Rumer displayed in that tenebrous programming room at the Mazzoni Center, though, gave me a new twinkle of hope. The people she was showing looked like they had chests as large as or larger than me in their before photos and their after pictures looked amazing! Maybe, just maybe, I would qualify.

●　●　●

I spent the subsequent weeks looking up patient-submitted photos of Dr. Rumer's work on TransBucket, a site for trans people to anonymously share photos of their surgery results. Photos are categorized by procedure type and surgeon, and posters often include details about their experience as well as contact information so folks considering the same surgeon can reach out with questions.

TransBucket is a great resource for finding a surgeon when you don't happen to run into one at a conference like I did. I used it as well as TopSurgery.net and top-surgery hashtags on social media to investigate other surgeons over the years. At the time, there weren't many surgeons in New York City whose results I had liked and since New York State's marketplace health insurance wouldn't cover transgender-related services until *after* I got top surgery, it made no difference in price for me to go out of state. Except, of course, paying for travel. Many people travel out of state, even across or out of the country, to get surgery from a doctor who delivers the kinds of results they want and a bedside manner they're comfortable with. These, in addition to price and whether they accept your insurance, are the key things to look for when you're researching a surgeon. You need to know what your priorities are in your results, check that you would get those results with this surgeon, and find out if their personality and that of their administrators matches yours. You're going to have a lot of logistical calls with the office ahead of time, and since this surgeon is literally going to be opening up your body while you're unconscious, you want to make sure to find one you can trust.

I emailed a couple of people I found on TransBucket who'd had top surgery with Dr. Rumer, asking about their experiences with her office, how satisfied they were their results, and if they would honestly recommend her. All their messages confirmed that Dr. Rumer's practice was the right fit for me and their results looked great—full, well-placed nipples, no sagging or misshapen pecs. I was sold.

As I was researching, I was also doing everything I could to make my body the perfect candidate for peri-areolar. I upped my workout regimen, kept a clean diet, and applied a cocoa butter lotion to my chest twice a day to keep my skin healthy.

One of the reasons I wanted peri-areolar so badly was because it was much easier for me to come to terms with parting with an actual piece of my body if I could think of it as just having some tissue sucked out of me. I've always had an irrational fear of losing a limb, and some of that fear translated into anxiety about top surgery, as badly as I wanted it. Without the thick, red scars left behind on my chest, I thought it would feel like part of my body had just lost some fat—and not like I'd actually had a part of my body removed. It was easier for me to process.

I was also aware that accurate information about transgender people was finally filtering into the cisgender world, and it probably won't be long before people at large know that two horizontal scars across a guy's chest means he's had a double mastectomy. One might be able to explain the scars with a vague medical excuse now, but in a few years they could clock me as trans at the beach or in the locker room— in the same way that a trans woman might be clocked by a protruding Adam's apple. I had also reasoned that I would rather have a few years of a less-than-stellar-looking chest while I received the revisions common to peri-areolar than have to live with prominent scars for the rest of my life. Most people's double-incision scars do fade substantially within a few years, especially if they take good care of them and are lucky enough to have skin that heals scar tissue well. Even without fading, your scars might be hidden under your pectoral muscles if you're super ripped, or chest hair if you've got a lot of it. Many people even get chest tattoos that obscure, or celebrate, the scars.

But I didn't want to hear any of those rational arguments at the time. I only had eyes for peri-areolar.

On my way to my consultation, I dressed up as Sirius Black and stopped by a Halloween festival at the Woodlands Cemetery in Philadelphia. Like you do.

So when I visited Dr. Rumer's office on a mild October day for my in-person consultation, in which I would hear the verdict on which procedure was best for me, I was a pile of nerves in the shape of a human. The friendly receptionist in the purple-painted lobby tried to put me at ease by offering me a bowl of violet-and-lilac-wrapped Hershey's Kisses.

Soon enough, I was led back to what looked like a normal doctor's office. A nurse asked me a few questions and then handed me a paper gown to put on, saying she'd be back with Dr. Rumer in a few minutes.

I remained upbeat and cheery on the outside, but inside my nerves were multiplying so rapidly that I ripped the gown down the middle when I tried to put it on.

While I waited for Dr. Rumer to show up, I looked down at my socked feet hanging off the side of the examination table and tried to practice some affirmational thinking. The moment of truth was almost here and I knew what I wanted to hear. *Peri-areolar*, I coached myself. *You're getting peri-areolar.*

The door squeaked open and Dr. Rumer bustled into the low-lit room, the nurse following behind her with a clipboard. Before she even sat down, she pulled open the front of the ripped paper gown and said brusquely, "All right, so you'll be double incision."

"O-oh?" I stammered.

"Yep, you'll have great results. So we'll let you get dressed again and then we can go over the logistics and you can ask me any questions you have."

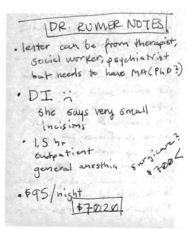

NOTES FROM *BEFORE* AND DURING MY CONSULTATION.

I tried not to show my disappointment, but I was crushed. I knew it had been a long shot. I was definitely borderline and five years of constant binding had adversely affected my skin elasticity, but I had still been hoping for a miracle.

In the months to come, I would ask Dr. Rumer again if there was any chance I'd qualify for peri-areolar and she told me I wouldn't be happy with the results. I trusted her. I'd seen a lot of results of peri-areolar on borderline candidates who experience sagging skin and misshapen nipples as time goes on. I just needed to get back to the mind-set of being content with the scars I would have from double incision.

Every now and then, I regret not getting a second opinion. I had done so much work to get to the point of meeting with Dr. Rumer and every other part of the plan—her price point, her practice's proximity to New York City—was so good that I didn't think to consider anyone else. I think the truth is that I probably thought my chest was a lot smaller than it was in reality, but I still sometimes wonder what would have happened if I'd talked to another surgeon.

CHAPTER TWENTY-FOUR

free my nipples

With my top surgery on the books for the start of January, I turned my focus toward saving up the money required to pay for the procedure and associated costs.

Top surgery costs in the $4,000 to $12,000 range depending on the surgeon you go to and the exact procedure you're getting. On top of that, there are the anesthesia fees, pre- and post-op care, facility fees, medications, travel and lodging if you're going out of town, money to cover the time you're not working if you can't get paid time off for the duration of your recovery, and more. Including airfare for my mom, stocking up on extra groceries, and all the incidentals from each day trip to Philadelphia for post-op checkups, my grand total came to just over $8,000.

While I was battling for *some* coverage from my health insurance company, I was prepared to cover all the costs out of pocket, just in case. I had been setting aside a little bit of money whenever I could for a couple of years, but with the date set, I turned my focus toward fund-raising in earnest.

I picked up video editing work and consulting jobs on top of my full-time job with the HPA. I sold a bunch of my old clothes. I launched a VHS digitization side hustle. I started selling merchandise under my YouTube branding. Eventually, after a lot of convincing from others, I launched a crowdfunding campaign asking for donations to help me cover the remaining few thousand dollars.

I dubbed this multiarmed fund-raising campaign Free My Nipples, a deliberate play on the Free the Nipple movement.

Free the Nipple, named after the 2014 film of the same name, aims to grant all people equal freedom and legal protections to bare their chests, whether they have breasts on them or not. The movement is pro–gender equality and anti–sexual objectification. While I personally might not have enjoyed having breasts on my own body, I remain committed to the fight for all people, especially those of marginalized identities, to be less objectified.

Though the movement is working to free nipples by reforming laws and challenging deep-set misconceptions about the primary purpose of breasts, I was freeing my nipples by having surgery to remove my breasts. It may seem counter to the Free the Nipple movement. Instead of joining their fight to free my nipples by bearing my breasts publicly, I only considered my nipples free to be seen by the public once my breasts were gone.

The whole idea of movements like Free the Nipple, however, is fighting for a world in which all people can express themselves in the way that most honors who they are. Part of the reason I was dysphoric about my chest is because breasts are so sexualized in our culture. I didn't like having giant gender markers attached to my torso, both because I didn't identify with the gender they were associated with and because I didn't like that they were associated with gender at all!

One person who has taken a stand against the gender-based sexualization of breasts is Courtney Demone, who launched #FreeAllBodies in 2015, as an inclusive addendum to the Free the Nipple movement. When she started hormone treatment, she posted daily topless photos to Instagram as her breasts began to grow. With each photo she asked Instagram, #DoIHaveBoobsNow? This project highlighted how nonsensical Instagram and other social media platforms' Community Guidelines are regarding torso nudity.

There are endless stories of breast-feeding mothers' and post-mastectomy cancer survivors' photos being taken down for being lewd or sexual. Meanwhile, cisgender men, some with breasts larger than some women, can post topless photos (and go topless in public!) with no problems.

And when you expand the field to transgender people, it gets even more complicated. Do platforms remove photos of trans men's breasts? What about flat-chested trans women? Trans people of all genders showcasing all sorts of chests have had different responses from social media platforms, so Courtney decided to see just how long it would take for her chest to be considered "feminine enough" to be censored.

Challenges to the authoritarian status quo like Courtney's #FreeAllBodies movement and the larger Free the Nipple movement create a safer world for all of us. By pushing people to question their preconceived biases, we open the floor for people of all different types to begin gaining widespread acceptance. Once we begin questioning why a parent can't post a picture of themself breast-feeding on Facebook, we're on the path to second-guessing all sorts of cultural "norms."

SKETCHING OUT POTENTIAL BRANDING FOR MY FUND-RAISING CAMPAIGN.

I wanted to acknowledge all these issues and keep them in the discussion as I went about fund-raising for my surgery, something that felt incredibly self-centered to me. In the end, over one hundred people donated to help me close the gap in my fund-raising goal. I was stunned and humbled by their generosity.

●   ●   ●

With finances squared away, it was time to start mentally preparing for surgery. Even though I'd been dreaming about having top surgery for years, I still had a lot of nerves about the procedure and a small amount of doubt at the back of my mind. I worried that the doubt meant top surgery wasn't actually right for me, maybe that I wasn't even actually trans. Fortunately, my therapist was there to set my mind at ease with his trademark rationality. He pointed out that this was a major surgery. I was preparing to permanently alter my body, take a huge step in my transition, and face a medical procedure on a scale I'd never had before.

"I'd be concerned if you *didn't* have doubts," he told me.

That made me feel better. I was still nervous, of course, but I was no longer nervous about *why* I was nervous. Like I often do, I turned to research as a salve for my anxieties. I looked up as much advice as I could find from people who'd had top surgery, prepping myself with knowledge of the risks and tips for any challenges I might encounter.

A major piece of advice I saw repeated over and over again was to have realistic expectations for how your chest will look. Just like starting hormones won't solve all your problems, getting top surgery won't fix all your dysphoria. You're not going to magically get a six-pack overnight. The rest of your torso is still going to look exactly like it did before the surgeon knocked you out. In fact, you'll probably notice your hips even more than you did before, so you should try to make peace with that beforehand if those are a particular source of dysphoria for you.

It's especially important to temper your expectations for the first time you see your chest. The stitches, dried blood, and possible bruising can be a shock to see on your own body. Even after the incisions heal, your chest will likely cave in a bit until you're recovered and start building up some fat and muscle. Everything will look better over time.

You do want to pay attention to anything that might look off as you recover, though. Two common complications are hematomas and nipple necrosis (if you had nipple grafts). A hematoma is a collection of blood outside a blood vessel that often looks like a nasty bruise. Nipple necrosis is when the tissue used for your nipple graft fails to develop new blood vessels.*

If you start seeing particularly dark bruising or your nipple turning black, call your doctor right away (really, call your doctor about anything alarming. Don't just trust some guy's memoir!).

Losing a nipple due to nipple necrosis is relatively uncommon, but it's understandably frightening. A friend of mine went to Bonnaroo very soon after his top surgery, where he indulged in some of the substances popular at music festivals. He was flopping around in a crowd of wild hipsters at a two A.M. Animal Collective show in the middle of a grass field when he felt something strange happening under the chest dressings he still had on. Remembering the top-surgery horror stories he'd heard, he was afraid his boisterous dance moves had knocked a nipple loose! Nipple grafts don't just fall off even when they do fail to connect to the new tissue, but the factual details of the oft-rumored "nipple death" aren't exactly common knowledge and probably weren't at the top of my friend's mind in that moment. As he recruited a bunch of nearby festivalgoers to get down on their hands and knees to rip up the grass in search of his lost nipple, he felt another classic top surgery

*Read FTM & FTN Nipple Grafts by Dr. Scott Mosser at genderconfirmation.com.

experience coming: the uncontrollable release after several pent-up days of painkiller-induced constipation. All he could do was laugh as he literally started pooping his pants while he and a group of strangers searched the ground for his nipple. Eventually, he thought to check under his wrappings and discovered that his nipple was still safe and sound, attached to his body—but at least he was going home with a good story.*

• • •

Another thing I discovered in my research was that it's not uncommon to experience temporary depression after surgery—any surgery, not just top surgery. Some think it may be a reaction to the anesthesia or painkillers, and sometimes it's simply your body coping with the trauma it's gone through. After all, in the case of top surgery, your body went to sleep one shape and woke up another. It's going to take your brain some time to process what happened.

A great piece of advice I found to combat the potential for this depression, especially if it manifests as dysphoria or your brain tricking you into feeling regret, is to write a letter to yourself before surgery. Remind yourself why you got top surgery and why you're an awesome person. Maybe even suggest a playlist, happy videos, or friends' phone numbers for your postsurgical self.**

---

*For more information about nipple death, see https://www.ncbi.nlm.nih.gov/pmc/articles/PMC4579172/.

**For more information about postoperative depression, see https://www.ncbi.nlm.nih.gov/pmc/articles/PMC4736276/.

Thanks for All the Good Mammaries!

I may not have loved them, but I had these breasts for more than half of my life. We went through a lot together.

- From sleeping on my stomach to try to stop them from growing to being able to deftly remove a bra with a shirt on while driving a standard-transmission car.
- Living in fear of feeling a bump during regular self-checks, but guiltily thinking that having to have a double mastectomy for medical reasons would make that part of life so much easier.
- Learning the pure joy of squeezing them like a sponge to get the water out of my bikini top when I got out of the swimming pool.
- Trying to figure out if I was supposed to act turned on the first time a starry-eyed boy touched my boobs. And being totally disappointed when smashing my own boobs against a woman's wasn't nearly as fun or sexy as I had thought it would be.

In addition to mentally preparing for the procedure, I wanted to make sure to say good-bye to my breasts. Even though I had never been a huge fan of them, they were still a part of my body that I was never going to have again. It took me years just to work up the guts to cut my long hair, and now I was preparing to slice off a part of my body in a span of two hours——or what would feel like an instant to me.

It took me a while to figure out a proper send-off with which I could feel comfortable. In the end, I settled on a body-painting party with a fellow trans friend. Painting my body with random acrylics or finger paints I had lying around the house had been a type of stress relief for me over the years—something I didn't realize until recently had probably been my way of feeling ownership and enthusiasm over a body that felt so foreign.

My friend came over, we turned on some queer punk tunes, we took our shirts off, and we danced around painting designs all over our bodies. It felt empowering to celebrate my body instead of trying to fight against it, but I also couldn't stop thinking of how much better this would be next time, when I had a flat chest.

PRE—TOP SURGERY BODY-PAINTING PARTY!

There was so much I couldn't wait for. Like for the day I could just take off my outer clothes and go straight to bed. Or even just fall asleep in my clothes! Before surgery, I had to go through the whole rigmarole of taking off my shirt to spring free from my binder and then put another shirt back on.

Soon I wouldn't need to worry about a binder showing through thin shirts or under tank tops. Soon I'd be able to change my shirt out in the open in the locker room and, the crowning glory, go swimming in just a pair of swim trunks—something I'd dreamt about since, well, my whole life really.

As my top surgery approached with just a few days left, I tried to stay calm and prepare for all possible outcomes, but it was difficult. All I felt was pure, unadulterated excitement. You could even say I was feeling *titillated*.

Finally, the day arrived. My mom flew into New York, and we drove a rental car to Dr. Rumer's office and recovery center in Ardmore, Pennsylvania. After checking in with Dr. Rumer, we did a test run of the drive from the recovery center to the hospital, noting how long it took and anything en route that might trip us up in the morning. Then we went to dinner at a tavern down the road, where I ate a huge, delicious meal before the cutoff time that evening when I would have to start fasting.

The next morning, we had to be up before six to check in at the hospital. Without being able to eat breakfast or even have a glass of water, I filled the time by doing a few push-ups to get rid of my nerves, knowing I wouldn't be able to do any again for several weeks. Afterward, I put on a binder for the last time in my life, posted an update to Instagram, and headed out with my mom for the hospital.

Throughout check-in and intake, everyone called me Jackson and used masculine pronouns even though I hadn't legally changed my name and gender yet. After we were led back to the preparation area, the nurses handed me a gown—cloth this time, not paper, so there was no risk of me ripping it—and told me to take off everything except my socks and underwear. Shortly afterward, Dr. Rumer arrived to discuss the procedure one last time and draw marks on my chest for where the incisions and nipple grafts would go. After her came the anesthesiologist. As she was inserting the IV into my arm, I told her that I'm prone to nausea and asked if she could add something to the anesthesia to help offset that—something I had read about during my pre-surgery research—and she obliged.

In what felt like hardly any time at all, I was saying good-bye to my

mom and being wheeled away by a whole team of people to the operating room. My view was mostly limited to the bright, white ceiling as
they transferred me from the bed to an operating table and finally made
me take off my socks, laughing when they discovered I was wearing
two pairs.

"It's cold out!" I protested, but I couldn't explain much further because someone was putting a mask on my face and, just like they do
on TV, telling me to count backward from ten. I blacked out somewhere
around six.

CHAPTER TWENTY-FIVE

mammary loss

Everything felt thick and heavy. I was aware of a group of people around me before I opened my eyes. How long had I been out of it? It felt like I had missed so much.

"Am I Rip Van Winkle?" I asked, my voice slurred and groggy.

Some laughter.

I lifted my head and looked down, seeing my chest wrapped up tightly in bandages. Oh, right. I had done it. I had really done it.

"This is awesome," I said. Then I dropped my head back down and passed out.

The next time I woke up I was back in the cordoned-off space where I had been before the operating room, but this time half of the curtains were open. I could see a desk of nurses and administrators not too far away from me. I was also suddenly aware that I might vomit.

I groaned, unable to do much else, trying to figure out if some up-chuck was on its way. This caught a nurse's attention and she came over to ask how I was doing.

I eventually managed to communicate that I was revoltingly nau-seated and also quite light-headed. She patiently fed me ice chips for who knows how long until I finally started feeling human again.

Within a couple of hours, my mom had come back to see me and I was cleared for discharge to the recovery center at Dr. Rumer's office.

After the initial nausea cleared, I was surprised by how alert I felt. I had an appetite, I had energy, and I hardly even felt cloudy from the pain-killers. I was relieved to discover that I had enough mobility in my arms to be able to use the restroom and brush my teeth without assistance, saving me from some embarrassing moments with my mom.

We stayed in the recovery center overnight, which was really just like a hotel of patients, and, after a quick checkup from Dr. Rumer the next morning, we were back on the road so I could recover in my own bed.

Recovery for me mostly meant several naps a day broken up by a bit of reading and a lot of Netflix. One of the most challenging things is the pure discomfort from the bandages. A lot of surgeons, Dr. Rumer included, wrap you up tightly in a compression bandage that you can't remove for the first several days. It's ironic, considering how much it's drilled into the heads of transmasculine people not to bind with com-pression bandages, that, when your breasts are removed, it's the first thing that happens to you.

The compression bandage is used to minimize swelling, help the skin tighten, and keep the nipple grafts safe from disturbance as they heal onto their new tissue. The bandage can make you pretty sore after a few days and is *seriously* itchy. The number-one item I recommend every person invest in for top surgery is a back scratcher. It might sound excessive, but you'll thank me later.

Top Surgery Recovery Checklist

Here are some of the items I found most helpful when I was recovering from top surgery:

- a caretaker or a rotation of a few people to help you out the first couple of days
- a neck pillow
- a back scratcher
- button-up shirts and zip-up hoodies (don't even think about pulling a T-shirt over your head for at least a week)
- bendy straws
- preprepared meals (either frozen or graciously cooked by friends)
- healthy snacks
- a notebook for recording nonurgent information you may want to tell your doctor
- books, podcasts, and a device loaded with lots of TV shows to stream
- a step stool (for reaching things with your T-rex arms)
- a table onto which you can put everything from high shelves until you regain mobility
- face/body wipes and dry shampoo (you can't shower for the first several days!)
- gauze, antibiotic ointment, acetaminophen, and other backup supplies as recommended by your doctor
- lots and lots of water
- one or two treats to cheer yourself up

In addition to the itching, the bandages and the general pain from the surgery can make it difficult to sleep in your usual position—and some surgeons even instruct you to sleep sitting up for the first couple of days.

Overall, the biggest thing to be aware of is not moving your arms too much or lifting anything heavier than a couple of pounds for the first week, especially while you have drains in. It can hurt a little to overexert yourself as you heal, and you also risk stretching out your scars, making them thicker as they heal.

Many surgeons require drains for about the first week, which are tubes inserted in your chest that empty excess fluids from under your incisions into a little plastic sack that has to be emptied a couple of times a day to help prevent swelling and fluid buildup. It's a little gross and unnerving to have these blood pouches attached to you, but honestly it's not that weird while it's happening.

My mom helped me with the drains and everything else I needed for the first several days—like making food, keeping the house tidy, and sometimes helping me put on my pants. But after a few days she had to get back to work.

Mom and me before I was wheeled back to the OR.

Fortunately, I had friends around who were willing to come take out my recycling and even drive me to Pennsylvania for my one-week follow-up appointment to get my drains out. As we drove down I-95 and rocked out to the playlist my friends had put together for the occasion, titled "Nipples or Bust," I thought about how lucky I was to have these friends who were so willing to drive me across state lines for a doctor's appointment on a weekday. More than that, how none of them thought my surgery was strange or unsettling, but rather something to celebrate. It was another moment I wouldn't have dreamt possible just a few years prior.

•   •   •

Not long after that post-op road trip, I did something else I wasn't sure I would ever do: I got a tattoo.

As an overthinker, I've always struggled with the idea of commitment and with permanence. That fear was a huge obstacle at every phase of my transition, because every part of it felt so permanent—cutting my hair, coming out to people, starting testosterone, and then getting top surgery.

Somewhere in the middle of all of that, though, I finally stopped fearing permanence. It is so scary to share your most vulnerable side with people, and to have to defend it over and over again. So much of existing as a trans person in this world feels like a fight that other things in life start paling next to in comparison. Like getting a tattoo. One small tattoo had nothing on the major surgery I'd just undergone. What was a little tattoo compared to that?

So I asked my friend to tattoo a small dagger on the back of my right ankle, on my Achilles tendon. I'm not generally a fan of violence, but I think of a dagger as a defensive weapon, a small knife one would keep just in case of danger; the kind of weapon Peter Pan had versus Captain Hook's sabers and cannonballs. I put the dagger on the back of my ankle so that, even on my Achilles tendon, the one place Achilles was unprotected, I am now protected. Even in my weakest spot, I can defend myself and rise to the challenge. I'm invincible. Not because I'm foolhardy, but because I choose to stand up and face my fears, head-on.

SKETCHING CONCEPTS
FOR MY TATTOO.

Once both the tattoo and my incisions had sufficiently healed and been cleared for submersion in water, I was ready for my first post-surgery swim.

There aren't many easily accessible indoor pools in New York City, nor are beaches up north open before Memorial Day, so my first opportunity to swim wouldn't come until March when I stayed at a hotel in Providence for the HPA's annual leadership conference, the Granger Leadership Academy.

My coworkers and I had been hard at work for months putting the conference together and that year I would even be giving a keynote talk, so there was a lot to be excited about, but I'd be lying if I said hitting the hotel pool wasn't toward the top of my list.

Unfortunately, when I checked in, tragedy struck: A flyer on the check-in desk informed me that the pool was closed for maintenance.

When I asked the receptionist if it was true, she confirmed my fears, but also added that guests were welcome to use the pool at one of their nearby sister hotels. It can be tough to find time to hit the pool during the hustle and bustle of a conference even when it's actually inside the hotel, but making time to travel to a whole other location just to go swimming was laughable.

Fortunately, I had two good friends with me at the conference who are always up for an adventure. We arranged our schedules and during one of the day's dinner breaks, we drove through the tar-blemished snowbanks of outer Providence to the other hotel. When we trudged in, tracking snow behind us, it was clear from the confusion on the hotel employees' faces that exactly zero other guests had made good on this offer. Probably thinking we were a bit odd for going to such lengths to go swimming in the midst of a New England winter, they nonetheless handed us a key and pointed us toward the indoor pool.

It wasn't the nicest pool we'd ever seen in our lives. The walls were yellowed in such a way that it was anyone's guess what their original color was. The tile perimeter of the pool was cracked and faded. The water itself was slightly cloudy. But we had come this far, so we were determined to at least try it out.

We all stripped off our winter coats and assorted clothing we'd layered on top of our swimsuits to keep warm. I hesitated for a second before pulling my shirt off. Both of my friends had known me before I transitioned and seen me in a bikini several times on previous hotel pool adventures. It felt a little strange to show off a part of my body I had previously kept covered around them. But my friends are chill and supportive; I knew that. They'd just driven all the way over here to swim in this sketchy pool with me. I shook off the nerves, pulled off my shirt, and took a second to enjoy the moment before cannonballing into the deep end to join my friends.

As soon as I'd resurfaced, I knew something was off. We all looked at one another in confusion, wet hair clinging to our foreheads.

"It tastes like bodies," one of them said.

He wasn't wrong. The water had a very *distinctive* taste and felt . . . greasy, almost? We tried to enjoy it for a few minutes, but ultimately it was just too unpleasant.

It wasn't the perfect first topless swim I'd always imagined, but at least it was memorable.

Once summer finally arrived, I had plenty more opportunities to go swimming in non-cadaver-scented waters. At the beach, I still had to put

a shirt on whenever I wasn't in the water because you're really not supposed to expose your scars to the sun for the first year, but having the
freedom to take it off otherwise made all the difference.

Swimming in just my trunks without a shirt on felt so immediately
normal that I barely remember all my firsts. In my joy at finally wearing
exactly what I wanted to go swimming, I tried not to concern myself too
much with what strangers might think about the two long scars lining my
chest.

I've yet to have anyone outright ask me, but I can see the path of
their eyes, the slight surprise followed by curiosity or confusion. My one
fear is kids. Unlike adults, who generally know it's impolite to ask about
scars on someone's body, a kid would just go for it. And while I have some
prepared answers for adults ("It's from a surgery. I don't like to talk about
it."), I'm more nervous about how to explain it to kids in a way that would
shut down the conversation before having to out myself and have *that*
conversation.

On a couple of occasions, however, the scars have been a source of
amusement for me.

In celebration of Valentine's Day just after my surgery, I did a special
edition of *Will It Waffle?* in which I made an anatomical heart using a gela-
tin mold and pretended to waffle my own heart. I kept up the charade of it
being my own heart for the whole video, including showing off one of my
surgical scars at the beginning when I claimed to have removed my heart
from my body myself. After I posted the video, I got one comment that
said, "That's the fakest scar I've ever seen." It remains my favorite hate
comment I've ever received.

I get so accustomed to seeing chest scars on all the transmasculine
people I follow online and hang out with in person that, on occasion, I'll see
a cisgender man without a shirt on and get really confused about where
his scars are.

That first summer after top surgery, I returned to the Philadelphia Trans Wellness Conference with increased confidence. I had made a few more trans friends in the intervening year, so we got a hotel room together, meaning I'd actually get to stay for the entire conference this time and attend more of the evening social events.

On the final night of the conference, I ended up with a group of about a dozen transmasculine people barhopping in Philadelphia's gayborhood. Going to clubs isn't typically my scene—I'm more of a pint-of-beer-at-a-dive-bar kinda guy—but with so many other trans-masculine people, I was having a blast. Toward the end of the night, we ended up at a club with a huge dance floor. All of us were pulling out our best moves and jokingly grinding up against one another. I don't know who started it, but eventually every person there who'd had top surgery had whipped off their shirt. I followed suit and got a kick out of the confused glances from people on the dance floor, no doubt wondering where this large group of short young men who all had the same exact chest scars had come from.

I would never have had the confidence to do that by myself, but once again I felt that power of being in a group. We weren't *the* majority in that club, but we were a large group, too large to be messed with, and we were claiming our space.

CHAPTER TWENTY-SIX

finding my (deeper) voice

Despite how overjoyed I was to have had top surgery—to feel the cotton of my T-shirts directly on my chest and back, to be able to run longer and faster without a binder restricting my breathing—I wasn't thrilled about how I looked with my shirt off.

The surgery results were great—don't get me wrong. My scars were relatively thin, the contour of my chest looked fantastic, and as weird as it sounds, I absolutely love how my nipples turned out. It was everything else about my body that I didn't love so much.

When my shirt was off, it was even more apparent just how wide my hips were—something that had bothered me even before top surgery. The occasional chub on my belly didn't help matters. Nor did I like how incredibly fair-skinned I am, or the dozen dark sizable moles dotting my torso. Maybe if I were tanner, had more chest hair, less belly fat . . . anytime I went down that self-conscious rabbit hole, I would pause and realize how *ordinary* those complaints were. Plenty of guys disliked their chest hair patterns or wished they had more muscle. Maybe I had one or two other trans-specific hang-ups, but for the most part my insecurities we're just like those of many other guys. Life was looking up so much that even my complaints made me happy!

And life *was* looking up. Bolstered by a renewed self-confidence, I had applied for and been accepted into YouTube's NextUp program, an annual initiative providing up-and-coming creators with a chance to attend a weeklong camp at one of YouTube's production spaces and receive a small grant to upgrade their equipment.

At NextUp, I got to talk to other creators and YouTube employees about best practices and emerging strategies for leveling up our channels. The camp inspired me to reevaluate the purpose of my YouTube channel and maybe start really taking it seriously. Since high school, YouTube had mostly been just a hobby. Over the years, it became a place to share my ideas with a small community and sometimes served as a kind of résumé, a place where people could see my work and maybe want to hire me to speak at an event or consult on digital media. But it never had a real purpose, a mission, a cohesive theme.

I still didn't have any delusions about ever being a full-time You-

Tube creator. The success needed to really make bank on YouTube required an alchemical potion of backbreaking work, exactly the right type of broadly appealing content du jour, and a heaping dose of luck.

But I did start thinking that maybe, if I started taking my channel more seriously and identified what I wanted to do with my career after the HPA, I could one day be a self-sustaining creator—not just a YouTuber, but someone whose income comes from many sources of their own creation. I continued percolating on what my purpose might be and meanwhile started going out for more opportunities like NextUp—grants, fellowships, anything where I would get to learn something new, and try out different ideas as I figured out what exactly I wanted to do with my life.

On a trip to YouTube's San Bruno office.

I interviewed for one opportunity I desperately wanted that I ended up not getting, largely because they correctly identified in the interview that I didn't know what I was doing with my work. I spent a lot of time thinking about my direction after that. What mattered to me? What did I care about enough that I wouldn't get tired talking about it? What had I tried before that had resonated with people?

I took a look at my video analytics and discovered that the last few episodes of *Will It Waffle?* had bombed in comparison to the spiking view counts and comments on videos I had made sharing my or other trans people's stories. I thought about all the messages I got every day from fellow trans people, from parents, and from teachers—all asking questions or sending their gratitude for something I had said in a video.

I had been hesitant to make my whole YouTube channel about being trans when I first came out, but it was becoming evident that, if I wanted a cohesive mission in my work, it was staring me in the face.

So I decided to lean into a mission of raising transgender awareness. I wouldn't quit making other videos on my channel, but I would ramp up trans educational videos and also start thinking about other ways I could spread awareness—through writing, speaking, designing workshops, and maybe even launching a podcast.

• • •

I got a chance to test this new direction when I was accepted into TED's Residency program. The TED Residency is an incubator for breakthrough ideas. Residents spend fourteen weeks working out of TED's offices in New York City and workshopping their ideas, and at the end of the program deliver an official TED Talk.

Even after spending fourteen weeks at TED's headquarters and being several years removed from the experience, I still sometimes can't believe it actually happened. Little ol' dorky me was handpicked by TED to workshop my ideas. It still doesn't seem real.

But it was. I had applied on an idea for a podcast that would share the stories of a diverse array of transgender, nonbinary, and gender-nonconforming people. Unlike many podcasts out there at the time designed for fellow trans listeners, I was targeting mine toward a cisgender audience—people who wanted to support transgender people, but maybe didn't quite understand things. Someone who might enthusiastically sign a petition for trans people to use the restroom that aligns with their gender, but wouldn't exactly be able to explain why it was so important for transgender people. There are so, *so* many ways to be transgender beyond the monolithic narrative you see in the media and I wanted to illustrate that. My goal was to break stereotypes, one episode at a time.

While I was hard at work on the podcast as well as the TED Talk I'd be giving, I got to experience office culture for the first time in years. TED's headquarters are in a gorgeous building in SoHo with skyline views, an in-house TED theater built right into the middle of the two-story open-plan office space, and—my favorite part—seltzer on tap.

For someone who had been working remotely from home for so many years, *getting* to commute into an office every day was a special treat. I had a blast decorating my desk and filling its drawers with candy and protein bars. I took breaks from working on my TED Talk to chat with my fellow residents, whose desks surrounded mine. They varied greatly in age, identity, and professional background. Among our ranks were coders, environmentalists, entrepreneurs—even an Emmy Award winner, a sleep scientist, and a Coney Island sword swallower. Needless to say, the water-cooler chats were never dull.

As I spent every day in this office, however, surrounded by progressive, compassionate people, I for the first time experienced some of the workplace micro-aggressions I had heard so much about from other trans people. It was nothing horrible—an awkward glance in the restroom, the *lack* of gender-neutral restrooms, the occasional incorrect pronoun, a few uncomfortable questions about my medical history—but it occurred to me that if I could experience those few uncomfortable inconveniences in a space as intentionally progressive as TED, how bad must it be for trans people in workplaces that are much less welcoming?

That realization only fueled me to work harder on my TED Talk and surrounding trans awareness projects. It was clear how even the most well-intentioned cisgender people could trip up due to their lack of exposure to trans people. People needed to understand how to talk to us, how to listen to us, and how to support us.

I worked hard over those fourteen weeks to launch my podcast and deliver the absolute best TED Talk I could. I played it really safe with the talk. I allowed myself a bit of sass, but I didn't want to alienate anyone by being aggressive or presumptive. My goal was to welcome people in. This resonated with cisgender people, who were largely moved by my talk. My queer trans friends, on the other hand, gave it such acclaim as "basic," "vanilla," and "boring."

Giving my TED Talk!

They're not wrong. Our movement, all movements, need people who are willing to rock the boat, to make some noise, to disrupt. I've never been very good at being that kind of activist. I care too much about being liked. But I'll defend the heck out of the rights and utility of louder activists. We won't ever take steps forward without people pushing us along.

Even with how vanilla it may have been, my TED Talk helped increase the number of opportunities coming my way to share my story and educate people on transgender basics on larger and larger platforms—platforms so large I still can't believe this li'l dweeb bagged an invite, but they were all too much fun not to share. Brace yourself for some #humblebrags.

I was invited to attend the inaugural Obama Summit in Chicago to engage with other activists and community leaders. I got to meet the Obamas and Prince Harry, but even cooler than that, I ended up in an emotional sing-along to TLC's "Waterfalls" led by author Angie Thomas.

I was also invited to be a Featured Creator at VidCon, the annual online video conference. I had attended the conference to run the HPA's merch booth for several years, but this was the first time I was invited by VidCon as myself to speak on panels about my experience being a transgender YouTuber.

Fellow (and full-time, unlike me) YouTuber Tyler Oakley invited me, alongside folks like comedian Joel Kim Booster, actress and author Jazz Jennings, actor Alex Newell, and activist Annie Segarra, on his channel to join a roundtable discussion about intersectionality over brunch.

I was invited to give a talk at YouTube to other creators about maintaining personal privacy while still being relatable. This one stood out to me, not just because it was a topic near to my heart, but because it was the first time I tried not telling any of the attendees of the conference that I was trans before giving my talk on the second day of the event. I don't usually like engaging in this kind of "gotcha" trick, but it does help people to reevaluate their assumptions of what trans people look like. When I showed old YouTube videos of me presenting as a girl during the talk, I had to stop to explain it because people didn't understand it was me. Especially for some of the attendees who weren't as familiar with transgender people, it was a really powerful moment.

From hiding my trans identity to wearing it loudly and proudly . . . I also got to pretend to be a model for a day, alongside other trans performers and activists, for a clothing company's Pride line.

Later that year, I even won a GLAAD Rising Star grant for the podcast, *Transmission*, I had launched during my TED Residency. They flew me and two other winners out to walk the red carpet and accept our awards at the annual gala in San Francisco. The three of us, with our thrifted and DIY formal wear (I had hand-sewn black buttons on my old shirt to make it look fancier), felt totally in awe and out of place all night. Grateful doesn't even begin to describe it. My head still spins when I think back on that whirlwind weekend.

Kids' blazer, safety-pinned pants, and DIYed shirt buttons. Making it work!

During this time, I left my employment at the HPA to focus on being a full-time creator and advocate. I had been fortunate to have the support of my coworkers on building this professional path while also working for the HPA over the years, but my outside work was growing into a full-time job unto itself and I needed to commit to one or the other. So I decided to leave my salary, my benefits, and a job I had loved for so long to venture out into a more uncertain life.

Fortunately, my YouTube channel was thriving from the singular focus I'd pivoted to and I was getting invited to speak at more schools and events. I relished the opportunity to explain concepts to people who seemed genuinely interested in learning, but even more so, I loved the chance to meet other trans people. At every talk, there would be at least a few in the audience who would come up to me afterward to share their own stories.

• • •

I wasn't completely making ends meet from all of this. I still had to pick up as much freelance videography work as I could and host pub quizzes once or twice a week to pay the bills. It was a ton of work. I was back in the lifestyle I had sworn off back before I started working at the HPA, when the infrequent paychecks from working on the documentary steered me deep into debt. But this time I was older and more financially prepared, not to mention much more confident and at home in my sense of self.

High school me would be thrilled I made it to New York, possibly intrigued by my living openly as a man. Depressed pre-transition me would just be in awe of my happiness, ease of self, and stability. To think I have so very little to be upset about this Christmas. I have challenges ahead, sure, and wish certain things like my weight or ability to see mom more were diffrent, but...
I have friends, opportunities, relative security.

DECEMBER 24, 2017.

Now in my late twenties, I was *feeling* older—or at least some new sense of maturity. I valued creature comforts much more, always being eager to get back to my own bed, my own coffeepot, and my own routine at the end of trips. I felt more self-assured in my decisions and made fewer foolish mistakes.

Even though I might have been feeling the effects of age, my outer appearance wasn't showing them. This is not an uncommon problem for transmasculine people. With my small stature, youthful skin, and barely visible facial hair, I was usually assumed to be a teenager. *Maybe* a college student on a good day.

I would get carded buying cold medicine and going to R-rated movies. Airport employees asked where my parents were. Administrators at schools where I was giving keynote talks would ask me if I was a lost freshman. At the time, I lived near a high school and, on more than one occasion, was reprimanded for leaving school grounds while I was passing by on the way home.

I know I'll be grateful when I'm older—that's what everyone says, and I'm sure I will. Both of my parents look great. But it messes with your head when everyone you encounter thinks you're only half your age. I don't ever actually think I'm a teenager, but I do sometimes feel like I'm breaking the rules. Sometimes I can tell I've been legal to drink for longer than the cashier asking me for my ID, but I still start sweating like I'm doing something delinquent and am going to get caught.

I'm lucky, though, that these are the kind of annoyances I have to deal with when I go out in public. Not being misgendered, not being harassed for being trans. Just being mistaken for an annoying teenage boy who's up to no good.

Looking back, I realize that I've followed the same pattern so many trans people, especially trans men, do. When I was consistently being read as male, when transition wasn't at the forefront of my brain anymore, I stopped being as much a part of the community. Sometime in between top surgery and the TED Talk, I had stopped going to my regular support group. I had even stopped attending therapy for the time being—at the recommendation of my therapist. He called it time for my "graduation."

It wasn't that I didn't want to be a part of the community. I absolutely did. It's just that transitioning wasn't constantly on my mind anymore. I didn't have anxieties and challenges related to transition that I felt I needed to work through with a group or a professional. That wired intensity had faded. I was just living. And life was all right.

CHAPTER TWENTY-SEVEN

ten-year reunion

There was never so big an example of my forgetting I was transgender as when I was preparing to attend my ten-year high school reunion.

I'd always imagined I would go to my high school reunions. Sure, I made fun of some school spirit stuff back in the day. I thought I was too cool for football games and homecoming. But even then, I secretly kind of liked some of the pep rallies and school traditions.

More than that, I had a good time in high school. Especially considering how fragmented and haunted by gender dysphoria my college years were, it's no wonder I look back on high school with much greater fondness. I didn't make any lasting friendships in college, but I remain in close contact with several of my friends from high school and was eager to catch up with the ones I'm not.

A lot of my friends moved away from our hometown. If not as far as New York City, then at least down to Austin. So even when one of us visits family back home, it's rare for more than a couple of others to be in town as well. We've had few opportunities for a bunch of us to be in one place since graduating. The reunion seemed like the perfect time.

Plus, cards on the table, I've always been one of those people who dreamed of showing up at my high school reunion with an awesome life that everyone would be jealous of. I didn't think I'd quite achieved *that*, but hey, I've done some cool things. I gave a TED Talk! I felt like I'd have a few bragging rights to bring to the table.

I was enumerating all these reasons for attending to a friend a few months before the reunion when they asked me, "Yeah, but won't it be weird now that you've transitioned?"

I stared at them.

"Oh, shit," I said. "I forgot I'm trans."

I mean, *clearly* I didn't completely forget. I had probably thought about it at least ten times that day in small, passing ways—twenty times if I had gone out in public. But it had never occurred to me in the context of attending my high school reunion.

Of *course* it would be a big deal. The last time most of these people had seen me, I had flowing, long blond hair and wore skirts to school. What would they think? Would they even all know I had transitioned? Would they make us wear name tags? Which name would I have to put on it? Would people make fun of me?

My mind was racing. I still wanted to go. I knew I'd always regret it if I didn't, but I needed to give this some serious thought.

I reached out to all the friends I'd kept in close contact with, ones I knew I could trust. I made a list of all the ones who planned on attending and asked them to act as my support system. They were all on board to lend an ear for my pre-reunion jitters, provide emotional support on the night, keep an eye out for anyone trying to make trouble, and even let me pretend to be one of their fake boyfriends if there was anyone who didn't recognize me and I wasn't comfortable outing myself to.

Support system confirmed, I booked my plane tickets back to Texas.

As I got closer to the big day, I imagined all my worst fears. One thing making me particularly uneasy was imagining what some of the guys I had dated or who'd had crushes on me would think. I hadn't talked to any of them since coming out. Maybe some of them didn't even know. I wanted to imagine the best in them, but it's got to be at least somewhat strange to see a "girl" you used to crush on now living as a man.

There was one guy I made out with in high school who I *knew* knew I was trans and was fine with it. We were good friends, and the few times we had made out were total flukes. It turned out he was gay but wasn't ready to come out while we were in high school together. He texted me on the day I posted my coming-out video and said, "Turns out you were the first guy I ever kissed!" It was one of the best coming-out responses I've ever received.

I also remain friends with some men that I'd dated in New York, all of whom are also perfectly cool with me being trans. Maybe it caused them a moment of questioning their identity, but they've never made that known. They've never been anything but supportive. Would the boys I dated in high school have grown up to be just as compassionate?

Part of what was giving me pause was knowing the religious and political ideologies they had subscribed to in high school, ones that say I'm confused or degenerate for being transgender. If they kept on the same ideological paths they did as teenagers, would they think that of me?

And beyond ex-boyfriends, what about all my other classmates? Texas is a red state, after all, one where I never felt supported or accepted as a queer person when I lived there. I would never judge all Texans based on its majority, especially not as someone who defied that majority. I knew all my friends, even the ones that still lived there, defied it too, and, logically, that our generation is more progressive than our parents' generation. But despite all that, I still had a much higher chance of encountering someone hopping on the transphobic bandwagon of their party in Texas than I did if I were attending an event in New York.

* * *

As I drove around town visiting old haunts with my support-system friends the afternoon of the reunion, I tried to keep count of how many Ted Cruz signs there were versus Beto O'Rourke ones for the upcoming 2018 midterm election. I wanted to gauge what kind of political climate I might be entering into that evening.

On the afternoon of my ten-year reunion.

We all gathered at one friend's house after our drive to clean up and get changed before heading to the reunion. I had fussed over what to wear when packing the day before. I had a pretty good handle on what kind of wardrobe I would've put together for this level of event in New York City, but in Texas? The fashions between the two were always just different enough to make me look out of place when I went back home. I was particularly nervous that something too stylish or hipster might make me look too feminine, or gay. I wanted to seem like as typical a guy as possible, but also look good. And also not stick out.

The class president's instructions of a "casual flexible" dress code were absolutely no help. What the heck does that even mean?

In the end, I settled on a plain blue button-down and some black wash jeans (pretty much the only jeans I ever wore back then). I last-minute decided on wearing a graphic tee under the button-down so I could have options—buttoned up or not.

Dressed and ready, we piled into the designated driver's car and headed out. The reunion was being held at a bar in Fort Worth, a larger town about a half-hour drive southwest of our high school. I got a little carsick on the drive there, so I took my glasses off, closed my eyes, and tried to calm myself for the rest of the ride.

After circling around for a while to find parking, we finally arrived. We were halfway to the bar when I realized I had forgotten my glasses in the car. The whole group turned around with me to retrieve them— they weren't leaving my side.

As I reached into the backseat to grab them, I considered just staying there. What was I doing? Why I had I paid all this money to fly halfway across the country to, what, be humiliated? How could anything good possibly come out of tonight?

I took a deep breath, closed my eyes, and put my glasses on. I *had* come this far, so I had to do it, if only because I had paid so much for the airfare. I shut the car door, and my friends and I repeated our journey to the bar.

It turned out the reunion was actually taking place mostly *outside* the bar, in a vast, dirt-covered yard with a pop-up bar and a large wooden stage usually reserved for live music.

There was a check-in booth set up at the entrance, where two smiling women I didn't recognize were distributing drink tickets and Mustang Class of 2008 pint glasses. One of them greeted me as Jackson. Just as I was trying to work out whether she had seen my name on the check-in sheet or actually knew me, and therefore I should've recognized *her*, a man came up from inside the event and asked her for a name tag.

"No one recognizes me," he explained with a laugh.

I believed it. There was something familiar about his eyes, but I had no clue who he was. Before I could see what he wrote on his name tag, several friends I hadn't seen in years spotted our group. They came over with broad smiles and open arms, buzzing about how weird the night already was. There were so many people we didn't recognize, or ones we had to squint at before we could figure out who they were. It was like that scene in *Hook* when the Lost Boy is squishing Peter Pan's face all around and staring into his eyes to try to recognize him.

Of course there were also plenty of people we probably straight-up didn't know since we graduated in a class of over six hundred students, which just made it more difficult to decide whether you were *supposed* to know someone when you went up to say hi. Difficult for my friends, anyway. *I* was not going to initiate conversation with anyone. I didn't want to put myself in any more of an awkward position than I was already in by having to explain myself. In those first few minutes, as I saw flashes of people from my past scattered all over the yard, I got so overwhelmed that I thought there was a good chance I might leave without speaking to anyone outside of this little group we had formed at the entrance.

As my friends went to claim a picnic table to camp out at, I dug my drink ticket out of my pocket and headed to the pop-up bar the venue had set up in a corner of the yard. The whole area was closed off for our ten-year reunion, but the bartender still insisted on carding me. To her credit, I *did* look younger than anyone else there. She joked that I could've been someone's hot date. Cool. I was the twink of the reunion.

A lot of my classmates had aged more than I expected. I swear half the men had second growth spurts in college. Everyone was just so much bigger and older-looking than me, especially all the men with their thick beards. I was embarrassed by how young, small, and unblemished I looked in comparison. I didn't look like I belonged.

Beer in hand, I joined my group of friends at the picnic bench they'd snagged. They had also swiped an entire tray of burritos and what looked like a veritable bucket of guacamole from the catering table. I tucked into the guac to avoid eye contact with the revolving door of classmates that kept coming over to say hi to people in our group.

It bothered me how antisocial and awkward I was being. I wanted to be enjoying this chance to see old friends and reminisce about the good times, but I was consumed by my fears of what they would think of me, what they would say to me.

So instead I made quick friends with everyone's spouses and fiancés who had not attended our high school. I could be my usual, extroverted self around these people who had just met me as Jack. As one of them was showing me photos of her and my friend's eight-month-old on her phone, I heard a voice call out, "Jackson!"

I turned and saw one of the guys I had briefly dated sophomore year. I really didn't want to talk to him, but he had used the right name, so I pasted on a smile and stood up to shake his outstretched hand.

We made pleasant conversation, sharing what we were up to these days, pretending that I wasn't standing there presenting as a different gender and using a different name than I had in high school.

This is when I realized something I hadn't been prepared for. I had been so preoccupied with how people were going to react to my transition that I had completely forgotten to think about how I would explain what I do for a living.

I can barely answer the question, "What do you do?" to a room of fellow freelance creatives, let alone old high school classmates who were all trying to one-up one another. I usually try to have a quick explainer prepared for different situations, but even then it's a crapshoot if they ask any follow-up questions.

It was almost laughable that days before, I had been lamenting the fact that all my brag-worthy accomplishments would be overshadowed by my transness, and now, given a chance to brag, I couldn't think of anything that sounded as impressive as a house someone had just bought for their new family with the steady income they were making from a job they could actually explain.

This kept happening. People would graciously greet me as Jackson, tell me about their wonderful lives, and then I would sputter that I, like, made videos and, uh, talked to people about how to do social media sometimes?

It was usually at this point that I would change the topic to something impersonal, like the beer selection at the bar or the latest Cowboys game. Fortunately, no conversation lasted too long because someone else would come over and the discussion would shift. As we were talking, I would scan the crowd, keeping an eye out for people I knew to be particularly hotheaded or fiercely homophobic. On one such scan, I noticed someone I had been certain wouldn't show up both because he lived pretty far south in the state and because he too was trans.

Since graduating, there have been two other classmates I'm aware of that have come out as trans guys. One of them even has the same birthday and had the same birth name as me. It's seriously eerie. He didn't go through as intense of a repression phase as I did in high school, so I used to watch him from afar, envying his short haircut and masculine everyday wear. As in awe as I was of him being himself, he's since told me that high school was hell for him. When I asked if he'd be attending the reunion so we could meet up and maybe even record a special episode of my podcast, he basically just laughed.

The other trans guy, however, had been a neighborhood friend of mine growing up. We lost touch in high school when our friend groups and extracurriculars set us on different paths, but we'd reconnected on social media after we both came out as adults. I saw him now, on the other side of the yard, jovially holding court with a whole crowd of people around him, and smiled. If he could do this, I could too.

I still let people come to me, rather than initiate any conversations, but I didn't try to avoid them anymore. Throughout the night, as more and more people from deeper and deeper into my past came by to chat, every single one of them greeted me as Jackson. I got zero questions about my transition. Not a single incorrect pronoun. Except for the few seconds of awkwardness after I heard my new name on their lips, everything felt completely like it used to.

Talking about a Trans Person in Past Tense

If an old classmate of mine was telling a story about a hilarious thing we did together in high school, should they have used my current name and pronouns or the ones I went by back in high school?

The simple answer: They should use my current name and pronouns.

That's not just my personal preference. It's the generally agreed-upon best practice for referring to all trans people in the past. You may encounter a trans person who has a different preference, but the gold standard is to always err on the side of validating the person's gender.

And it may seem weird at first. Maybe you were looking at the photos of me wearing dresses earlier in this book and found it odd to refer to me as "he."

Or maybe you know someone who directed a movie, wrote a book, or performed in a band under a different name before transitioning. Even though their old name is out there in the world, they'd probably prefer that you use their current name when referencing those projects.

The important thing to remember is that it's very likely that, at least on some level, the trans person in question has always felt like the gender they are. It wasn't something "new" that they "changed" once they came out and shared with everyone. When I think about my childhood, it feels more true to my experience to think of myself as having been a little boy, even though most people saw me as a little girl.

By referring to a person the way they identify now, even when talking about the past, you're validating their gender and recognizing that they didn't just "change" genders when they decided to tell the world about it.

Hearing that old name and pronouns might be really disorienting, even anxiety-inducing, for some people. You might also be putting their safety at risk. Are you sure that everyone you're talking to knows this person is trans? If you switched to their old pronouns and birth name to tell a pretransition story, would you be outing them against their will? Outing someone as trans is not only incredibly disrespectful but can also be dangerous if some of the folks who find out are transphobic and choose to act on that transphobia with violence or forms of disenfranchisement—like getting the person fired or removed from their housing.

Yes, sometimes this means there might simply be stories you can't tell if you're in a mixed group where some people aren't aware of the person's trans status. Does the story involve them using the restroom of another gender, being a Boy Scout, or attending an all-women's event? Ask the trans person in question how they would prefer you share those stories ahead of time. In some cases, they may be okay with your outing them for the sake of the story. Other times, they might request you bend the truth—change Boy Scout to Girl Scout, for example. Often, they might ask you to just not tell the story at all, or pretend it happened to someone else.

Going to all this trouble is not unlike the niceties we all perform for other people in our lives—making sure not to offend or reveal information about friends' past relationships, family secrets, personal medical histories, etc.

And again, it can really differ for some folks. Depending on their gender identity and relationship to their transition, it might be important to them to make those distinctions between the different genders they presented as and were treated as at various points in their life. For example, in some of my more feminine stages of adolescence, especially when talking about topics like how I was treated by men, I think it can be important to bring up the gender I was presenting as.

But those sorts of nuances and opinions are down to each person to decide for themselves. Your role as an ally is to defer to the most respectful assumption until you're told otherwise.

It's possible there *were* some people there who disapproved of me, but I successfully avoided them and they didn't try to start anything. All my real friends acted like it was no big deal at all. They were so great, I even started wondering if I would've been able to pull off transitioning in high school.

• • •

I daydream about that kind of thing every now and then—what my life would be like if I had transitioned at this age or that age. How would my life have played out differently if I'd had the guts to come out?

Then again, as someone who's read a lot of time travel sci-fi, I tend to be wary of *actually* changing anything in the past for fear it will mess up the present and future too much. If I somehow got to go back in time and transition as a fourth grader, would that later cause my hand to disappear in the middle of my sick guitar solo at my parents' high school dance?

Time travel paradoxes aside, I honestly think that my college years were so bleak and empty that transitioning earlier might have improved things. I would've had access to the support and resources at the campus LGBTQ centers as well as all the different youth programs I had aged out of by the time I actually transitioned at twenty-five. With my dysphoria being proactively dealt with, I probably would have been a better student and made more friends. But perhaps being happy with my life and focusing on transition would have distracted me from becoming so involved with the Harry Potter fan community and with YouTube, both of which laid the foundation for this weird, difficult-to-describe career that I love.

Maybe not, though. Watching YouTubers was a key part of my coping mechanism both before and during transition. I'm sure I would've decided to start keeping my own video log during my transition, like so many others. I might've even been a bigger player on the scene earlier on. And even if I didn't end up working for the HPA, I think being more sure of myself would've led me to something great, even if it's not on the same path as where I've ended up now.

As wonderful as that all is to dream about, if I'm being really honest with myself, I just don't think it would have been possible. I went through a lot, even gender aside, in my first several years out of high school. Looking back on it all, I didn't give myself enough credit for how much tragedy I experienced and how uprooted my life was. I wouldn't have been able to thrive in my transition without a stable base on which to do it. I had to build myself back up, climbing through the hardships and gender dysphoria, before I could reemerge on a firm launchpad from which to take flight.

J. K. Rowling said in her Harvard commencement speech when discussing losing her job shortly after her divorce and the seemingly endless tunnel of darkness that followed, "I was set free, because my greatest fear had already been realized, and I was still alive . . . and so rock bottom became the solid foundation on which I rebuilt my life."

• • •

Having faced my greatest fear—letting people in on my Big Dark Secret and living openly as myself—I can finally move forward.

For so many years, my mind was monopolized by thoughts and worries about my gender. Now, my mind has calmed down. I have the mental space to think about other things——my family, my friends, my passions, and my future.

I think that's why my high school reunion ended up being a bit of a gut punch in a totally different way than I had expected. I realized that I wanted some of the things my classmates had. Everyone defines and values success in different ways. Recently I've been redefining it for myself, veering more toward wanting stability and family life—and not so much focusing on the shiny events and career accolades. Ideally a balance of both would be nice, but my reunion was a wake-up call for how far behind I am on one part of life I would very much like to have.

It's pretty common for LGBTQ+ people, especially trans people, to be a little behind on these milestones. We often don't get to be ourselves until early adulthood, if then. We have to work out a lot of things that cis or straight people worked out earlier in life. We have challenges when it comes to employment, housing, medical needs, mental and emotional health, and relationships.

So I shouldn't be so hard on myself. And honestly, if the one slightly heavy thing to come from my ten-year high school reunion was a completely common feeling of envy that several other people probably left with, I'm totally okay with that. I'm so glad I didn't exclude myself from a milestone I'd always looked forward to just because of the possibility that some people wouldn't have wanted me there.

I refuse to live my life in fear. I already did that for the first twenty-five years of my life. I need to be aware of the real risks I face as a transgender person, yes. I will never stop being trans, even if I do have the privilege of forgetting every once in a while. I'm proud of how far I've come, of what I've been through. But I'm ready to start looking forward, not back.

I know it's not all smooth sailing from here. I'm sure there will be many more challenges to come as I enter adulthood in earnest—more medical procedures in my future, maybe starting a family, hopefully homeownership one day, but also losing more friends, perhaps illness, watching my parents get older—all kinds of trials and road bumps I can't even imagine now. But I'm ready for the next phase of life. Unlike when I turned eighteen and allegedly entered the adult world, this time I know who I am. I'm better at tackling challenges head on. I have a rock-solid base. I haven't cracked all the secrets to life or even all the secrets of my own life, but I can at least say that I've sorted things out . . . for now.

acknowledgments

I'm a collaborator at heart, so from the zine to the publication of the book you hold in your hands, I have *a lot* of people to thank.

First, my family. My brother Austin and my parents Dave and Janice—as well as each of their new families, who have barely ever known me as anyone but Jackson and, in that happy coincidence, have given me new homes to be myself in.

Thank you to Sam Ford for inviting me in to that first meeting at Tiller Press. To my editor Anja Schmidt for sharing my vision and handling my story with as much care as if it were her own. To my agent Kevin O'Connor for never giving up on me. And to the whole team at Tiller for working so hard to bring my book to life.

A huge thanks is owed to the team at FRESH Speakers, especially to Courtney Martin for coaching me through the publishing world and to Vanessa Valenti for her unceasing mentorship.

When I wasn't sure if my little zine was really good enough to become a book, there were a few people without whose encouragement I wouldn't be here. So thank you to Sue Jay Johnson, Katie Salisbury, and Ash Hardell for helping me believe in myself and my story.

Thank you to everyone at the Harry Potter Alliance and Mischief Management for giving me so many opportunities over the years and for creating welcoming spaces for queer and trans kids to be themselves, without that being the sum of their being. A special thank you to Taekia Blackwell for answering my first email to the HPA, setting me on the path that would define my career—and for giving me the title to chapter twenty-six.

Thank you to Katie Riley for originally coming up with the title of this book, but mostly for feeding me while I wrote it.

To RV Dougherty for providing essential encouragement and creative ideas when I was first writing the zine—and for being a solid pal in so many ways before and after my top surgery.

A big thank you to everyone whose emails I missed, deadlines I pushed back, and plans I flaked on. Especially to Allison Jungkurth for putting up with me while I was writing. I'll go take the recycling out now.

To everyone who gave me a chance and believed in me, even when I couldn't see it for myself: Paul DeGeorge, Carolyn Forbes, Alora Lanzillotta, Michael Morgan, Renato Verdugo, and, most of all, Eric Selbin.

To my patrons, YouTube subscribers, and the original donors of this zine. I would not be here without your love and support.

And finally, to every trans, nonbinary, and gender-nonconforming person who came before me and fought hard so that I could live the life I have now—and to future generations, may the fight get easier but your resilience never waver.

sources

Bergman, S. Bear, and Kate Bornstein. *Gender Outlaws: The Next Generation*. New York: Seal Press, 2010.

Bongiovanni, Archie, Tristan Jimerson, and Ari Yarwood. *A Quick & Easy Guide to They-Them Pronouns*. Portland, OR: Limerence Press, 2018.

Cho, Jin-Woo et al. "Nipple-Areola Complex Necrosis after Nipple-Sparing Mastectomy with Immediate Autologous Breast Reconstruction." *Archives of Plastic Surgery* 42, no. 5 (2015). 601–7. doi:10.5999/aps.2015.42.5.601.

Erickson-Schroth, Laura. *Trans Bodies, Trans Selves: A Resource for the Transgender Community*. New York: Oxford University Press, 2014.

"Expert Q & A: Gender Dysphoria." American Psychiatric Association. https://www.psychiatry.org/patients-families/gender-dysphoria/expert-q-and-a.

Feinberg, Leslie. *Transgender Warriors: Making History from Joan of Arc to Dennis Rodman*. Boston: Beacon Press, 2005.

Frey, Jordan D., Grace Poudrier, Michael V. Chiodo, and Alexes Hazen. "A Systematic Review of Metoidioplasty and Radial Forearm Flap Phalloplasty in Female-to-Male Transgender Genital Reconstruction." *Plastic and Reconstructive Surgery—Global Open* 4, no. 12 (December 4, 2016). doi:10.1097/gox.0000000000001131.

Ghoneim, Mohamed M., and Michael W. O'Hara. "Depression and Postoperative Complications: An Overview." *BMC Surgery* 16, no. 5 (February 2, 2016). doi:10.1186/s12893-016-0120-y.

GLAAD Media Reference Guide: 10th Edition. New York: GLAAD, 2016.

Green, Jamison. *Becoming a Visible Man.* Nashville: Vanderbilt University Press, 2006.

Grinker, Roy Richard. "Being Trans Is Not a Mental Disorder." *New York Times*, December 6, 2018. https://www.nytimes.com/2018/12/06/opinion/trans-gender-dysphoria-mental-disorder.html.

"Guest Post—Tragic Tropes: Transgender Representation in Contemporary Culture." *Geek Melange*, March 21, 2014. http://www.geek melange.com/2014/03/tragic-tropes-transgender-representation/.

"How Common Is Intersex?" Intersex Society of North America. http://www.isna.org/faq/frequency.

"HRC." Human Rights Campaign. https://www.hrc.org/state-maps/transgender-healthcare.

"Hudson's Guide: FTM Testosterone Therapy Basics." Hudson's FTM Resource Guide. http://www.ftmguide.org/ttherapybasics.html.

"International Classification of Diseases." World Health Organization. https://www.who.int/health-topics/international-classification-of-diseases.

"Intersex Definitions." Interactadvocates. https://interactadvocates.org/intersex-definitions/.

Ira. "Chest Binding 101—FTM Binder Guide | FTM Binding, Chest Binder, Breast Binders." TransGuys.com, September 25, 2018. https://transguys.com/features/chest-binding.

"It's Time for People to Stop Using the Social Construct of 'Biological Sex' to Defend Their Transmisogyny." *Autostraddle*, December 28, 2016. https://www.autostraddle.com/its-time-for-people-to-stop-using-the-social-construct-of-biological-sex-to-defend-their-transmisogyny-240284/.

Kennedy, Pagan. *The First Man-Made Man: The Story of Two*

Sexes, One Love Affair, and a Twentieth-Century Medical Revolution.
New York: Bloomsbury, 2007.

Kotula, Dean. *The Phallus Palace: Female to Male Transsexuals.*
Los Angeles: Alyson Publications, 2002.

"LGBTQ Definitions." Trans Student Educational Resources. http://
www.transstudent.org/DEFINITIONS/.

"Making a Case for a Singular 'They.' " AP Definitive Source. https://
blog.ap.org/products-and-services/making-a-case-for-a-singular-they.

"Mapping Transgender Equality in the United States." Movement
Advancement Project. http://www.lgbtmap.org/mapping-trans-equality.

Mardell, Ashley. *The ABC's of LGBT.* Coral Gables, FL: Mango Media, 2016.

Meagley, Desmond. "Your BIGGEST Questions about They/Them
Pronouns, Answered." *Teen Vogue,* October 17, 2018. https://www
.teenvogue.com/story/they-them-questions-answered.

National Health Service. "A Guide to Hormone Therapy for Trans
People." https://www.gires.org.uk/wp-content/uploads/2014/08/doh-hormone
-therapy.pdf.

Page, Morgan M. *One from the Vaults.* Podcast audio.

Reitz, Nikki. "The Representation of Trans Women in Film and Television." *Cinesthesia* 7 (2nd series), no. 1 (December 14, 2017). https://
scholarworks.gvsu.edu/cine/vol7/iss1/2/.

Serano, Julia. *Whipping Girl: A Transsexual Woman on Sexism and
the Scapegoating of Femininity.* Berkeley, CA: Seal Press, 2016.

Skidmore, Emily. *True Sex: The Lives of Trans Men at the Turn of
the Twentieth Century.* New York: New York University Press, 2017.

smith, s. e. "Does Informed Consent Mean 'Hormones on Demand' for Trans People? Not So Much." *Rewire.News,* July 10, 2018.
https://rewire.news/article/2018/07/10/informed-consent-mean
-hormones-demand-trans-people-not-much/.

Snorton, C. Riley. *Black on Both Sides: A Racial History of Trans Identity*. Minneapolis: University of Minnesota Press, 2017.

Standards of Care for the Health of Transsexual, Transgender, and Gender-Nonconforming People. Vol. 7. Minneapolis: World Professional Association for Transgender Health, 2012.

Stryker, Susan. *Transgender History: The Roots of Today's Revolution*. New York: Seal Press, 2017.

"The Gender Unicorn." Trans Student Educational Resources. http://www.transstudent.org/gender.

"They | Definition of They in English by Oxford Dictionaries." Oxford Dictionaries | English. https://en.oxforddictionaries.com/definition /they.

Unger, Cécile A. "Hormone Therapy for Transgender Patients." *Translational Andrology and Urology*, December 2016. https://www .ncbi.nlm.nih.gov/pmc/articles/PMC5182227/.

Urquhart, Evan. "Should Trans People Need a Doctor's Permission to Medically Transition?" *Slate* magazine, March 11, 2016. https://slate.com/human-interest/2016/03/transgender-patients-and -informed-consent-who-decides-when-transition-treatment-is-appro priate.html.

Vamos, Jorge. "How to Date a Transgender Person: 5 Essential Tips for Starting a Relationship with a Trans Woman or Trans Man." PairedLife, May 21, 2018. https://pairedlife.com/gender-sexuality/How -to-Date-a-Transgender-Person-5-Tips-for-Starting-a-Relationship -With-a-Trans-Woman-or-Trans-Man.

Vancouver Coastal Health, Transcend Transgender Support & Education Society, and Canadian Rainbow Health Coalition. *Hormones: A Guide for FTMs*. https://apps.carleton.edu/campus/gsc/assets /hormones_FTM.pdf.

"Victims or Villains: Examining Ten Years of Transgender Images on Television." GLAAD, January 12, 2017. https://www.glaad.org /publications/victims-or-villains-examining-ten-years-transgender -images-television.

Wilkinson, Willy. *Born on the Edge of Race and Gender: A Voice for Cultural Competency*. Oakland, CA: Hapa Papa Press, 2015.

Wong, Brittany. "What It's Like to Date Online as a Trans Person." *HuffPost*, April 9, 2019. https://www.huffpost.com/entry/what -its-really-like-to-online-date-as-a-trans-person_n_5b848aace4b0 cf7b002e467b?ncid=engmodushpmg0000000.

further learning

Books
Holy Wild by Gwen Benaway
A Quick and Easy Guide to They/Them Pronouns by Archie Bongiovanni and Tristan Jimerson
To My Trans Sisters edited by Charlie Craggs
Trans Bodies, Trans Selves by Laura Erickson-Schroth
Becoming a Visible Man by Jamison Green
The ABC's of LGBT+ by Ash Hardell
Whipping Girl by Julia Serano
Transgender History by Susan Stryker

Young Adult and Middle Grade Books
Some Assembly Required by Arin Andrews
Beautiful Music for Ugly Children by Kirstin Cronn-Mills
Symptoms of Being Human by Jeff Garvin
George by Alex Gino
Rethinking Normal by Katie Rain Hill

Children's Books
I Am Jazz by Jazz Jennings
One of a Kind, Like Me/Unico Como Yo by Laurin Mayeno
Who Are You? The Kid's Guide to Gender Identity by Brook Pessin-Whedbee and Naomi Bardoff
The Boy & the Bindi by Vivek Shraya
Jack (Not Jackie) by Erica Silverman
From the Stars in the Sky to the Fish in the Sea by Kai Cheng Thom and Kai Yun Ching
It Feels Good to Be Yourself: A Book about Gender Identity by Theresa Thorn

Other Media

One from the Vaults, a podcast on transgender history by
   Morgan M. Page
Gender Reveal, a podcast by and for nonbinary folks by Molly
   Woodstock
The Gender Unicorn, transstudent.org/gender
Transgender Oral History Project, alliedmedia.org/tohp

For Trans, Nonbinary, Gender-Nonconforming, or Questioning Individuals

CenterLink, lgbtcenters.org
Health Coverage Guide, transequality.org/health-coverage-guide
Transgender Suicide Prevention Hotline, translifeline.org
The Trevor Project, 1-866-488-7386

For Parents, Loved Ones, and Friends

My Kid Is Gay, mykidisgay.com
PFLAG, pflag.org
TransYouth Family allies, imatyfa.org

For Students and Educators

Campus Pride, campuspride.org
GLSEN, glsen.org/students/tsr
Live out Loud, liveoutloud.info
Trans Student Educational Resources, transstudent.org

Legal Assistance and Advocacy

American Civil Liberties Union, aclu.org/issues/lgbt-rights
   /transgender-rights
GLAAD, glaad.org
Lambda Legal, lambdalegal.org
The National Center for Transgender Equality, transequality.org
National LGBTQ Task Force, thetaskforce.org
Transgender Legal Defense and Education Fund, tldef.org

MORE RESOURCES AND FANTASTIC BOOKS ARE COMING OUT
EVERY DAY. FOR AN UP-TO-DATE LISTING AS WELL AS
NUMEROUS RECOMMENDED VIDEOS, SEE THE AUTHOR'S
DIGITAL RESOURCE PAGE AT JACKSONBIRD.COOL/RESOURCES.

photo credits